SUCCESSFUL
CIVIL LITIGATION

How to Win Your Case
Before You Enter
the Courtroom

SUCCESSFUL CIVIL LITIGATION

George

Prentice-Hall, Inc.

How to Win Your Case
Before You Enter the Courtroom

Vetter

Englewood Cliffs, New Jersey

Prentice-Hall International, Inc., *London*
Prentice-Hall of Australia Pty. Ltd., *Sydney*
Prentice-Hall of Canada, Ltd., *Toronto*
Prentice-Hall of India Private Ltd., *New Delhi*
Prentice-Hall of Japan, Inc., *Tokyo*
Prentice-Hall of Southeast Asia Pte. Ltd., *Singapore*
Whitehall Books Ltd., *Wellington, New Zealand*

*Successful Civil Litigation: How to Win Your
Case Before You Enter the Courtroom*

George Vetter

© 1977, *by*

PRENTICE-HALL, INC.

Englewood Cliffs, N.J.

Second Printing . . . . . September, 1977

This publication is designed to provide accurate and authoritative information in regard to the subject matter covered. It is sold with the
understanding that the publisher is not engaged in rendering legal, accounting, or other professional service. If legal advice or other expert assistance
is required, the services of a competent professional person should be
sought.
... *From the Declaration of Principles jointly adopted by a Committee of
the American Bar Association and a Committee of Publishers and Associations.*

Library of Congress Cataloging in Publication Data

Vetter, George,
   Successful civil litigation.

   Includes index.
   1. Pre-trial procedure--United States. 2. Pleading
--United States. 3. Trial practice--United States.
I. Title.
KF8900.V4   347'.73'72   76-28525
ISBN 0-13-860205-0

Printed in the United States of America

A Word from the Author

How to win cases? How to make the best of a weak case? How to get an edge on the opponent?

There are no air-tight answers to guarantee those results. But there is an answer that comes as close as possible to a guarantee. It lies in thinking the case through, handling it professionally, and preparing it thoroughly as though it were headed straight for a courtroom battle.

That's what this book is about. But it's not just another book on the subject.

For an overview consider the value of the following five themes in the book:

• The book approaches litigation as an exercise in persuasion which orients you at the outset to pursue that goal from start to finish.

• It deals with litigation "like it is"—how the courts actually treat situations, not how they often say they do—and gives you pointers on how to cope with such situations.

• It exposes hidden pitfalls of practice so that you can spot and avoid them.

• It tackles some of the tough "no answer" problems and gives you the thinking and techniques to handle them best.

• By examples and explanations it illuminates the reasons why things should be done in certain ways, which equips the reader to solve problems when they arise.

Now consider the following 15 specific, practical features of this new volume:

—It furnishes checklists and step-by-step guidelines on the key phases of trial preparation for ready reference in the day-to-day work on a case.

—It reveals the "theory of the case" formula for winning cases, illustrating the several kinds of theories of the case and showing how to develop them.

—It explains the "trial book" technique—the flexible way of organizing cases to guarantee thorough preparation and a professionally conducted trial, with models for such important items as witness sheets, the analysis of the issues, and the outline of proof.

—It covers the use of pleadings to achieve long-range goals, and the framing of allegations to express precise positions.

—It shows how to use motions as weapons to gain tactical advantages in an overall winning strategy.

—It shows how to plan and conduct an investigation—including tips on interviewing witnesses so as to dig out all the facts—and how to dovetail investigation with discovery to enhance the value of each.

—It reveals litigation-tested techniques in the use of each discovery tool, both as a means to collect facts and as a source of proof for the trial.

—It shows how to multiply the benefits of discovery by the artful use of the discovery tools in combination with each other, with illustrations in different kinds of cases.

—It sets out in schedule form the fine points of responding to interrogatories and requests to admit as a guide for analysis in practice.

—It puts expert testimony into context by giving the evidentiary basis for expert testimony—with the provisions of new Federal Rules of Evidence keyed in with the common law rules—and then shows how to use expert testimony for maximum effect with least risk.

—It illustrates and explains how to use modern litigating techniques—videotape depositions, the several types of demonstrative evidence with an evidentiary analysis of each, demonstrative evidence tied in with expert testimony, and others.

—It shows how to develop medical proof to win cases in areas of litigation where the use of such proof is often overlooked.

—It deals with damages with a view to maximizing the recovery for the plaintiff or minimizing it for the defendant.

—It describes the several different types of procedure referred to under the name pre-trial, and the varying attitudes of judges toward pre-trial, and then explains how best to handle each of these situations to gain advantage at trial.

—It approaches direct and cross-examination as critical matters that must be carefully thought through before trial, and shows how to add an extra dimension to this phase of preparation by incorporating an evidentiary analysis.

The realistic approach to civil litigation outlined in this work can produce many individual benefits, not the least of which is the prompt resolution of cases that should not be tried, and probably won't be, with a solidly prepared case evident to the opponent.

George Vetter

CONTENTS

Chapter 11   PREPARING DEMONSTRATIVE EVIDENCE
THAT WILL CONVINCE JURORS *(continued)*

Chapter 12   USING THE PRE-TRIAL CONFERENCE TO
GET THE UPPER HAND AT TRIAL

Chapter 13   HOW TO PREPARE YOUR WITNESSES FOR A
DIRECT EXAMINATION THAT WILL PROVE
YOUR CASE AND WITHSTAND CROSS-
EXAMINATION—WHEN TRIAL IS
IMMINENT

1

How to Win the Case
with a Theory of the Case

1.1 How to Use a Theory of the Case to Persuade Jurors

A hit-or-miss approach to a case is an invitation to disaster. You might miss or glide over strong points. You might expose or emphasize weak points. Worst of all you probably will not try the case with an eye focused on persuading the jury. To make sure that you do try the case that way, you must try the case with a theory of the case.

In the broad sense, the theory of the case is how you hope to win the case. It is your plan of action. It is the perspective you want the jury to view the case from. It is your formula for persuading the jury to find in your favor. It is the persuasive theme you integrate the case with.

The definitions vary because there are different kinds of theories of the case. All of them, however, have a common foundation in the realistic view of what actually takes place at a trial. At a trial the jury finds facts, and then applies the law to the facts it finds. The critical point is how the jury goes about doing this. In finding facts the jury does not travel back in time to see and hear what happened as it happened. What the jury does is reconstruct what it thinks happened from what is presented to it at the trial.

In most cases there are serious disputes about the facts. Each side has its version. If you can get the jury to accept your version you will win. A theory of the case can be instrumental in accomplishing this as the following case illustrates.

Plaintiff was driving south on the inside lane of a busy four lane street. Defendant pulled out of the parking lot at an ice-cream parlor, intending to turn left to join the south-bound traffic. The two cars collided. Plaintiff testified that she was in her lane and defendant turned into her. Defendant said that plaintiff had crossed over the center line and hit her (both parties were women) as she momentarily paused to let plaintiff's car go by.

The accident was trifling. It would have amounted to nothing except that plaintiff claimed it triggered an epileptic condition.

There were no independent witnesses. The marks on the cars were inconclusive. But plaintiff had a couple of extraneous factors going for her. At the time of the accident defendant had been a teen-ager. She and a car full of girl friends had been celebrating a high school football victory at the creamery. On the other hand, plaintiff was a middle-aged practical nurse.

Then two crucial facts came to light about plaintiff. Her medical record revealed that she had tunnel vision, and that she had not indicated this condition on her application for a driver's license.

At the trial counsel hammered home through experts that without peripheral vision plaintiff could not truly judge whether she had driven over the center line. He produced a Department of Motor Vehicles employee to testify that had she disclosed the condition she would not have been licensed to drive. The court sustained plaintiff's objection to the question but the jury got the point from the question.

Defendant's theory dominated the case. It kept plaintiff's theory about sky-larking kids and an inattentive driver from getting off the ground. It helped blunt sympathy for an injured person. And most important, it let counsel attack plaintiff's testimony on the basis of capacity and not veracity.

The theory persuaded most of the jurors. But the God of Trials is capricious. The jury hung. Sensing there was insurance in the case one or two jurors held out for plaintiff to get her medical expenses.

This case shows how a theory of the case can help persuade the jury to accept one among several disputed versions of the facts. A theory of the case can also help persuade the jury to accept one among several disputed inferences to be drawn from undisputed facts. The case of the Frugal New Englander shows how this works.

The settlor of a substantial inter-vivos trust lived in Newport, Rhode Island. However, he had New York attorneys draw the trust, he executed the trust deed in New York, and he conveyed the trust res to trustees located in New York. The settlor's brother-in-law was an officer of the corporate trustee.

By the terms of the trust the settlor gave the income to his wife for life and then to his daughter. The wife out-lived both her husband and her daughter, who never married, by many years. Over its long life the trust received substantial stock dividends on securities in the portfolio. The trustees held the stock dividends in a suspense account, not allocating them to either principal account or income account.

The trust deed did not provide for the allocation of stock dividends. It did not designate the law of any state as controlling. This left the stock dividends "up for grabs" when the wife died. If stock dividends belonged to principal of the trust they passed under the distribution clause in the trust. If the stock dividends belonged to income of the trust they passed under the wife's will.

The law presumed an intention when settlors did not provide for allocation of stock dividends. The problem was which law applied. If New York law did, the lion's share of the stock dividends went to income account. If Rhode Island law did, all of the stock dividends went to principal account.

The trustees brought a construction suit in New York. The income group argued that the many New York contacts indicated that the settlor wanted New York law to apply. Besides, they said, allocating stock dividends was a matter of administration governed by the law of the situs.

The principal group had a more subtle theory. The theory of the income group, they argued, boiled down to the question, "Why would the settlor have chosen New York if he didn't want New York law to apply?"

"Easy," they replied. "He wanted to give his brother-in-law a handsome piece of business."

But theory did not end with this riposte. A person creates a trust in order to distribute money to certain people according to a certain plan. To say that the distribution of substantial sums is a mere matter of trust administration does not make sense, but to view it as a matter of interpreting intention does. On questions of interpretation the law of the domicile applies. It bases presumptions about intention upon the habits and characteristics of its inhabitants. "Notoriously," the theory wound up, "New Englanders don't spend principal!"

Both theories made virtue of necessity. But a good theory will set counsel off on a hunt to support it. A file search through 40 years of trustees' records did not turn up any hard facts about intention. It did let counsel put together a nice packet of documents, locking the settlor up as a born and bred New Englander. Those materials were stipulated into evidence along with basic facts about dates and places and births and deaths, the drafting of the deed, etc.

If Empire State parochialism ever was a danger, the result belied it. The courts held that the issue involved interpretation and that Rhode Island law applied. A fine theory of the case furnished a key to what the undisputed facts meant.

1.2   The Different Types of Theories—How to Tell What Type Fits Your Case

1.2.1   Straight Proof of the Issues

In some cases, the issues and facts are plain and uncomplicated. There is no need for a sophisticated theory. There is little or nothing from which to formulate a special point of view. The obvious approach, therefore, is the best approach—straight proof of the issues.

A recent patent suit illustrates this. The patent office had granted a patent on a principle as old as the cuneiform seal. The seal with raised figures would be rolled on a soft clay. When the clay dried the impression became fast.

In this case, defendant used a roll to emboss electrical cord. The cord would be fed into and travel in a continuous line through a high-temperature vulcanizing chamber. Seconds after entering the chamber it would become soft enough to receive an impression. At this point it ran between two rollers, the uppermost of which embossed the familiar legend seen on electrical cord. When the cord left the chamber it cooled, and the impression became fixed.

Plaintiff commenced an infringement action against a large manufacturer of rubber cable. Defendant defended on three grounds: unpatentability since the technique was as old and as common as the Babylonian seal; vagueness in the patent, especially an alleged formula about exactly where the roll should be placed in terms of softening of the rubber; prior commercial use based on use in a vulcanizing chamber process before the patent.

The facts supported defendant so counsel simply bored in. He developed the case through investigation and discovery. He honed the facts to a sharp edge for trial. He proved each issue crisply at trial. He won on each issue.

1.2.2   The Critical Factor Approach

Sometimes a case will stand or fall, or can be made to stand or fall, on one crucial point. The case hinges on whether the jury accepts your interpretation of the facts on one crucial point. This insight is the key to the critical factor type theory of the case. It is a kind of force play. You force a point—a strong one in your case or a weak one in your opponent's case—into the position of a fulcrum on which the entire case turns.

The case of the Traumatic Epileptic discussed in section 1.1 illustrates this. Defendant's counsel forced plaintiff's tunnel vision into the center of the case. He cross-examined plaintiff and her doctor at length about it, pushing it into prominence. With the buildup, he had a firm foundation for his defense experts. And to keep the focus, he did not call defendant who had previously testified in plaintiff's case under the adverse witness statute.

A word of warning about this technique, however. The critical factor must be able to stand up at trial. If it cannot, the technique might backfire and the other side reap the benefits.

1.2.3   The "Red Herring" Theory

"Diversionary tactics!" The purists may splutter, but such tactics are part of litigation. A red herring dragged across the trail sends the hounds off the scent. An adroit ploy at the trial can get the jury off the path of doom for your client.

One species of red herring has been enshrined, preserved in brine might be a better metaphor, by the plaintiffs' bar in negligence cases. When liability is thin, but damages are heavy, the theory of the case is clear: carry liability by playing on the jury's sympathy for the plight of the plaintiff.

The plaintiffs' bar also makes much of the target defendant. The greater the gap between the big, rich corporate defendant and the poor, little plaintiff, the better the chance that the jury will overlook the fact that there may have been no wrongdoing at all.

By no means do defense counsel scorn the red herring. In fact, case-hardened defense lawyers instinctively look for an overreaching plaintiff. Take the following case:

Traffic was stop-and-go one cold, wintery morning. In a fitful surge of traffic, defendant bumped into the rear end of plaintiff's car. It was a tap at best. After some breast-beating, everybody went to work. The cars had minimal damage. All seemed well. But appearances can deceive. Plaintiff claimed a permanent back condition.

Defense counsel had serious doubts. The condition did not tie in with the accident. Plaintiff's own doctor seemed to hedge in his reports. Still the case looked hopeless, and plaintiff would not settle reasonably.

Then counsel got a break. Plaintiff's counsel served interrogatories just before trial. In preparing answers defendant made the startling revelation that when he put on the brakes, his car slid on a patch of ice into plaintiff's car. "Unavoidable accident." Not much perhaps but at least a defense to talk about.

The trial started out predictably enough—clear negligence with just a question of how much. But plaintiff began to play up his condition. He went beyond his own medical reports. He almost seemed to whine. Sensing that the jury saw this, counsel baited plaintiff on cross-examination. Plaintiff took the bait. He went on about his condition even more.

Cross-examination of plaintiff's doctor turned the case around. The doctor stuck to the letter of his medical reports and acknowledged the subjective nature of the complaints.

By the close of evidence, counsel had set the case up for a crushing final argument. He tested the jury with a remark or two on malingering. He saw a couple of jurors nod in agreement. He sharpened his attack. He saw more jurors begin to nod. By the time he finished, he had every juror nodding.

Plaintiff's closing fell on deaf ears. After a few minutes' deliberation, the jury returned a verdict for defendant. The case illustrates the red herring theory. In fact the judge called the result a miscarriage of justice. But was it? If the jury did not think plaintiff had the back condition he claimed he had, did they not do justice? What may seem a red herring may not be a red herring after all.

1.2.4   Theme and Variations

In some cases you will set a theme for your presentation. You seek to impress a point of view upon the jury, a perspective through which you want them to view the facts and assess what the case is all about.

Defense counsel have a stock theme in medical malpractice actions—the Healer. Some cases lend themselves to a variation on this theme—the Ungrateful Patient. Combined as a theme and variation, they can be lethal—the dedicated physician who has done all he could for the patient who in disappointment at a less than perfect result lashes out at the person who tried to help him. The case of the Implanted Dentures illustrates this.

Plaintiff had lost all of her teeth. And, she had a problem. The roof of her mouth was too shallow to hold a plate properly. Defendant had become world-famous for a technique of implanting prosthetic teeth. Because the mandible is a strong bone, lower

jaw implants enjoyed great success. Because the maxillary is less
sturdy and subject to degeneration, upper jaw implants had a more
limited success.

When plaintiff came to the doctor, he explained the procedure. He warned her about the reduced chance of success with
an upper jaw implant. She elected to undergo the procedure. For a
while her hopes soared. Then slowly, as the implant began to fail,
her hopes faded. Finally, the implant failed. She sued the doctor.

The theme and variation rang true for the case. By the close
of evidence, defense counsel knew the jury saw the case this way
too. He wove his summation around it. For his final remark, in a
hushed voice and with the trace of a throb, he reminded the jury
that "There has only been one perfect healer."

He won!

1.2.5   Reconstruction of Events

Imagine the *Titanic* sinking without anyone having seen the
iceberg. Speculation about what had happened would itself have
been titanic. A case like that at trial stands or falls on whether
speculation can attain to the status of reconstruction. In seamen's
litigation, for example, the Supreme Court has held that minimal
circumstantial evidence about an unwitnessed death can be the
basis for inferences about what happened.

Even in cases with more concrete facts to go on, the process
is the same. From the known facts the parties draw inferences, and
often use scientific proof to create a hypothesis about what
happened. Sometimes the hypothesis can get into evidence only
through expert opinion testimony.

In a "Migrating Plane Crash" case, two light planes, a
Beechcraft Baron and a Cessna 150, collided in mid-air on
approach for landing at an uncontrolled airport. Five people died
in the fiery crash. At uncontrolled airports, Federal Aviation
Administration regulations require that all turns be to the left.

The Cessna belonged to the airport. At the time, an instructor and student pilot were practicing touch-and-go landings.
Several witnesses, all airport people—proprietors, employees,
pilots, and so forth—claimed to have seen the collision. They said
the Cessna was flying south on final approach for landing,

descending and heading straight toward the runway which ran almost due north and south. The Beechcraft, they said, came in fast from the northwest in a shallow right bank to line up with the runway. They added that it smashed into the rear of the Cessna at a point about 100 yards from the end of the runway and on a direct line with it.

One witness, probably the only truly independent one—he was a state employee who worked in the radio facility at the airport—had a substantially different version. He had seen the Beechcraft flying straight south on a direct line with the runway from a great distance out. At the same time he made this observation, he also had seen the Cessna flying west on its base leg. This meant that before the left bank from base leg to final approach, the Cessna had been flying at right angles to the line of flight for final approach. By looking no more than 45 degrees to their right, the pilots could have seen the Beechcraft coming in on final approach from their right. And the manuals emphasized that a pilot should keep his "head on a swivel." Since the Beechcraft was at a higher altitude, and was a low wing plane, the Cessna could have been in its blind spot.

Still, for the Beechcraft, it was several witnesses to one. Something had to be done to supplement and bolster the radio operator's testimony. Taped radio messages seemed to be the answer. The Beechcraft had flown into the state on instruments, following established airways. The control tower taped and timed each conversation with the plane. From these tapes the course and speed of the plane could be plotted to the point where the pilot could see the airport and went off instrument flight onto visual flight. A line projected from this point on the same bearing as the line of flight intersected a line projected on the bearing of the runway at a point more than 3 miles from the end of the runway.

The significance of this was enormous. A right bank 3 miles out for a straight-in approach from 3 miles out violated no regulations. Furthermore, calculations of the usual speed of a Beechcraft Baron on approach for landing dovetailed with the time of the crash. Expert testimony explained that with the considerable crosswind at the time, the left wing of the Beechcraft would have been up to compensate for it. This tended to explain the right bank observation of the airport's witnesses.

The theory had another virtue. It was consistent with the points of impact as reconstructed from the wreckage during the on-scene investigation. About 8 feet of the outer part of the left wing of the Beechcraft had become embedded into the right rear part of the Cessna cabin. The Cessna interests contended these impact marks proved a rear-end collision. The Beechcraft theory tied them in equally well with the independent radio operator's testimony—the Cessna banking in front of the faster moving and descending Beechcraft.

What about these two theories? Which was the stronger? The answer is obvious. The Cessna theory had three distinct advantages. First, this was a rear-end collision. Second, the Cessna had more eye-witnesses. Third, the theory had the virtue of simplicity.

The Beechcraft theory had to be more complex. It had to fit in with the incontrovertible points of impact. It had to explain how the collision took place in terms of an understandable, acceptable, and probable maneuver of the planes. And it had to buttress the testimony of its one eye-witness with respectable technical proof. It did these things. The next section will relate what happened when the Beechcraft interests changed their theory at trial.

1.3   The Six Bench Marks of a Winning Theory

Successful theories regardless of type share certain features. Six of these features have become bench marks for working up a winning theory for a particular case.

First, the theory must have a firm foundation in strong facts and the fair inferences to be drawn from the facts.

Second, if possible, the theory should be built around the so-called "high cards" of litigation, incontestable or virtually incontestable facts, such as self-certifying documents, patently undoctored pictures, admissions against interest, the testimony of independent witnesses, clear scientific facts, and so on.

The principle behind this rule should be mentioned. The jury reconstructs what happened from the evidence. Often the evidence is in sharp conflict. Naturally, then, the jury will seize upon the facts that seem fixed and certain and true. These facts then serve three functions. They, themselves, become part of the foundation for the jury's reconstruction. They become the means by which the jury tests other facts and inferences. And they become the basis for inferences.

Third, and as a corollary of the second bench mark, the theory should not be inconsistent with, or fly in the face of, incontestable facts.

Fourth, the theory should explain away in a plausible manner as many unfavorable facts as it can. In the plane crash case, for example, the Beechcraft theory explained away the rear-end theory of the Cessna by its notion of the Cessna turning left into the line of flight without looking.

Fifth, the theory should be down-to-earth and have a common-sense appeal. It must be readily acceptable by a jury. A theory gets an "A" if it persuades a jury to say, "Yes, that's the way it is."

Sixth, the theory cannot be based on wishful thinking about any phase of the case.

The events at the trial of the Migrating Plane Crash show the importance of these bench marks. At trial the Beechcraft interests abandoned the theory described in the last section. They substituted a theory that moved the place of the actual collision 100 or so yards to the west; that is, no longer on a direct line with the runway.

The new theory had several hypotheses: that the Beechcraft had been about to enter a pattern of flight paralleling the runway to the west by 100 yards; that the Cessna was being flown by the student, and that he had mistakenly flown 100 yards past the point where he should have turned left for a straight-in approach; that the Cessna then turned left and began to angle back left toward the runway, and consequently flew into the Beechcraft's line of flight from the right!

The new theory scrapped the testimony of the radio operator. Instead it relied on the testimony of four boys out of a group of five who had seen the planes just before the collision. The four boys said they saw the Cessna to the west of the Beechcraft. The fifth boy disagreed.

For awhile the new theory held its own at trial. Then the roof fell in. The Cessna interests unveiled a mock-up of the actual wreckage. The court let counsel simulate the accident by moving the segment of the Beechcraft wing, which was mounted on a dolly, into the rear cabin area of the Cessna.

The demonstrative evidence also neutralized the testimony of the Beechcraft's expert on how the collision took place. He had to put the Cessna into a stunt maneuver, one technically possible for the plane to execute but complicated and unusual, and highly improbable even for an experienced pilot.

The Cessna won. It probably would have in any event. The point, though, is the merits of the three theories. You can judge for yourself the extent to which each met the bench marks.

1.4 How to Tailor-Make a Winning Theory of the Case from the Facts of Your Case

There is no magic formula on how to develop a theory of the case, but there are guidelines.

To start with be sure you understand the theory behind the concept of a theory of the case. At the risk of repetition, you must appreciate that first, last, and always a trial is an exercise in persuasion.

Next, get a feel for the different types of theories. Start looking at cases in terms of theories. After awhile you will find yourself instinctively fitting cases into the various categories.

The formulation of a theory for a particular case usually happens in one of two ways. Sometimes a theory becomes obvious as the contours of the case emerge. In those instances, your main job is to test and re-test the theory against the bench marks.

If a theory does not spring to mind, you must construct one step by step.

First, isolate the legal and factual issues in the case. Be sure about the nodes on which the case will turn. In cases where the legal principles are broad, much of the analysis will be factual. In cases where the legal principles are narrower, the analysis will be a mix of law and fact.

Next, take an objective look at the proof pro and con on these issues.

Third, pin-point the critical areas. This means assessing and weighing the results of the analysis on the first two points in terms of the presentation at trial. At this stage, you must begin to think about how to exploit your strong points and your opponent's weak points, and how to shore up your weak points and attack your opponent's strong points.

Fourth, come up with a tentative theory and check it against the five bench marks. If it falls way below the marks, scrap it. If it partially passes muster, set about strengthening it. This usually means searching out further facts or getting expert testimony.

Fifth, as you strengthen and develop the theory, keep checking it against the bench marks.

Finally, from the time you begin to develop a theory try it out on a colleague. It is too easy to miss the forest for the trees deep in the preparation of a case.

2

Maximizing
the Hidden Potentials of Pleading

2.1 How the Veteran Litigator Uses the Pleadings to Get Leverage for His Case

At common law the pleadings dominated procedure. Except for the bill of particulars, discovery was virtually unknown. In modern procedure this is changed. Discovery is the moving force and the pleadings simply "ain't what they used to be." But they are not dead. Together with the rules on joinder of claims and joinder of parties, they still play a pivotal although more subtle role.

The test for the scope of discovery is relevancy to the subject matter of the action. The pleadings establish the subject matter of the action. Consequently the pleadings set the broad limits for discovery. A case involving a "disgruntled distributor" shows how important this can be in practice.

The distributor had fallen down on the job. Neither the carrot nor the stick approach seemed to do much good. Finally

35

the manufacturer gave up and canceled the distributorship. The distributor lashed back with an anti-trust action. And he planted a bomb in his complaint. He alleged a lot of history—when the defendant company was formed, how it grew through mergers, certain landmarks in its career, and so forth.

A complaint like this would give plaintiff a field day with discovery. He could start with the deposition of the chairman of the board and work his way down.

Defendant moved to strike this archeological material. The motion took work, a lot of work really, considering the antipathy of the courts to this kind of motion. But the work paid off. The court granted the motion.

For many a defendant, a broad complaint is the opening gun in a campaign of harassment by discovery. The cost and inconvenience softens him for a settlement. Of course it can work the other way too—more than one well-heeled defendant has exhausted his opponent's war chest through discovery.

These are abuses of discovery, but the differences between abuse and legitimate use is a matter of degree; and either way, how the pleadings are couched matters a great deal. Other things being equal, if you have more to lose than gain by broad discovery you should try to set limits to discovery. For the plaintiff this means a sniper rather than a shotgun complaint. For the defendant it means admitting allegations liberally and venturing motions to strike. If you have more to gain than lose by broad discovery, the opposite is true.

The pleadings also play a pivotal role in forum shopping. In many cases for many reasons a plaintiff will be better off in the state court than in the federal court. The trick comes not in starting the case in the state court but in keeping it there. Defendant might be able to remove it to the federal court. You can block removal in three ways. You can allege damages of $10,000 or less. You can take pains to name as one of the defendants a party with the same citizenship as plaintiff. Or you can make sure that one or more of the defendants is a citizen of the state in which the action is brought. For diversity and removal purposes, a corporation is a citizen of the state of its incorporation and of the state where it has its principal place of business. See 28 U.S.C. § 1332, 1441, et seq.

This fact of jurisdictional life has given rise to the phenomenon of the Distributor in the Middle. In many products liability cases, plaintiff takes dead aim at the manufacturer as the responsible party. With the aid of the long-arm statutes, he usually can get jurisdiction in the state court over an out-of-state manufacturer. On the merits he might have no reason to sue the local distributor. When the distributor and plaintiff enjoy the same citizenship, plaintiff may sue him too, simply to prevent removal.

The third pivotal role grows out of the tie-in between pleadings and parties. The case of a "drowned pilot" shows how important this can be. The Warsaw Convention and Montreal Agreement limit recovery for death or bodily injury to $75,000 on scheduled international airplane flights. The verbiage of the protocols, however, refers to suits against the air carriers. In the struggle to escape the limitation, counsel have started to name the pilot as an additional defendant.

The pilot and the passengers sank together with the plane to the bottom of the sea. The pilot did not live in the forum state. However, an insurance company underwriting the airline did business there. The state direct action statute permitted suit against the insurer of a deceased assured if at the time of suit the estate of the deceased assured had not been probated.

Under the insurance policy covering the airline, the pilot was an additional assured. At the time of suit his estate had not been probated. So what did plaintiff do? He sued the insurance company as well as the airline.

These examples are not exhaustive but they do spotlight the importance of the pleadings even in the era of discovery.

2.2   How to Impress the Court with Craftsman-like Pleadings

The first thing the court reads in the case are the pleadings. A clear pleading, one that is crisp and to the point, will impress the court. In a field like litigation where imponderables abound, a good first impression is invaluable. Also, "bulls-eye" pleading lets the court instantly grasp your position. A busy court will not spend much time searching for hidden meaning in a long-winded document.

Good pleadings do not just happen. They have to be thought through and organized, and then pled according to certain canons.

A pleading should be organized in its legally logical order. It is convenient to discuss this in terms of a complaint but it applies to counterclaims and cross-claims, and any defenses that have to be spelled out.

First, ascertain the requirements or jurisdiction and venue. In an action in the federal courts, jurisdictional allegations are crucial.

Next, determine each claim or basis for recovery that you can and intend to assert arising out of the situation.

Isolate and list the component elements of each claim, noting next to each element the fact supporting it.

Next, decide upon the damages or other relief that you seek.

Finally, double-check any special requirements for pleadings; for example, alleging fraud, mistake, special damages, and (in an answer) breach of a condition precedent with particularity.

A one-draft complaint is a one-way ticket to mediocrity, or worse. For very simple cases this may be an over-statement, but for most cases it hits the mark. You should go over the first draft and each succeeding draft until you can do no better.

The professional prides himself on this kind of craftsmanship. He does not pretend to predict how the extra time and effort sometimes can pay off. He knows it does though, sometimes in unexpected and often dramatic ways. To illustrate, take the following damages case.

An embossing roll fractured during a calendaring operation in plaintiff's plastic plant. The flammable coolant circulating in the roll spewed out and ignited. The fire caused substantial property damage and deprived plaintiff of the use of the calendar for some time.

The embossing roll resembled a giant rolling pin. It consisted of a hollow cylinder with a head and journal plugging each end. Plaintiff contended that it had ordered a roll to be manufactured according to a drawing calling for a one-piece construction of the head and journal; i.e., machined from one large piece of steel stock. In fact defendant had made the head and journal from two pieces, welding and shrink fitting the journal into the head. One of these welds failed. Plaintiff claimed that defendant had changed the design without plaintiff's knowledge.

Plaintiff did not inspect the roll when received. A visual inspection could not readily have revealed that the roll was of two-piece instead of one-piece construction. An embossing roll had an average life of over 20 years. The fracture occurred after about seven years of normal use.

On these basic facts counsel worked up seven theories sounding in warranty, strict liability, and negligence, and sought damages for both property damage and business interruption.

An embarrassment of theories? Far from it. They turned out to be barely enough.

The court ruled that damages for business interruption could not be recovered under strict liability. It dismissed the warranty counts on the grounds that the limitations period had run. It dismissed the *res ipsa loquitur* count.

Then the court gave the case to the jury for a special verdict. In substance the questions put to the jury embraced the two theories of strict liability and the two theories of negligence.

The jury found for plaintiff on the negligence theories only (negligence in failing to check on operating data before making the design change, and negligence in fabrication)!

The point of the example is "What if?" What if counsel had not squeezed every possible theory out of the facts? What if he had not pled each element of each theory so that the negligence counts had not stood up?

Thinking the case through and structuring the pleading according to its legal logic is only half the job. Presenting it professionally is the other half. Here is a checklist for craftsman-like pleading.

1. Allegations should be simple, concise, and direct. The object of a pleading is to communicate. Plain English communicates best.

2. Be brief. Assert the legal elements of the claim or defense and stop. Unproved allegations can be argued by opposing counsel in summation. Allegations in a pleading can be used as judicial admissions in other cases.

3. Define long terms and names, and use that definition thereafter. For example, "Plaintiff, The Society to Prevent the Spread of Rocky Mountain Fever (hereinafter "Rocky Mountain") . . .".

4. Separate different claims or defense in separate counts or defenses.

5. Paragraph freely. By and large every element of a claim should be in a separate paragraph. Apart from this, good syntax serves to limit a paragraph to a single set of circumstances.

6. Number each paragraph, and number the paragraphs sequentially throughout the pleading. Count 1, for example, might consist of paragraphs 1 through 10. Count 2 should start with paragraph 11. This practice makes for ease of reference.

7. Do not repeat allegations previously made. Incorporate them by reference. For example, "Repeats and realleges paragraphs such and such." The rules even permit other pleadings to be incorporated by reference.

8. Attach documents to the pleading if they are not too bulky and cannot be briefly but accurately paraphrased. An exhibit is a part of the pleading for all purposes. It controls over any characterization of it in the pleading.

9. Double-check that you have properly pled special matters such as fraud, mistake, condition of mind, time and place, special damages, etc.

10. Place the demand for judgment at the end of the pleading, not after each count or defense. Where the counts all seek the same relief: "Wherefore plaintiff demands judgment of defendant for . . ., interest and costs." Where the counts seek different relief: "Wherefore plaintiff demands judgment against defendant on count 1 for . . ., on count 2 for . . ., and on count 3 for . . ., interest and costs."

11. Do not verify a pleading unless required to do so. Since a verification is an affidavit, the affiant can be impeached by it on cross-examination.

12. Sign the pleading. Your signature certifies that to the best of your knowledge, information, and belief, there are good grounds to support it. This means you must check the facts. When you rely on "secondhand" facts, you should seriously consider making allegations "upon information and belief."

2.3   How to Maximize Results by the Proper Timing of Suit

Sometimes you have no choice about the timing of suit. An exigency has to be met—the imminent running of the statute of limitations for example. When you have time to breathe, you have two groups of considerations. Is the case ready for suit? Are there other factors to be taken into account?

As a rule-of-thumb you can file suit when you have satisfied yourself on four points:

• That you have buttoned up the facts by statements and investigation as well as can be expected in the circumstances.

• That you have a good grasp of the law.

• That there are no gaps you will find impossible to fill. In a products liability case, for example, you must be sure you can produce testimony on causation.

• That damages have matured to the point that you have at least a general idea of what to sue for.

The "other factors" are numerous.

The time between filing and trial has an important bearing on when to start suit. If the delay runs into years, you will want to start suit as soon as you can. If the court races through its docket, you should make sure you exhaust *ex parte* preparation before filing.

Whether you should try to settle the case before filing depends on the type of suit and the nature of the parties. The good offices of counsel might be all that is necessary to settle a commercial dispute between businessmen unaccustomed to litigation. In an insurance case, on the other hand, a case-hardened adjuster can talk settlement as easily with suit pending as without. Other things being equal, since settlement talks can run on, when you are ready to file suit you might as well do so. The small case where even the costs of suit would cut into the recovery might be an exception.

One last point. The client considers the case under way when he gives it to you. Postponing suit increases the delay in the

client's mind. As time drags on, the client may get his hackles up
about having to wait so long.

2.4   How to Precondition the Court with the
           "Story" Complaint

The rule in pleading is to be brief. Sometimes, though, you
should flesh out the bare bones of the complaint. Take this
situation. You have a case in a sensitive area. It presents a close
question of law and an unusual fact situation. You anticipate that
your opponent will move to dismiss. You realize that his motion
will have a surface appeal, so you want the court to get the full
picture right at the beginning. You want the complaint to tell the
story, perhaps even anticipate defenses. A case involving belliger-
ent brothers illustrates the why and how of the story complaint.

Union members refer to each other as brothers. But wish
does not always give rise to fact. Here one brother assaulted four
other brothers at a union meeting with a carving knife. The State
brought charges of criminal assault. The victims freely testified in
court.

The employer fired the culprit. The union filed a grievance.
From this the employer surmised the assaultor stood in much
better with the union than the victims. Surmise gained certitude
when three of the victims refused, though under subpoena, to
testify at the arbitration unless assured of no retaliation by the
union. The other victim said he did not want to testify against a
fellow member of the union.

The employer sued in the state court, against the men to
testify in compliance with the subpoenas, and against the union to
enjoin retaliation.

The complaint had two burdens to carry. It had to state
claims that could withstand minute and possibly hostile scrutiny
by the court. It also had to get across the reality beneath the legal
surface.

The court had no option but to compel the men to testify
pursuant to the subpoenas. However, the employer wanted reasonably cooperative testimony. This meant the men had to be assured
of no retaliation.

Plaintiff based its case on the integrity of the collective bargaining agreement. The union could not invoke the agreement then frustrate its operation. The problem was that counsel knew of no direct threats to the men. Finally counsel hit upon a formula. The men had testified in court shortly after the incident and before the disciplinary action and the grievance. However, they refused to testify after the disciplinary action and the grievance. Based on this, counsel alleged upon information and belief that in the premises the three victims had good reason for their fear of union retaliation.

With this nut cracked the complaint fell into place. Starting at the beginning, counsel told of the assault, the criminal hearing, the disciplinary action and the grievance, the refusal to obey the subpoenas, and so forth.

The complaint stood up under an all-out attack by the union. The court granted the entire relief sought. The men testified at the arbitration and the company won the arbitration.

The story complaint paid off.

2.5   Tips on How a Defendant Can Meet the Unrealistic Demands of Answering

The defendant's lot in pleading, like that of the policeman in *The Pirates of Penzance* "is not a happy one." He must meet the averments of the complaint, admitting what he can, denying what he must, and so forth. This works fine when as the rule requires, the complaint consists of a short and plain statement of the claim. The trouble is that the courts do not monitor the rule. In fact they undercut it by discouraging motions attacking the pleadings as pleadings.

The upshot has been a widening stream of garrulous complaints often with allegations that are "wrong-headed" at best or distorted at worst. What does a defendant do when faced with a pleading like this? He cannot use the general denial which the rules have killed for practical purposes. If he attempts to pick out each item and answer it precisely he ends up with a pleading monstrosity, admitting or denying or "d k i -ing" individual words and phrases and not just sentences and paragraphs. And he might not be able to deny having knowledge or information because he does have general knowledge of the subject.

One technique recommends itself. Although not mentioned by the rules, it has been tacitly accepted. Defendant alleges his own version of the facts alleged in the paragraph being answered.

> "Answering paragraph _____ of the complaint, alleges that [set forth counsel's version]; except as so alleged, denies the allegations of that paragraph."

Note: The express denial is crucial because averments not denied are deemed admitted.

Allegations of law can be troublesome. The rule requires that a party must admit or deny the averments "upon which the adverse party relies." A party who makes an allegation of law by definition relies on it, and so it must be answered. However you will rarely agree with either the applicability or formulation of the allegation. You usually can deny it.

Then there is the problem of cases with multiple defendants. Any one defendant might have to deal with allegations or counts not addressed to him. The problem arises for defendant because the rule requires a defense "to each claim asserted," not "to each claim asserted against him."

So technically a defendant has to answer material addressed to another defendant. And of course the rule about answering each averment lies. Admitting the liability of another defendant makes no sense. However, there may be allegations which if not denied might be thrown up into defendant's face by a capricious court. Still defendant does not want to spend a lot of time digging out facts to answer allegations directed at others. A defendant can either deny having knowledge or information sufficient to form a belief, or use the following form:

> "Counts (or paragraphs)—to—do not apply to this defendant but insofar as any allegation therein does refer to or may apply to this defendant, denies each and every such allegation."

Here are five more brief tips about answering.

Admit what can be admitted. You give up nothing. You may narrow the scope of discovery. You avoid being forced from a frivolous denial at pre-trial. Also, allege admissions in the answer. Though a failure to deny constitutes an admission, the pleadings are easier to work with if you allege that you admit such-and-such paragraphs or averments.

Be sure to deny performance of conditions precedent, or to allege lack of capacity specifically and with particularity.

When documents are characterized in a pleading or attached as an exhibit, deny the characterization and allege that the document speaks for itself.

Do not answer an allegation by stating, "Neither admit nor deny the allegations of paragraph ____ but leave the plaintiff to his proof." The courts have held this not to be a denial, and have deemed the allegations admitted.

The paragraphs of a complaint do not have to be answered separately. If you have like answers to several different paragraphs, consolidate the answers; e.g. "Admits the allegations of paragraphs 3, 5, 7 through 9 of the complaint. Denies the allegations of paragraphs 1, 2, 4, and 6 of the complaint."

2.6   How to Counterattack in the Answer

You should cover three key topics when you go over the case with the defendant. Are there any jurisdictional or other preliminary motions to be made? What are the facts to meet the allegations of the complaint? Are there any affirmative defenses or counterclaims?

The theory behind asserting a counterclaim goes beyond the compulsory and permissive counterclaim provisions of the rule. A solid counterclaim puts pressure on the plaintiff. By exposing the plaintiff to liability it gives the defendant a bargaining tool. And needless to say it may set the stage for a recovery by the defendant.

In short, defendant must use the answer as a sword as well as a shield. This tactic has become so ingrained that in certain kinds of cases particular kinds of counterclaims have become virtually routine. For example, a seller sues for the price of a piece of

equipment. The buyer counterclaims for damages for breach of
warranty. Or a manufacturer sues for amounts due upon cancellation of a distributorship. The distributor counterclaims for violations of the anti-trust laws. Faced with counterclaims like these,
plaintiff can see the costs escalate and the dangers multiply.

You usually have to probe for the counterclaim. You cannot
expect the client to know the significance of the facts. If you
defend assureds through insurance carriers, you must be constantly on guard about this. The insurance investigation cannot be
relied upon to uncover counterclaims. To illustrate how alert
counsel must be:

The *Walloping Window Blind* and the *Pinafore,* two fine, big
yachts, collided during a major race on the high seas. Both vessels
were on the first windward leg of the race. The *Pinafore,* the last
boat in the prior race, was on a starboard tack. The *Window Blind,*
the lead boat in the succeeding race, was on a port tack and
overtaking the *Pinafore.*

As the burdened vessel, the *Window Blind* yielded the right-
of-way. As the privileged vessel, the *Pinafore* should have maintained
her course and speed. Instead, according to the *Window Blind,* the
Pinfore began and continued to bear off to leeward, steering
directly into the course of and thwarting the efforts of the *Window
Blind* to avoid a collision. With full sail up but with speed much
reduced, the *Pinafore* could not correct her ill-fated leeward swing.
The two vessels collided.

Events at the protest committee need not concern us. The
decision of an insurance adjuster, doubtless a landlubber, does. It
led to a suit in admiralty for damages by the *Pinafore.* The
nominal plaintiff was the owner of the boat; the real party in
interest was the insurance company which had paid for repairs.

The owner of the *Window Blind* turned the case over to his
insurance carrier for defense. Counsel saw nothing in the file on
the obvious repairs to the *Window Blind.* From the assured
counsel ascertained that there had been substantial repairs with
more to come. He alleged a counterclaim. With the both-to-blame
rule of damages in effect in admiralty at that time, he almost
certainly had cut exposure to a minimum. If both vessels are at
fault, and the fault of one is not *de minimus,* the damages of each
are added, divided by two, and half awarded to each.

Then plaintiff served interrogatories. In discussing them the assured happened to mention that the resale value of a yacht, especially one with a reputation as a racing machine, can be affected if she has been in a collision. Counsel thus had the possibility of a second counterclaim for loss of market value.

2.7 How to Spot an Affirmative Defense

An affirmative defense has to be pled affirmatively, or else it is waived. Consequently you must know an affirmative defense when you see one. There are three ways to do this.

An affirmative defense is a confession and avoidance. It says in substance that even assuming plaintiff's allegations are true, he cannot recover for a given reason; e.g., that the statute of limitations has run.

Anything that merely controverts the elements of the plaintiff's *prima facie* case is negative, and need not be set forth affirmatively. Stated otherwise, anything within the scope of the old general denial is a negative.

You have two crutches. Rule 8(c) lists 19 affirmative defenses: accord and satisfaction, arbitration and award, assumption of risk, contributory negligence, discharge in bankruptcy, duress, estoppel, failure of consideration, fraud, illegality, injury by fellow servant, laches, license, payment, release, *res judicata*, statute of frauds, statute of limitations, waiver. In addition, the courts have held the following to be affirmative defenses: circuity of action, comparative negligence, active and passive negligence, election of remedies, exception or exemption created by statute, exclusion in an insurance policy, failure to mitigate damages, immunity, failure to raise a compulsory counterclaim in an earlier action, lack of authority, justification, novation and release, patent litigation defenses (e.g., late claiming, prior use, misuse), prescription, ratification, defamation litigation defenses (e.g., privilege, retraction, truth, fair comment, etc.), unclean hands, failure to comply with statutory provisions, wrong party.

You must guard against one pitfall in diversity actions. State substantive law governs the elements of the *prima facie* claim. For example, state law may require a plaintiff to prove freedom from

fault as part of this case. There are federal cases holding that
nonetheless defendant must plead contributory negligence.

The long and the short of it is that an affirmative defense is
what the court says it is. The moral is that when in doubt plead a
defense affirmatively.

2.8   To Implead or Not to Implead—The Pros
and Cons of Third Party Practice

A defendant may bring an action against a person not a party
to the action who is or may be liable to him for all or part of the
plaintiff's claim against him. This is the heart of the rule.
Strikingly, it is not mandatory. By not impleading, a defendant
does not lose his right to sue later for contribution or indemnity.

The upshot is that defendant has maneuvering room. Here
are some of the tactical considerations.

The third party defendant may contribute toward a settlement. Being in a suit exerts more pressure on a party than the
threat of a future suit.

If the plaintiff fails to sue a logical party defendant—e.g., a
joint tort-feasor—at the trial, the defendant can heap the blame on
the absent party and perhaps get out scot-free.

Sometimes a third party defendant will team up with a
plaintiff to beat the defendant on a claim for which impleader
does not lie.

A defendant might bring a third party defendant in to get his
help. The case of the Lonely Retailer illustrates this. The plaintiff
sued the retailer but not the manufacturer in a technical products
liability case. Apart from the cost of hiring an expert witness,
defendant faced the problem of even being able to find one. He
brought the manufacturer into the case primarily to insure a solid
technical defense.

In admiralty a defendant can bring in a third party defendant
and demand judgment against him in favor of the plaintiff. On the
civil side, a plaintiff can assert a claim against a third party
defendant that arises out of the occurrence on which the claim
against the defendant is based. By offering up the "big enchilada,"
defendant might induce plaintiff to make such a claim. Or he

might manipulate the trial so that plaintiff willy-nilly tries the case against the third party defendant.

Along these lines, a defendant might be tempted to bring in a "target" party as a third party defendant. If defendant thinks he might lose, he offers up the target party to the jury as the one who will actually pay the plaintiff. The case of the Vanquished Victor will show how this works in a moment.

Impleading can snarl a case up in two ways. First, you have another lawyer in the case to live with and cope with. This new boy on the block might be an ace who will do you in if your interests are antagonistic. Or the new boy might be a boob who will pull a boner that ruins the defense even if your interests are the same.

Second, the third-party defendant might complicate the case with counterclaims and cross-claims. A third-party defendant *must* assert compulsory counterclaims against the defendant. He *may* assert permissive counterclaims against a defendant, or he *may* assert cross-claims against other third-party defendants.

Then there are the imponderables. For example, the third-party defendant might be a person for whom the jury will feel sympathy. You must assess how this would affect the case. Also, bringing in a third-party defendant makes him an adverse party. If you had to call him as a witness anyway, making him an adverse party would let you cross-examine him.

These are illustrative of the imponderables and fine points. It would be entertaining to speculate about them, except for the danger of missing the forest for the trees. The fact is that impleading can be a tricky business. It is so tricky, that many case-hardened litigators do not implead unless the reasons for impleading are clear and strong.

The case of the Vanquished Victor illustrates how tricky impleading can be. Plaintiff sued the manufacturer in the federal court and the distributor in the state court on the same products liability claim.

The manufacturer won on a jury verdict in the federal case.

The distributor impleaded the manufacturer in the state action. The manufacturer moved for summary judgment on the grounds of *res adjudicata* or collateral estoppel. The court denied the motion. Since this was not a final order, the manufacturer

could not appeal. At the trial the plaintiff recovered against the
distributor, and the distributor recovered indemnity against the
manufacturer.

The manufacturer appealed. The appellate court affirmed!
Rule 14 says that a third-party defendant *may* assert against the
plaintiff any defense the defendant has to plaintiff's claim. The
court read "may assert" to mean "must assert." It held that the
manufacturer should have pled the defense of *res adjudicata*. The
court said that if the defense were not pled, the distributor would
be stripped of its right to indemnity.

The court's reasoning falters on analysis. But that is not the
point. The point is twofold. Defendant's offering up of a target
party paid off, and third-party practice cannot be taken lightly.

2.9   A Pleadings Checklist for Plaintiff and Defendant

As counsel for either plaintiff or defendant, you will profit
by this checklist. At one glance you can see what you and your
opponent have to consider. You will protect yourself from
overlooking something. You can see options open to your opponent and guard against them. You can spot if your opponent
overlooks anything.

Checklist

Limitations Periods—in statutes, regulations, ordinances,
contracts, insurance policies, etc.

Conditions Precedent to Suit—demands, administrative
claims, claims against an estate, notices, return of service *non
est inventus* for direct action suit against insurer, corporation
registered within state, etc.

Notice of Appearance

Choice of Laws

Class Action Possibilities

Claims—assertion of all possible claims and theories
(e.g., counts in negligence, breach of warranty, and strict
liability).

Joinder of Claims—all claims arising out of the same transaction must be joined.

Joinder of Remedies

Parties and Joinder of Parties:

    Necessary Parties

    Permissive Parties

    Suit in Name of the Real Party in Interest

    Direct Action Suit Against Insurer (Check for Conditions Precedent).

    Capacity of Party to Sue or Be Sued

Pleading Special Matters Under Rules 8 and 9 in the Complaint, and in the Complaint and Answer.

Jury Demand in Complaint

Need to Post Bond

Jurisdiction:

    Subject Matter

    Personal

    Diversity of Citizenship in Federal Diversity Action

    Jurisdictional Amount

    "Long Arm" Statutory Jurisdiction

    Collusive Jurisdiction 28 U.S.C. 1359

    Removal to Federal Court and Remand to State Court

    Venue, Transfer to a More Convenient Forum, *Forum Non*

Conveniens

Service:

    Personal

    Substituted

Provisional and Extraordinary Remedies—Attachment, Arrest, Temporary Restraining Order, Etc.

Motions Before Answer Under Rule 12.

Compulsory and Permissive Counterclaims and Cross-Claims

Affirmative Defenses

Limitation of Liability in Admiralty (Note: Can be asserted as a defense by a defendant, and in a complaint by a plaintiff.)

Jury Demand in Answer
Third-Party Practice
Reply to Counterclaims or Answer to Cross-Claims
Motions to Attack Insufficient Defenses
Excess Letter to Assured
Intervention
Interpleader
Motion to Sever or for Separate Trials
Certification by the Federal Court of a Question of State Law to the State Court

3

How to Make Your Motion Practice
Pay Dividends

3.1 How to Decide Whether to Make a Motion:
The Risk/Return Ratio

In some ways, modern procedure can be called "motion madness." The rules provide for dozens of different motions. The average case provides dozens of opportunities to make a motion. The bar has not let these opportunities slip by.

Because a motion can be made does not mean that it should be made.

There is a test for whether to make a motion, the risk/return ratio. How do the risks of losing the motion compare with the gains of winning it? There are several corollaries to this test.

The first corollary is especially important. With many motions there is no appreciable down-side risk. If the motion is denied, the case reverts to the *status quo ante.*

In the case of the "Old Woman" who died, counsel made a motion with no down-side risk, realizing that he probably would lose the motion but hoping that the motion would provide the key to unlock a legal riddle.

Wall Street knew the New York, Ontario, and Western Railway as the "Old Woman." Others, from the logo on her 46 diesel locomotives, knew the road as the "O & W." The main line of the O & W ran between Oswego, New York, its northern terminus on Lake Ontario, and Cornwall, New York, on the Hudson River; trackage rights over the West Shore Division of the New York Central gave it a southern terminus at Weehawken, New Jersey. Altogether the O & W operated on 541 miles of track.

The O & W had been conceived in 1870 to connect the Great Lakes with the port of New York. However, as *The New York Times* put it, "Experience quickly proved what a look at the map might have shown: that Buffalo, giving water-level access to all the Midwest, was many times better as an outlet in that direction than Oswego, from which shippers could reach the heartland only by climbing around or over Niagara Falls." For that and other reasons, from virtually the beginning, the O & W struggled to make ends meet.

In fact, the O & W did not make ends meet. For 19 years the road had been operated in a railroad reorganization proceeding under section 77 of the Bankruptcy Act. In those 19 years only four plans of reorganization had been submitted to the Interstate Commerce Commission. However, also in those years approximately $100,000,000 in operating deficits had been run up. Of this, over $7,000,000 was for federal taxes, interest, and penalties, including over $2,000,000 in withholding taxes which by law are trust funds. The Internal Revenue Service estimated that withholding tax was accruing at a rate of $800,000 per year. To make matters worse, the I.R.S. had received complaints that some O & W employees had received income tax refunds.

The railroad's future looked as bleak as its past, and the Government could not let the state of affairs go on forever. Yet the problems seemed insuperable. The towns along the right of way wanted the O & W to continue in operation, as did the trustee. The judge in charge of the reorganization proceeding by statute had to bend his efforts towards effectuating a reorganization. (The statute optimistically contemplated the elimination of delay in the reorganization of railroads. More optimistically yet, it contemplated that railroads could be reorganized; it had little to say about what happened if a railroad could not be reorganized.)

The biggest problem was that the O & W, running as it was with annual deficits in the millions of dollars, could not pay its taxes, federal, much less state or local, and stay in operation.

The Government finally lurched off dead center. Government counsel moved in the reorganization proceeding for an order requiring the trustee to segregate and hold separately all withheld taxes as they accrued, and to pay them over quarterly when due.

Counsel expected to lose the motion, and he did. The judge said that although the proposed order had no greater effect than the provisions of the law itself, he was sure the trustee would attempt to comply with the order. He was equally sure, he added, the trustee would be unable to do so, and "that operations of the Road would cease."

The motion had no down-side risk. If lost, the *status quo* continued. In fact, the motion served notice that the *status quo* could not continue for long. And it did not. Within a few weeks the ICC refused to approve pending plans of reorganization. It found that no plan of reorganization was possible then or in the foreseeable future. It recommended that the court dismiss the proceedings. Arguably, the exposure of the tax situation by the motion had a bearing on the recommendation.

From that point events moved rapidly, the engine still being the insupportable tax situation. An outright dismissal of the proceedings would have led to a rash of foreclosure actions. However, there had been no pre-existing equity receivership proceedings as a receptacle into which the assets could be conveyed. Counsel solved the problem by proposing commencement of a foreclosure action and the appointment of receivers under the Internal Revenue Code. The reorganization court modified its standing order to permit that action. The Government commenced it. The foreclosure court appointed receivers. The reorganization court dismissed the reorganization proceeding and ordered the trustee to convey the O & W's assets to the receivers.

The receivers liquidated the O & W. Several years later the receivers sent the Government a check for close to $4,000,000. A good day's work for a motion with no down-side risk.

The second corollary is that the lack of an appreciable

down-side risk has given rise to a dangerous "nothing ventured, nothing gained" approach toward motions. This is ill conceived for two reasons.

Litigation has become expensive. The cost of handling many cases has outstripped the value of the cases or the ability of the client to pay. It becomes a matter of allocating scarce resources. So, cost as well as risk must be weighed against benefits in deciding to make a motion.

The approach also breeds carelessness. Each motion has to be thought through. Though with many motions there is no down-side risk, the loss of an ill-conceived motion can be a major setback. An admiralty case illustrates why.

In admiralty certain types of claims give rise to a maritime lien. A lien claim supports a suit *in rem* against the vessel. Service is effected by seizing the vessel with a warrant of arrest.

Admiralty also recognizes suits *in personam* against the owner of the vessel. A claim giving rise to a maritime lien can be brought both *in rem* and *in personam.* But a claim not giving rise to a lien can only be brought *in personam.*

In an *in personam* action, service can be made in two ways. If the defendant can be served within the district, service must be by personal service. If the defendant cannot be found within the district, and only if this is so, service can be by seizing the vessel by a writ of foreign attachment.

Attachment in an *in personam* action confers jurisdiction. It also affords security for a judgment but only as an incident of acquiring jurisdiction. Regardless of a need for security, attachment does not lie in an *in personam* suit which was or could have been commenced by personal service within the district.

This wrinkle has led to a clever tactic. If a threat of attachment exists, the owner of the ship will file a notice of appearance in the action or otherwise subject himself to personal jurisdiction in the district.

These intricate rules provide the framework for the case styled the "Elusive Maritime" Lien.

Defendant was a foreign corporation with headquarters overseas. Its sole asset was a 16,000-ton cargo vessel. Plaintiff claimed that extensive negotiations had resulted in a charter of the vessel.

Defendant disputed this. In any event defendant did not deliver the vessel.

Later, on a tip that the vessel would put into a certain American port, plaintiff commenced a damage action for breach of charter, alleging a lien claim *in rem* against the ship and a claim *in personam* against the owner.

Then the fun began. The clerk refused to issue two processes. No district judge could be reached to straighten the matter out. By chance the clerk issued the warrant of arrest.

This set up a brilliant defense strategy. Within hours after the arrest, defendant filed a notice of appearance. Though defendant denied a charter party, it also contended that at best it was an executory contract. Breach of an executory contract does not create a maritime lien!

So that the ship could sail, defendant posted a letter of undertaking without prejudice.

The ship sailed and the parties took a deep breath for the battles to come. Plaintiff opened with a motion for summary judgment based on affidavits and hundreds of Telexs.

Defendant countered with a motion to vacate the arrest and revoke the undertaking. It argued that the charter was executory, and consequently no lien arose to support an action *in rem* and the warrant of arrest.

This was the key motion. If defendant won the motion for practical purposes, it won the case. Plaintiff would still have a suit but would not have any security for a judgment. In the nature of things this meant a worthless judgment. The ship was the sole corporate asset. At best and if lucky, plaintiff could seize it in some remote port. At worst defendant could put it out of reach entirely by selling it.

Plaintiff responded with a motion for issuance of a writ of foreign attachment *nunc pro tunc* on the ground that the clerk had a ministerial duty to issue it.

Then defendant moved for arbitration under the arbitration clause in the charter (the arbitrators have power to decide if a charter exists), and to stay proceedings pending arbitration.

The court granted the motion to arbitrate and to stay. It also refused to rule on any of the other motions.

A risk/return analysis would have revealed the danger. This last motion gave the court a perfect solution. The law favors arbitration. If the arbitrators found no charter had been fixed, that ended matters. If they found that a charter had been fixed, then the court could tackle the jurisdictional problems.

The third corollary is comparing the utility of the motion with the utility of different courses of action. Pleading a rule 12(b) defense, for example, keeps the threat of that defense alive up to the trial. This might accomplish more than raising the defense by motion. If the motion is lost, the threat recedes to a mere point on appeal.

A fourth corollary is that sometimes the risk/return ratio has to be measured in technical terms. A motion may be necessary to make a record or preserve a right to take a later step in the action.

3.2   Forecasting How Your Motion Will Do in Court

Three factors explain how motions fare in court: the rules are designed to achieve certain ends; judges have different predilections and work habits; by and large the courts are busy.

Discovery motions provide a good example of these factors in practice. Discovery is the moving force in modern procedure. But it can be abused. Consequently, the rules provide for objections and protective orders. Nevertheless, to make the rules work discovery has to be favored.

Also the scope of discovery is broad. On a discovery motion the court tends to assume relevancy. It rarely will go beneath the surface to determine relevancy. Part of this is due to bedrock theory. Part is due to the work load imposed by the huge number of discovery motions. Part is due to the judicial attitude that handling discovery motions is coolie work.

And at times part is due to judicial predilection. In the case of the Predisposed Jurist, defendant refused to produce a witness statement on the ground that it was work product, that it had been taken orally, etc. The judge gave short shrift to defendant's arguments. He ruled for the plaintiff, commenting, "I interpret the discovery rules to favor plaintiffs."

Other things being equal, motions seeking to limit discovery must be well-grounded.

Motions attacking the pleadings as pleadings are not favored. As mentioned before, the consequence is a raft of sloppy pleadings. The courts apparently believe this is the price of not reintroducing the common law technicalities of pleading.

The rules also seek to avoid a multiplicity of suits. To achieve this they provide for the liberal joinder of parties and claims. But joinder run wild can cause complex trials. So the rules also provide for severance and separate trials. Once a true degree of complexity is reached, motions to sever tend to stand or fall on the nature of the complexity. The confidence of the judge in his ability to handle a complex case plays a covert role.

Motions seeking final resolution of the case face one big hurdle. Most judges believe a party should have his "day in court." This explains the common fate of the motion to dismiss. The court grants it with leave in the plaintiff to replead within "x" number of days. More often than not plaintiff makes up the deficiency in the amended complaint.

Summary judgment will be discussed later. For present purposes, it is enough to point out that the courts do not favor summary judgment in cases where credibility plays a role in determining the facts. In the case of the Phantom Tank Cleaner, for example, a seaman claimed he sustained a lung ailment while cleaning tanks. The ship's records proved that plaintiff did not work in the tanks on the days he claimed he did, or indeed ever had on any but a very few days. Defendant moved for summary judgment. The court denied the motion on the literal ground that the case was a negligence case.

Occasionally, an unmeritorious suit can be "deep-sixed" on motion. In the case of the Seagoing Lawyer, a seaman sued *pro se*. The court dismissed the action on defendant's motion but gave the seaman leave to replead. This happened several times. Finally, on defendant's motion to dismiss the fourth or fifth amended complaint, the court got plaintiff to admit there was nothing to what he said.

"But now," the court asked him, "is there anything else you claim the ship did to you?"

The seaman pondered. Then his face brightened. "Yes, your honor," he said, "The captain threw my law library overboard."

One last point. Some judges are bullet-biters. They will decide tough motions. Other judges are duckers and weavers. They will avoid deciding tough motions. And they can get away with it. Appeal from the denial of a motion is limited. This is one reason you should judge shop when you make a motion. The other reason is to get an able and impartial judge.

3.3　The Tactics of a Successful Motion Practice—How to Spot the Pivotal Situations Where a Motion Will Help Win the Case

A lot of motions are waste motion. Whether they are made or not, and whether they are won or lost hardly make a ripple in the case. But sometimes a particular motion or a series of motions can affect the outcome of the case.

This much is obvious, but there is more to it than that. There are certain situations that recur in litigation. They crop up often enough to be recognized as pivotal and as requiring a motion. Five of these situations can be mentioned:

- To shape the course the case will take.
- To compel or resist essential discovery.
- To get leverage in the case.
- To prove that the moving party means business in the prosecution or defense of the case.
- As the step on which the case will be won or lost.

3.3.1　How to Shape the Course of the Case into Favorable Channels

A widow sued under a state wrongful death statute. Her husband had been killed while making repairs to a vessel within the navigable territorial water of the state.

The Supreme Court had recently held that the general

maritime law provided the exclusive remedy. The court did not go into the elements of damage. It left that to be fashioned by the courts below observing that they would be guided by the Jones Act, the Death on the High Seas Act, and the various state wrongful death statutes.

The plaintiff preferred the state wrongful death statute. It based damages on loss to the decedent's estate. It also provided that economic trends could be taken into account in calculating damages.

The defendant preferred the general maritime law. The two maritime statutes and most state wrongful death statutes based damages on pecuniary loss to the beneficiaries. This rule of damages generally nets any recovery out lower than loss to the decedent's estate.

Defendant's counsel saw that he had two crucial motions. To dismiss and, after plaintiff filed a new complaint, move for an order setting forth the elements of damages under the general maritime law.

Plaintiff consented to the first motion but after filing a new complaint fought like a Turk on the second motion. The reference to state wrongful death statutes, she insisted, required adoption of the key concept of the particular statute, loss to decedent's estate. Defendant argued pecuniary loss to beneficiaries.

After some "waffling" the court ruled in defendant's favor. It asked the parties to submit orders. Plaintiff's order recited that pecuniary loss to beneficiaries was the applicable rule. But it defined the rule in terms of the state wrongful death statute.

The court signed plaintiff's order!

Defendants' counsel sized up the situation instantly. Either the court had made a mistake or the difference between the two rules of damages had not been made clear. Counsel moved to resettle the order. In support of the motion he filed a detailed memorandum. It traced the history of wrongful death actions. It elaborated the differences between the rules. It listed the elements of the different rules. And it pin-pointed the errors in the order entered by the court.

The court granted the motion and entered a proper order.

3.3.2   How a Motion Can Crucially Affect
          Discovery

The wrongful death case also illustrates the need for a motion on important discovery.

After the enormous effort the case seemed headed in the right direction. Defendants had to wait for the ruling and order before they could serve interrogatories on damages. Before that interrogatories on how plaintiff calculated damages would only have elicited answers framed in terms of the state wrongful death statute and not the general maritime law.

Defendants served the interrogatories. For answers plaintiff attached the report of an economist prepared in terms of the state wrongful death statute. To boot she did not identify which sections of the report related to specific interrogatories.

Defendants had to move to compel responsive answers. Without the information they would go to trial blind in this vital area. But "once bitten, twice shy." Defendants spelled out the travel of the case, and exactly how the answers fell short of the mark.

The court granted the motion.

3.3.3   How a Motion Can Give Leverage in the
          Case

Litigation often is a see-saw affair. First one side then the other has the initiative, depending on which side has taken the last step. But sometimes counsel has to seize the initiative. He has to get leverage and force his opponent's hand. A well-conceived motion many times is the answer.

In the case of a "Million Dollar Tanker" a bank foreclosed a first-preferred ship mortgage on a once proud but now venerable tanker. The judicial sale of the vessel came during an acute shortage of bottoms. The ship sold for almost twice its appraised value. The administration costs advanced by the bank, the balance due on the mortgage, and the claims of third parties came to $1,000,000.

The distribution of proceeds should have been simple. But some creditors would not scale down their claims. Others tried to escalate their claims into a lien status. One or two implied that collusion between the mortgagee and owner invalidated the mortgage as to third-party claims.

But worse for the bank, its claim was huge compared to even the largest of the other claims. The major creditor began to stall. He hoped delay would put pressure on the bank.

Counsel for the bank spotted the Fabian tactics. He knew that in time the other creditors, especially crew members with claims, would press for distribution. He also knew the court would not spend days passing on claims in a case that would settle itself but for an intransigent party.

The key was to let the matter ripen. Despite importuning from the bank itself, counsel held out. When the creditors became restive he hatched two motions. One was for reimbursement from the sale proceeds of administration expenses. (This was an undisputed top priority claim.) The other was for payment to the bank on account the mortgage debt of the remaining proceeds, except for an amount representing the total of the creditors' claims. The creditors could not deny the debt of the owner to the bank.

The bank made the first motion for administration expenses. The hold-out creditor snapped up the bait. It opposed the motion, filing a memorandum that nit-picked the account of administration expenses.

The court roared. It told counsel to present a plan of distribution within a month.

In one stroke counsel for the bank got the whip-hand. He surfaced his plan—payment of administration expenses to the bank; payment to each compromising creditor in the full amount of the compromise; holding in the registry of court an amount representing the total of the claims of non-compromising creditors; payment of the balance to the bank on account of the debt.

The case settled without a hitch. Counsel first got the crews' attorney, a realistic litigator, to agree on a formula. With one major creditor in line, he readily got the others to follow suit, even the hard-nosed ones.

3.3.4   How to Use Motions to Make the Other
Side Realize It has a Fight on Its Hands

To illustrate by way of an example, a woman plaintiff bowled a duck-pin record. The bowling pin manufacturer got her to pose for a publicity photograph. Then, through a mix-up, it used the photograph in a national advertising brochure without getting plaintiff's written consent.

Plaintiff sued in the federal court for invasion of privacy. The state did not recognize that cause of action.

The federal court had several times sustained new theories on the ground that if presently faced with them the state courts would do likewise. Also, on a choice-of-laws analysis, the court could choose the law of another state to sustain the claims.

Still defendant moved to dismiss. If defendant won the motion, plaintiff was out. If defendant lost the motion, defendant had a point on appeal hanging over plaintiff's head. And, won or lost, defendant made clear its intention to fight the case all the way. Defendant lost the motion.

All the while defendant had another motion in the wings. Plaintiff had no damages. A federal case on all fours had dismissed a like claim for failure to meet the jurisdictional amount. Plaintiff's deposition confirmed her lack of damages.

Despite the favorable authority, counsel knew he stood less than an even chance to win even this motion. In fact, defendant lost this motion too. But the strategy paid off. Plaintiff's counsel saw still another forbidding point on appeal. He faced an expensive and tough trial. He knew that at best plaintiff's damages were marginal.

The case settled for a reasonable figure.

3.3.5   How a Case Can Stand or Fall on the
Outcome of a Motion

The instances where the whole case stands or falls on a motion tend to be obvious. Many of these instances involve temporary restraining orders or preliminary injunctions. If a threatened action is not stopped or the status quo maintained for practical purposes, the case is lost. A case involving a strike makes this point.

An employer announced that on a certain date a certain policy would go into effect. The local union threatened a strike.

The employer sought a temporary restraining order. It alleged three key points: that the collective bargaining agreement contained a no-strike clause and an arbitration clause; that the grievance over the new policy was arbitral; that an illegal walk-out would harm the employer more than an injunction would harm the union.

The local union was given notice of the application for the temporary restraining order. It did not appear. After a short presentation, the court granted the temporary restraining order. Counsel for the employer served it immediately.

The wild-cat strike never materialized. The union agreed to continuance of the temporary restraining order indefinitely. Ultimately, the union agreed to a permanent injunction. And it never even processed a grievance!

3.4   How to Double the Benefits from a Motion for Summary Judgment

3.4.1   Summary Judgment in a Nutshell

Summary judgment pierces the pleadings to see if there is a genuine issue as to any material fact. If there is not, there is no need for a trial. The court need only look to the substantive law. It can enter judgment for the moving party if the law favors him. It can also enter judgment for the non-moving party—if instead the law favors him.

The court can do three further things. It can enter partial judgment on phases of the case. For example, it can enter judgment on liability but require a trial on damages. It can enter judgment for one or more but not all of the parties to an action. It can enter what is essentially a pre-trial order that certain facts are not in controversy at the trial.

A motion for summary judgment must be based on material that would be admissible in evidence. These materials include depositions, answers to interrogatories, admissions, and affidavits. The rule spells out the form of affidavit.

A party against whom a motion for summary judgment is made may not rest upon his pleadings. He must controvert the motion by affidavits and other evidentiary materials. If an adverse party cannot get affidavits, he may file an affidavit setting forth the reasons why.

Summary judgment in the rule and summary judgment in the court are two different things. The rule applies to all types of cases. The courts draw some important distinctions.

In the first place, summary judgment deprives a party of his day in court. It should, of course, if there is no fact in controversy. But as mentioned earlier, a number of judges shy from such radical surgery. This is especially true where one party is an unsophisticated litigant.

In the second place some types of cases lend themselves to summary judgment more than others. Where the nature of the facts are such that cross-examination and assessing the witnesses are important to finding the facts, trial not summary judgment is appropriate. Where the critical facts are within the control and knowledge of one party, summary judgment may not be appropriate either.

On the other hand where the facts are firm, for example as in an action on a contract or a lease or on book account or a note, summary judgment more readily lies.

One further preliminary point. If matters outside the pleadings are considered on a motion to dismiss for failure to state a claim or on a motion for judgment on the pleadings, the motion must be treated as one for summary judgment.

3.4.2   How to Win Outright or Gain a Tactical Advantage with Summary Judgment

These basic points furnish the guidelines for the use of summary judgment.

It can be used where clearly the moving party should win.

The so-called partial summary judgment is a flexible tool. It fills a considerable gap in the rules. It appears to be the only way to knock out individual affirmative defenses where facts must be adduced. The case of the Exploding "T" illustrates this.

A steam line burst in the tenant's premises. A surge of steam shot into the line causing a rupture at a "T" intersection of pipes. Steam and water caused hundreds of thousands of dollars worth of damage to the tenant's inventory.

In an affirmative defense in its answer, the landlord pled a clause in the lease. The clause, a familiar one in landlord-drawn leases, exculpated the landlord from its own negligence. The courts of the state had narrowly construed such clauses. Unless such clauses were explicit they were nugatory.

The tenant did not want that clause in the lease or that defense to be brought up before the jury at trial. To knock it out, the tenant had to move for summary judgment (or for partial judgment on the pleadings if there is such a thing), appending the lease to the tenant's affidavit.

The tenant won the motion.

Summary judgment can smoke out an opponent from an ambiguous position because he must file affidavits. The case of the Waffling Denial typifies thousands of cases in the courts every year. Plaintiff sued on a note. Defendant would not admit, but he could not deny or deny having knowledge or information sufficient to form a belief. So he pled the notorious waffling defense, "Neither admits nor denies but leaves the plaintiff to his proof."

This averment amounts to an admission since it is not a specific denial. But many courts do not enforce the rule. Counsel can buy time and perhaps a discounted settlement with the waffling defense.

Here, counsel for plaintiff did not fool around. He got defendant to admit his signature. Based on the admission, he moved for an obtained summary judgment.

The case of the Improvident Option shows the strength of summary judgment to smoke out an opponent in more sophisticated situations.

A lease gave the tenant an option to buy the property at any time during the term of the lease or any renewals at a price fixed in the lease. The lease also gave the landlord power to cancel the lease on 180 days' notice plus certain payments.

The landlord gave notice that "I will terminate the lease" on such and such a date (which was 180 days from the date of the notice).

Before the expiration of the 180 days and the date in the notice, the tenant exercised his option to purchase.

The landlord refused to convey. Over the many years of the lease and renewals, the value of the property had sky-rocketed from the fixed price. The tenant sued for specific performance. The landlord filed an ambiguous answer. However, the landlord did agree to a stipulation of facts.

The tenant moved for summary judgment on the stipulation. The landlord filed an affidavit in opposition. In it he tried to raise ambiguities to justify parole evidence. The court denied the motion. In its opinion the court seemed to say it found no issue of fact, but was not altogether clear on the point.

The landlord took heart from the opinion. Abandoning his attempt to create an ambiguity, the landlord moved for summary judgment. The court granted this motion. The court stated that it based this and its prior decision solely on the lease, which it said was not ambiguous, and not on the landlord's affidavit.

On the surface it might look like the tenant had made an ill-conceived motion. However, the one reported case on the point in the country favored the tenant, as did general principles of lease law. The tenant appealed. The Court of Appeals sustained the appeal and issued a mandate for the court below to enter judgment for the tenant.

The motion for summary judgment here forced the landlord to take a position. In making it the tenant had no down-side risk. And very important, the tenant avoided a trial. At a trial, especially in a non-jury case, the tenant would have run the risk that the court would have let in parole testimony of the landlord. Because the lease had been executed years before, the tenant would have had difficulty finding the employees who had negotiated and entered into the lease.

3.4.3   How to Stop a Motion for Summary Judgment in Its Tracks

There are four lines of defense to a motion for summary judgment.

The first and strongest is to show or create a genuine issue of material fact. This means filing affidavits and other material in opposition to the motion.

The second line is to expose the invalidity of the materials in support of the motion, for example hearsay in the supporting affidavits.

The third line is adroit exploitation of the nature of the case. This works best obviously when the case hinges on crucial facts involving credibility.

The fourth line is to emphasize (if such be the case) the moving party's nearly exclusive knowledge and control of the facts.

4

How to Streamline
the Preparation of the Case
and Organize It
for Fingertip Presentation
at Trial—The Trial Book
Technique

4.1 The Trial Book—The Secret Weapon the Top Litigators Use to Win Trials

The smooth performance at trial of the top trial lawyer does not just happen. He has prepared his case down to the last detail. He has the entire case at his fingertips during trial. The trial book technique is a major key to his success. It is the basic tool in preparing the case as well as in trying it.

The trial book contains all of the material you will need at the trial. It also tells you where anything you need to refer to may be found. It organizes that material into appropriate categories for instant use at the trial.

The trial book is also an aid in preparation. To reap its full benefits, you must start it early. You have to think the case through to decide upon the categories you need for both the preparation and trial of the case. As the case progresses, you can eliminate or consolidate categories, or add new ones.

There is no hard-and-fast rule about the contents of the trial book. The hallmark of the technique is flexibility. The amount of preparation and how that preparation is organized will vary with the case and the lawyer. Because of their importance, however, certain matters have become standard for inclusion in the trial book. Others almost as important have become standard options. As will be seen often, categories can be merged. The following list contains both the standards and standard options:

 a. The preparation agenda.

 b. The analysis of the issues.

 c. The outline of proof.

 d. Notes for the selection of jurors.

 e. Notes for the opening statement.

 f. A list of witnesses pro and con.

 g. Witness sheets for direct examination.

 h. Notes for cross-examination.

 i. Index of discovery material to be used at trial.

 j. Notes and briefs on law and evidence, and trial motions.

 k. Requests for charge.

 l. Notes for final argument.

 m. List of exhibits and exhibit file.

 n. A master index and cross-indices.

 o. The trial agenda and "do list."

Special categories can be added when needed: a "medical brief" capsulizing medical information in a personal injury case

(Chapter 9); a section on technical matters in a products liability case; a section on damage calculations in a wrongful death action or contract action.

4.2   The Format and General Use of the Trial Book—Litigation-Tested Methods for Setting Up and Using the Trial Book

The heart of the trial book is an 8-1/2 x 11 inch three-ring loose-leaf binder with separators. The separators are tabbed with the categories you intend to use. The loose-leaf feature provides flexibility in adding or subtracting categories.

You will also need folders to hold materials generated during preparation—correspondence, memoranda, exhibits, etc. One of the folders will bind-in copies of court papers that are tabbed and indexed as they are sent and received. A conventional jacket or accordion file is used to store the folders.

There are two keys to unlocking the benefits of the trial book.

The first is memorandize everything. It prevents duplication of effort. It keeps ideas from getting lost. It facilitates preparing the trial book in final form for use at trial.

Memorandizing ranges from jotting down an idea to preparing a memorandum of law. For example, during preparation you get an idea for the opening statement. Jot it down in the section on the opening. When you sit down to prepare the opening, the idea is there. Or you may look up some cases on a point. Note them in the trial book, or dictate a memorandum for filing in the memorandum file.

The other key to the successful use of the trial book is to work on all phases of the case. In other words, do not unduly postpone doing things that have to be done. The format of the trial book helps here. It keeps all of the categories constantly in front of you.

Memorandizing and pacing the work make the trial book valuable in two other circumstances. If the court unexpectedly calls the case for trial or a pre-trial conference, you will not be caught short. Or if a dormant case comes to life, you do not have to go back and pick up pieces.

You can make notes and store material in the notebook or in the folders, whichever suits your convenience. All of the preparation is utilized when you put the trial book and its supporting devices into final form for use at trial.

The pay-off for the trial book technique comes at trial. The notebook lies unobtrusively on the counsel table or lectern. It does not obtrude itself between you and the court and the jury. The exhibits are organized and stored for ready access. Nothing is misplaced. Nothing has been overlooked in preparation.

The contrast between the lawyer who impresses the jury with a crisp presentation and the "one-armed paper hanger" can be dramatic. The case of the Cumbrous Counsel is a good example.

One attorney tried the case from a thick loose-leaf binder so bulging with papers that the rings barely closed. He had every question and answer written out. He examined each witness by reading each question.

Then, inadvertently, he knocked his trial book to the floor. It burst open, spewing papers in every direction.

Like a flash his opponent leaped to his feet.

"Your Honor," he said. "We need a recess. Mr. Schmidlap just lost the script."

Laughter cascaded from the jury.

4.3　The Preparation Agenda—How to Keep Track of What Has to Be Done

At the beginning of the case, you must plan how you intend to prepare it. The preparation agenda is the list of these steps, in the order you intend to take them in. Often you should set deadlines for taking certain steps.

As you take a step, check it off. As other steps occur to you, add them to the agenda.

The preparation agenda is more than a mere list. It is the blueprint for preparation.

The discipline of working up a preparation agenda thus confers the benefits of rational planning. The early analysis of the case gives you a good idea about the costs of preparation. The listing prevents you from overlooking small but important things to do. An up-to-date list with steps checked off reveals the status of preparation at a glance.

4.4   The Analysis of the Issues—How to Make Sure That You Know Each and Every Issue in the Case

The pleadings and facts determine the issues in the case.

There is a distinction between the existence of an issue and its status as a disputed issue or an undisputed issue. For example, the answer might admit a jurisdictional allegation in the complaint. However, you still must be aware that jurisdiction is an issue, and whether it has to be proven or not.

"Pleadings" is used in the broad sense of all court papers. For example, a pre-trial order or an answer to an interrogatory might eliminate a disputed issue from the case.

Occasionally, issues will be implicit in the facts but not explicit in the pleadings. The last clear chance doctrine is an example.

The Analysis of the Issues starts with the pleadings in the broad sense. Issues implicit in the facts are worked in. The analysis should be prepared early in the case. As new issues develop, and old issues become undisputed, the analysis must be updated.

The Analysis of Issues does several things. It forces you to formulate vague allegations into precise issues. It provides you with guidelines for discovery and investigation. It pin-points which issues have to be proven and which do not, and thus serves as the basis for the vital Outline of Proof. It lets you refresh your recollection about the issues on the eve of trial.

The format is simple. Each separate allegation in the complaint is identified and numbered. The number is indicated in column 1. The substance of the allegation is set forth in column 2. The answering allegations in one or more answers are set forth in columns 3, 4, etc. Material pertaining to the issue in another court paper (pre-trial order, answer to interrogatory, etc.) would be set forth in still another column.

The following example is an excerpt from the Analysis of Issues in the case of the Man-Made Cove, a suit against a boatman for trespass upon a private, man-made cove on Long Island Sound.

Until the turn of the century, the area had been a salt marsh with a small creek meandering through it. Then dredging operations commenced for sand. They continued intermittently over the years. Finally, a large cove was formed with an opening to the Sound.

Boatmen used the cove for many years. With the upsurge of boating, the cove became a popular spot. Of a weekend hundreds of boats would use it, many mooring overnight. Vandalism and dangerous boating began to get out of hand. The owner of a large part of the cove (Parcel A) had to hire a policeman to patrol it.

One boatman would not recognize the owner's right to patrol the property. The boatman contended the waters were navigable in law and in fact, and that in any event a prescriptive right had arisen in the public.

The dispute spiraled in intensity. One day the boatman defied a request of the officer who thereupon issued a police court summons. The owner also sued for trespass. The boatman counter-claimed for assault by the officer.

The case turned on the nature of the cove. If artificial the public easement of navigation did not attach to the waters, if natural the easement did. A fine point involved the former creek. If it had been navigable, the cove might be deemed the expansion of navigable waters, and hence navigable itself.

EXAMPLE OF AN ANALYSIS
OF THE ISSUES

Issue #	Issues Raised in Complaint	Answer
1	Plaintiff owner, and in possession of Parcel A, ¶1	DKI ¶1
2	Parcel A originally consisted of lowlands, marshes, meadows, ¶2	DKI ¶2
3	Plaintiff and his predecessors in ownership of Parcel A caused dredging of cove and opening to Sound, ¶3	Deny ¶3

4	Defendant frequently used Parcel A from _____ to _____ as an anchorage, and used the beach for swimming and picnicking, ¶4	Admit ¶4
5	This use was without plantiff's consent and over his objection, ¶4	Deny ¶4
6	Defendant's use was unlawful, wilful, wanton, and over plaintiff's objection, ¶4	Deny ¶4
7	Defendant threatens to continue such use, ¶5	Admit intention to use. Deny unlawfulness. ¶5

Issues Raised in Answer

19	For more than 36 years, public has used Parcel A for boating, fishing, swimming, etc., ¶5
20	For more than 36 years, commercial fishermen have used Parcel A as harbor shell-fishing area, and harbor of refuge, ¶6
21	Parcel is navigable in fact and in law, ¶7
22	Defendant's frequent use of Parcel A has been peaceful, ¶8
23	From _____ to _____ no one attempted to prohibit defendant or any member of the public from using Parcel A for boating, fishing, or swimming, ¶9

...

Issues Raised in Counterclaim	Reply
27	Plaintiff supplied the patrolmen with a police badge,

revolver, whistle, and summons
book, ¶14   Admit ¶1

Issues Raised in Answer
_____

28   On [date the police court
            summons was served] the
            patrolman put defendant and
            members of his family in
            apprehension of physical harm
            while on his (defendant's)
            boat, ¶15   Deny ¶2
29   The patrolman's actions were
            done on instructions from
            plaintiff in order to frighten
            defendant and his family, ¶16   Deny ¶3

Issue #   Issues Raised in Answer
_____   _____

30   Defendant and his family sus-
            tained damages of $____, ¶16   Deny ¶3

                        . . .

Issues Raised by Affirmative Defense in Reply
_____

31   On [date the police court summons was
            served] the patrolman served a summons
            on defendant upon advice of plaintiff's
            counsel to protect plaintiff's property,
            and without malice, ¶4

**4.5   The Outline of Proof—The Ironclad Way
          to Make Sure You Know What Proof You
          Need to Prove the Issues, and That You
          Have This Proof**

The Outline of Proof is a key section in the trial book.
Virtually the entire preparation of the case goes into preparing
it—the analysis of issues, witness statements, discovery material,
documents, demonstrative evidence, legal research.

To prepare the Outline of Proof you must analyze each issue in the case in terms of the component facts to prove that issue, and in turn analyze each component fact in terms of the proof (evidence) and rules of evidence necessary to establish that fact. The Outline of Proof thus sets forth:

a. each issue in the case,

b. each fact necessary to prove each issue,

c. each item of proof (evidence) available to prove each fact, and any pertinent rule of evidence.

The Outline of Proof helps you in many ways. It forces you to marshal the evidence. It lets you assess the strengths and weaknesses and gaps in the proof. It shows what you must do to shore up the proof. It warns you if you should settle the case as, for example, where a vital piece of proof cannot be found. It facilitates your decisions about the order of proof at trial. It helps you prepare the witness sheets and trial agenda.

An excerpt from the case of the Man-Made Cove illustrates the format of the Outline of Proof.

EXAMPLE OF AN OUTLINE OF PROOF

. . . . . .

ISSUE NO. 2

Parcel A originally consisted of low-
lands, marshes, meadows. Complaint ¶ 2
Answer DKI ¶ 2

LAW   Waters navigable in fact are navigable in law.

Exception if waters though navigable in fact are made by artificial means on private property.

Query if a stream navigable in fact and law is expanded by artificial means into a larger body of water navigable in fact?

FACT	WITNESS/FOUNDATION	EXHIBITS
Issue as stated above	Ancient document rule, Request to Admit	Dongan Patent 3/18/1685

Deposition of custodians   [Maps, charts,
of documents   and deeds
                                  going back to
                                  Colonial times]

Jolyon Jones

[an octogenarian who
remembered Cove before
dredging]

Dr. Carl Anders   His charts show-
                                  ing area at
[an expert geologist and   four stages of
cartographer]   development

ISSUE NO. 3

Plaintiff and his predecessors in
ownership of Parcel A caused dredging of Cove and opening to Sound.
Complaint ¶3   Answer Deny ¶3

LAW   Same as Issue No. 2

FACT	WITNESS/FOUNDATION	EXHIBITS
Dredging commenced	Plaintiff	His Dredging Contract
for fill and continued intermittently for years	Jolyon Jones Dr. Carl Anders	

The case of the Fraudulent Freight Receipts shows how an Outline of Proof might have staved off loss in the case of probable liability.

Plaintiff, a Japanese import-export firm, undertook to handle the importing of newsprint from an American shipper to several Japanese publishers. Plaintiff obtained irrevocable letters of credit in favor of the shipper. The letters of credit required that drafts drawn on them had to be supported by bills of lading showing merchandise on board the vessel as of a cut-off date.

The vessel scheduled to carry the shipment was delayed. She would not reach port until after the cut-off date in the letters of credit. At the shipper's request, the carrier issued bills of lading indicating the merchandise had been loaded as of the cut-off date. The shipper obtained payment on the basis of the pre-dated documents.

The newsprint was loaded and shipped after the cut-off date. It did not meet specifications. Plaintiff sold it in batches for a net loss.

Plaintiff sued the steamship company for fraud. The measure of damages for fraud is pecuniary loss sustained as a result of the wrong. Plaintiff readily proved the basic facts, and what it had paid for the shipment.

The proof of what the goods sold for fell apart. A witness had come from Japan. He did not bring the original documents and books of account reflecting the various sales. Instead he brought summaries especially prepared for the trial.

The court dismissed the action.

The Outline of Proof would have exposed this gap in the proof. It would have set forth the law on the measure of damages. It would have set forth the evidence necessary to prove each element of the measure of damages. It would have pin-pointed the existence and inadequacy of the summaries.

4.6   Notes for the Selection of Jurors—How to Reduce the Risk in a Chancey Business

You should not leave selection of a jury purely to chance. You should think it out beforehand and record your ideas in the trial book.

Some of the more important topics to be covered are:

• The "boilerplate" questions you intend to ask the jury on *voir dire*. Has any juryman been a party in a lawsuit? Does any juryman know any of the parties, counsel, or witnesses in the case? And so forth.

• Types of jurors you want and do not want in light of the nature of the case.

• Biographical data about the jury panel if it is available.

• Specific questions based on the nature of the case that you must ask each juror.

• The theme and scope of your remarks to the jury about the case on *voir dire*. This is the first glimpse the jury has of the case and of you. You want it to be a favorable one.

Where the judge conducts the *voir dire*, you must submit questions you want asked in writing.

The selection of the jury in the case of the Vanishing Damages discussed in Chapter 2 illustrates the point. The defendant had not manufactured an embossing roll according to the drawing supplied by plaintiff. The drawing called for a one-piece construction of the head and journal. Defendant manufactured the roll with two-piece welded construction.

A weld failed, a flammable coolant sprayed out and caught fire.

A steamfitter was selected for the jury. One of plaintiff's claims was that the weld was insufficient in size and strength. Another was that defendant should have checked back with plaintiff on operating pressures and stresses if it intended to use a welded two-piece construction.

Defendant's counsel quizzed the steamfitter whether he could impartially decide about the weld. He tried to get the court to challenge the juror for cause. The court refused; in fact, the court asked questions itself.

A steamfitter obviously knows about pressure vessels and welding. Counsel might or might not want a person with this or other technical knowledge on the jury. A decision about this beforehand helps counsel guide the *voir dire*. The point is that the mere asking of questions about the weld indicated to the jury a concern about the weld.

4.7   Notes for the Opening Statement—How to Maximize the Impact of This Important First Step at Trial

The opening statement at a trial, like the statement of facts in an appellate brief, is all important. It must be effective advocacy. To achieve this you must analyze the case, organize the material for maximum effectiveness, and polish it for a lucid presentation.

The end product should be included in the trial book.

How you record the material depends on how you want to use it. Most counsel will want to have it in paragraph-by-paragraph form, well-spaced and with wide margins, typed in block letters perhaps, for use as notes in making the opening.

4.8   How to Keep Track of Who Will Testify to What—A List of Witnesses Pro and Con

During preparation a section of the trial book should be devoted to notes about witnesses. Here you will put down things you have learned or surmised about a witness and his testimony. You might note that the witness is hard of hearing, how he or she stood up and came across during a deposition as an indication of performance on the stand, parts of his story that seem thin, and so forth.

Material about witnesses will find its way into other parts of the file too—in witness statements, in depositions, in memoranda about a witness and his testimony, as part of answers to interrogatories, even in your memory.

These materials do not constitute the testimony of the witness. They are the raw materials for that testimony. You must work this raw material into final form for use at trial.

You also must make a number of important decisions about the presentation at trial:

• Which witnesses to call.
• The order in which to call them.
• The order of the story of each witness so as to present it in a clear and effective way.
• What exhibits are to be introduced through which witnesses.
• At what point(s) material is to be introduced from depositions, requests to admit, stipulations, etc.

This endeavor is one of the main steps in organizing the case for trial. The result of the work will comprise several sections of the trial book, principally the List of Witnesses Pro and Con, The

Witness Sheets for Direct Examination, The Notes for Cross-Examination, and The Trial Agenda.

The List of Witnesses Pro and Con serves a checklist function at trial. Some counsel dispense with it but incorporate its features in other sections of the trial book.

The list consists of the witnesses you intend to call in the order that you intend to call them, with a note next to each name of the topics on which the witness will testify.

You can note comments about each witness next to his name. (You may find these comments more useful if you make them on the witness sheet.)

You should also list probable opposing witnesses. Thinking about the case from the other side's viewpoint can give some surprising insights. Also, at trial the list reminds you what you think your opponent's case should logically consist of. If your opponent does not call a probable witness, you should hear an alarm bell ringing and investigate.

4.9   The Witness Sheets for Direct Examination—How Best to Insure Complete and Compelling Testimony

The witness sheet records everything you must elicit from the witness in the order you will elicit it.

On top of the first page, type the witness' name in block capital letters.

Immediately under this note what you want to bear in mind about the witness during his examination—physical infirmities, mannerisms in testifying, areas to be avoided, special points in handling him on the stand, etc.

The testimony can be organized in two ways.

One, write out each question and answer. It is cumbersome when used for the entire testimony of a witness. Nor is it necessary assuming you can ask clear questions. Reading questions makes for a stilted presentation at trial.

Occasionally, you must write out important questions in order to ask them exactly. Hypothetical questions, for example, should be framed beforehand.

Two, the most effective form of witness sheet, is the point-to-a-paragraph summary. It consists of the narrative of the testimony in the order of presentation broken down into independent paragraphs for each idea, thought, point, or fact.

The paragraphs are single or double-spaced, in regular or all capital typing, on the right-hand half of the page, with triple or quadruple spaces between paragraphs. On the left-hand side, notes to the testimony can be keyed in at given points; for example, "Introduce contract as exhibit." During trial, this clear space provides room for counsel to jot down ideas.

This format gives you at-a-glance control at trial without letting your notes get in the way. At a glance you get the full point but just that point. You can easily frame a spontaneous question. At a glance you can see whether the answer covered the point completely. If it did not, at a glance you can couch a follow-up question.

The content of the witness sheet usually tracks what the witness in fact testifies to. This frees you from the need to take notes of the direct testimony. When the witness does add something not on the sheet, you can jot it down on the wide left margin.

The brief example that follows illustrates the format. It is an extract from the witness sheet for Jolyon Jones, the very old man in the case of the Man-Made Cove who remembered the area before dredging. The example picks up after biographical data.

EXAMPLE OF A
WITNESS SHEET

JOLYON JONES

Note: Jones' memory about the condition of the Cove is clear. He gets confused about dates. Speak somewhat lodly and slowly in examining him.

. . . . . .

         I lived on my father's farm which was about 5 miles from the Cove.

	My older brother Ben and I used to hunt in the area.

My older brother Ben and I used to hunt in the area.

Sometimes we would come after school. Most of the time we would go on the weekends.

We did this for many years while we were growing up.

The area consisted of salt marshes with a little creek running down into the Sound.

There was no Cove at all, just the little creek.

Show witness Dr. Anders' Chart No. 3 [the area as it was just before dredging].

This is how the area looked. The creek ran like it is shown, and emptied into the Sound at about that spot.

The creek was very shallow and twisty, and a boat could not use it.

4.10   Notes for Cross-Examination—How Not to Get Caught Short with an Adverse Witness

The cardinal rule about cross-examination is, "Don't. Not unless you have to."

You have to make the final decision about cross-examination at trial after the direct examination. To do so you must ask yourself four questions:

- Has the direct testimony hurt my case?
- If so, can I impeach the witness or his testimony?
- Can I obtain testimony helpful to my case?
- Do the probable benefits sufficiently outweigh the possible dangers to warrant cross-examination?

You have to answer these questions in a three-fold context: the direct examination; an analysis made before trial about whether any of the classic ends of cross-examination will be served; how the direct examination affects the pre-trial analysis.

The topic of cross-examination is covered in Chapter 10. Suffice it to say here that you should include your pre-trial analysis, your notes for possible cross-examination, in the trial book.

Typically, you would make notes for each witness. These notes would include your observations about the witness, the nature and location of any impeachment material (e.g., portions of depositions, exhibits, certified copies of convictions, etc.), helpful new facts to be elicited, and so forth.

4.11   Notes on Discovery Material to Be Used at Trial—A Fail-Safe Way to Avoid Overlooking Discovery Material

In modern trials, you routinely use discovery material as part of your case or on cross-examination. Somewhere you have to record what you intend to use and when you intend to use it.

The trial agenda will indicate what items of discovery you intend to use when. If the material is not extensive, you can note the references to the particular portions right on the trial agenda.

If the material is extensive, you should record the references in a special section of the trial book. For example, for depositions you should list every page and question-and-answer reference. The depositions themselves are stored separately.

4.12   Notes and Brief on Law and Evidence, and Trial Motions—A Tested Technique for Winning Legal and Evidentiary Points That Arise at Trial

You must be prepared on the general principles of law and evidence that apply to the case, and on particular points that may arise at the trial.

Your general research, which has been embodied in memoranda, notes, or case abstracts, you need only index. This index in the Law and Evidence section of the trial book gives you fingertip access to the material at trial.

However, you also have to anticipate specific points of law and evidence that may arise at trial. To take care of them you should prepare separate briefs on each point. If the point arises, you have a brief and authorities ready for the court. Keep the original and copies of the briefs in the storage folder. List the briefs in this section of the trial book.

The case of the Surprise Subpoena shows this technique in action. The case was complex and involved a number of parties and lawyers.

One of the parties was a foreign corporation. It was a one-asset company—the vehicle that was lost in the accident. It had no presence in the state of suit. It was in the case only by virtue of long-arm tort jurisdiction.

At one point counsel for an opposing party insisted the corporation had certain records. Counsel for the corporation assured him the corporation did not.

Counsel for the corporation sensed trouble: a subpoena *duces tecum;* a hurry-up search that again would turn up nothing; eye-rolling and posturing by his opponent when he reported that.

That night counsel for the corporation hit the books.

The next morning opposing counsel produced a subpoena *duces tecum.* He dramatically served it on the corporation's trial counsel. The latter moved to quash this patently bad service. The court indicated it was inclined to uphold the service.

Then counsel for the corporation produced a memorandum with a case squarely in point. The judge digested the memo and quashed the subpoena.

4.13   Requests to Charge—How to Get the
          Court to Support Your Side of the Case
          in His Charge to the Jury

A section of the trial book should cover the instructions you want the court to charge the jury.

The importance of the charge cannot be over-emphasized. The jury is bound by the judge's pronouncements on the law. The jury gives great weight to whatever the judge says. Even if the jury does not understand everything the judge charges them, they put great stock in the impression he conveys.

The charge is the framework in which the jury decides the case. You want to slant the framework your way if you can. If you cannot, you at least want to make sure the charge is fair. At all costs, you do not want the charge to be slanted the other way.

Consequently, you must prepare the requests meticulously.

They must cover every facet of the substantive phase of the case.

They should also cover "boilerplate" items (basic instructions on negligence, burden of proof, etc.) even though the court may have standard charges of its own.

The requests must cover any special procedural or evidentiary points. The "empty chair" charge (failure to call a witness within a party's control) is an example.

Each request must accurately reflect the law, and be supported by citations. A court is more apt to give an accurate request verbatim. On appeal the appellate court will support an accurate request if the court below gave it, or possibly reverse if the court below failed to give it or gave an inaccurate one instead.

Each request must be accurate but also be couched as favorably to your case as possible. The time you spend in drafting accurate but favorable charges can be the margin of victory. You should frame and submit two or three versions of essential charges. If the court rejects one it may give another.

You should submit the request in writing to the court. You can keep track of what charges the court gives and those that it does not give or modifies. This can be important for the taking of exceptions to the charge.

Custom or local rules of court will determine the form of the requests. In some jurisdictions, each request is placed on a separate page. In other jurisdictions they will be typed on the usual legal cap, one following the other. In still other jurisdictions, the court will require inclusion of the requests to charge in the pre-trial memorandum.

You can keep your copy of the requests in the trial book, or bind it into the legal papers file. The key is accessibility.

4.14   Notes for Final Argument—How to Maxi-
mize the Impact of This Key Argument

The gist of what was said about Notes for the Opening Statement applies here (§4.8 above).

During preparation and trial, jot down ideas about the closing in this section. At the close of the evidence, you will pull it all together—the notes you have jotted down, your trial notes, your thinking about the case, etc.

The end product is your outline for the closing argument. Record everything in this section of the trial book in the form you find most convenient.

4.15   List of Exhibits and Exhibit File—How to
Have Fingertip Control of the Documents
in the Case

The documents and exhibits must be organized and indexed before trial.

The nature of the index can vary but a reasonably complete one would:

a. Identify the document with a thumbnail abstract of its contents;

b. Give the code number of the document if a coding system is used;

c. Indicate the location of the document in the storage file;

d. Note how the document is to be used at trial.

The categories counsel selects to organize and index the documents will depend on the requirements of the case. The simplest is by the name of the item. A cross-index or cross-indices by topics or by witnesses who will be using the documents might be a helpful tool. In simple cases, the keying of the documents into the witness sheets can serve as a cross-index.

The thumbnail abstract of the contents of the documents takes time to prepare but can pay for itself where there are voluminous documents. At a glance you can get the gist of the document without having to retrieve it.

There are seven "Dos and Don'ts" in using documents in litigation:

• Don't mark or mutilate originals.
• Work with copies of important documents.
• Don't file original documents with depositions. Stipulate for the substitution of copies.
• Safeguard important documents in a safe.
• Obtain original documents from the client, not copies.
• Insist that the opponent produce original documents, not copies in discovery.
• Indicate the source of each document. A simple way is to write the source on a slip of paper and attach it by paper clip. Don't staple the slip on.

4.16   The Index and Cross-Indices

The nature of the case will determine the nature and number of indices you will need. Often the lists and indices in particular sections of the trial book will be sufficient. In complicated cases you may need master indices.

In huge cases nowadays, you should look into hiring a computer expert to program the material.

4.17   The Trial Agenda and "Things to Do"
          List—The Blueprint for Trial

The trial agenda replaces the preparation agenda in the trial book for use at trial.

The trial agenda is the blueprint for trial. It is the complete outline of the things you plan to do at the trial in the order you plan to do them. It starts with the very first thing and ends with the very last thing.

A typical agenda would start with preliminary matters—a motion for a view; a ruling on an anticipated line of prejudicial testimony; stipulations; any matters in short, to be taken up at the outset.

The agenda would then list the *voir dire* and the opening.

It would go on to list the plan for the presentation of the

evidence; the witnesses in order; exhibits to be introduced other than through witnesses (e.g., a certified document); discovery to be read.

It would list matters in conclusion—exhibits marked for identification as full exhibits; submitting requests for charge; final argument; exceptions to the charge; checking that all exhibits go to jury.

The agenda must be flexible. A witness may have to be called out of turn. Developments at the trial may call for other steps. These changes can be inked into the typed agenda. The format, a well-spaced list down the page with wide margins, lends itself to notations.

Following the trial agenda in the trial book, you should have a page for a "Things to Do" list. Here you note things that come up at trial that have to be done. In the heat of trial, you may scribble a note on a convenient piece of paper. Every day after trial you should pull these notes together into a list.

— 5 —

Your Own Investigation
Still Wins Cases—
How to Plan It
and How to Conduct It

**5.1   What You Must Know About the Nature
of Investigation, or Why You Cannot Let
Discovery Become a Crutch**

    Your own investigation, *ex parte* investigation,
and discovery are two sides of the same coin, investigation in the
broad sense. You should dovetail the use of each to achieve four
well-defined purposes: to get the complete factual picture; to turn
up evidence for use at the trial; to obtain impeachment material;
to elicit admissions.

    An investigation resembles a shuttle traveling back and
forth on a loom, weaving a fabric as it goes. You start with certain
basic facts. From these you form working theories and derive

leads. You check these out through investigation. From the investigation you test the working theories, form new ones, and derive further leads. You keep this up until you have as complete a set of facts as you can get, and as sound a network of theories as you can expect.

There are two kinds of *ex parte* investigation. One, in-house investigation, consists of getting facts and evidence from the client. The other, outside investigation, consists of getting facts, evidence, admissions, and impeachment materials from others.

There are also two investigative uses of discovery: obtaining facts, etc. from the other parties in the case, a unique power of discovery; obtaining facts, etc. from others not parties to the case. You might get such latter information on a voluntary basis. Discovery gives you the power to compel it, but at the price of notice to the other side.

To illustrate how counsel's own investigation, and it alone, won the case, take the following intersection collision: One driver, who became the defendant, contended plaintiff had run a stop sign. Nonetheless, the other driver sued.

Defendant's counsel wondered what was up. He got the answer at trial. Plaintiff denied there was a stop sign at the intersection!

Defendant's counsel bided his time. Then, in his own case, he pounced. He produced photographs taken within days of the accident by an independent photographer that unmistakably depicted the intersection. In each the stop sign loomed as big as life.

5.2   How to Blueprint an Investigation That Will Produce All of the Facts

The first step is to get a grounding from the client. An investigation cannot be planned without basic facts.

How much the client can contribute varies. Sometimes it will not be much. The widow of the decedent in a wrongful death action often only knows the contours of the tragedy. You may have to get the start-up data from others.

The second step is to visit the scene and inspect the objects involved. A knowledge of the physical aspects of the case put it into context. It helps you orient your thinking and evaluate the facts.

At the scene you must note and record a number of things: the topography; lines of vision; measurements of distances; physical indicia of the event. Similarly with an inspection of an object—how it operates; where it was damaged; safety features.

The third step is to pin down each principle of law involved. You plan your investigation to find facts that satisfy or rebut these principles.

This preliminary work prepares you for the fourth step, blueprinting the investigation. Six topics should be covered:

—General areas to be investigated.

—Specific questions to be answered.

—Leads to be explored.

—Sources to be tapped.

—Methods of investigation: discovery, *ex parte* investigation, both.

—Who will investigate what topics: counsel, his associates, professional investigator, experts in the fields involved.

In the case of the Unfortunate Fisherman, a decedent had been a crewman on a fishing trawler. One evening, after the vessel had tied up at a pier, he and several others had gone ashore. They had dinner, quaffed a few beers, shot some pool. The others left for the ship. He stayed behind.

The next morning the crew missed him. He was not aboard ship. Ashore the tavern people only recalled that he had left the tavern.

Then one of the crew spotted his hat floating between the ship and the pier near the foot of a ladder built into the side of the pier. The renewed search found his body submerged at the same spot.

The official reports fleshed out the widow's brief account of the tragedy. Diagrams in the reports gave counsel a good grasp of the scene. He had the basic facts but had to work up the facts on negligence or unseaworthiness, and causation.

Counsel spent some time on research. He found a line of authority holding that circumstantial evidence could support a *prima facie* case for an unwitnessed death. The cases also furnished guidelines for the type of circumstantial evidence that would stand up at trial.

Counsel swiftly drew up a blueprint for the investigation. An excerpt follows:

Areas of Investigation and Specific Questions

The dock. Condition. Lighting. Structures on it. Materials on it.

The ladder. Condition. Defects. Marine growth on rungs exposed to water.

The ship. Any gangway or mode of egress. Railings. Lighting. Structures. How tied up.

The weather, tide, and wind. How far ship from dock. Relationship of railing/ship to pier/ladder.

Decedent's activity ashore.

Customary and available modes of egress on trawlers.

Sources

The captain and crew.

The tavern people and patrons.

Other possible witnesses.

Other vessels and seamen (on modes of egress).

Charts, tide tables, weather reports.

Leads

None as yet.

Method of Investigation

Ex parte. Much of the information will come from potential defendants. The investigation of the pier and the vessel depends on them.

Investigator. A professional investigator might do better with seamen and fishing village people than a lawyer.

5.3   Six Tips to Guarantee a Successful Investigation

5.3.1   Promptness Pays Dividends

Promptness does pay dividends. The intersection collision case dramatizes windfall dividends. Counsel took photographs of the scene within days of the accident. Had he delayed, the stop sign might have already been removed.

But even the usual dividends more than compensate for the effort of a fast start. Witnesses will still be around. Files will be complete. Evidence will not have disappeared. Memories will be fresh. Painful or embarrassing events will not have had time to color recollections. Opposing counsel will not have had the opportunity to have schooled his witnesses.

A main purpose of the investigation is to get witness statements for use at trial. The closer they are in time to the event, the more powerful they are for impeachment or refreshing recollection at trial.

5.3.2   Interview All of the Witnesses

You unquestionably will interview friendly or neutral witnesses. You should not shy away from interviewing hostile witnesses for several reasons:

• You might discover that the witness is not really hostile at all.

• You might be able to explain the hostility away.

• You might find that the source of the hostility is a basis for impeachment.

• You might be able to use an absolute refusal to talk as a basis for impeachment.

• You might pick up useful information even in an aborted interview.

• You can get an idea if you should take the witness's deposition.

• You might be able to use the witness's statement of "no knowledge" as a basis for impeachment.

You should not forgo interviewing a hostile witness because you think that he will not give you a written statement anyway. Even if he does not give you a written statement, you can impeach him from your recollection of the interview, or better yet from your notes of the interview. For example, if a hostile witness testifies to an event he told you he knew nothing about, on cross-examination you could ask him about his statement of "no knowledge" to you at the interview.

This brings up the point about who should interview a hostile witness. As an attorney, you might not want to pit your word even by implication against his. In fact, a court could sustain an objection to a question assuming the fact and content of your interview, unless you assure the court you later would establish these facts. You can avoid this problem by having someone with you when you conduct the interview or by having your investigator conduct the interview.

5.3.3   Collect Documents and Pictures and All Material That's Needed

You should collect everything you can lay your hands on. You must especially insist that the client furnish you all of the documents and files on the case. You, not he, must determine relevant from irrelevant material.

Also, only you, not he, can fully appreciate how carefully materials must be examined. In one case on the front of an accident report form, the assured reported what seemed to be a minor rear-end collision. In a space headed "Injuries," also on the front of the form, the assured had answered "None." The back of the form had a space headed "Describe injuries." The assured answered, "One dead."

Also, many a case has been won by a painstaking search through mountains of material that turns up a key item. As an example, see the case discussed in section 5.6.

In modern litigation, physical things and demonstrative evidence play a central role. You must be aggressive about getting these things—documents, pictures, the objects involved, recordings, and so forth. The camera and the measuring tape, as much as a pad and pencil, are the tools of the modern investigator.

5.3.4   Put It in Writing

Record each step in the investigation. Your memorandum should cover at least six points: the date and place of the interview or investigative step; the circumstances; the names and addresses and capacities of everyone present; the information and data obtained (this may be a witness statement); the background of the witness; your appraisal of the witness, of the value of the evidence, etc; other relevant material.

Chapter 4 on the Trial Book discusses how you should work these materials up for use at trial.

5.3.5   Be from Missouri—Assume Nothing

In trial work you cannot assume a gosh darn thing. You cannot take anything for granted. Everything has to be checked and double-checked. The pieces have to be played with and put together in different ways. The drift of things has to be tested whether it makes sense or not.

Your instincts make you wary about the other party but often not about your own client. However, your instinct to trust your client can play you false at times. You must put your client's story to the same acid test as you put that of the other party.

By way of example, in one case a leading concern had achieved a technological breakthrough on a major product. The product virtually swept its competition from the market. No competitor had the know-how to match it.

The general manager of a small manufacturing company thought he knew the secret. He developed equipment that in the shop at least seemed to work. The equipment was complicated, and took skill to operate, but he had no trouble in selling it to an eager buyer.

After weeks of attempted start-up, the buyer claimed the equipment did not work. The general manager accused the buyer of wanting push-button equipment, and of not cooperating in learning how to operate it.

The parties reached an impasse. The buyer sued for rescission.

Counsel's initial investigation bore out the general manager's story. Defendant's on-site, start-up engineer related many instances of indifference. Defendant's salesman who acted as a trouble-shooter verified this.

This defense blinded counsel for awhile. As the investigation wore on though, bits and pieces began to bother counsel. Would a buyer be so indifferent about equipment that it would put it back into the market? Could not a big-shot type like the general manager easily have puffed about a push-button operation? Did the general manager really misplace samples of the product from an allegedly successful on-site run? How did the general manager always contrive to be around when counsel interviewed others? Why did the on-site engineer get vague on certain topics?

Counsel knew he would get nothing from the general manager or the on-site engineer. He decided to tackle the salesman with whom he had built a good relationship. One evening he invited the salesman to dinner. At what he hoped was the right time, he put forth the question point-blank.

"Did the equipment work?"

"I'm no engineer," the salesman replied. After a moment's reflection he added, "But you might ask them about all the time they spent fussing with the scrubber."

The scrubber performed a vital function in the equipment.

Counsel followed up with the general manager but got nowhere. He could and did change his tactics though. At the hearing he boldly assumed the equipment worked. He hammered at the buyer's indifference and lack of cooperation.

The tactic paid off. The court awarded rescission. However, it did not award interest or consequential damages, both of which were substantial.

5.3.6   Keep Control of the Investigation but Don't Always Do It Yourself

You must block out and direct the examination. However, you should not necessarily do the investigating yourself. You must decide who can get the best results on different phases of the investigation.

By and large you or your associate should handle or supervise an in-house investigation. Client relations and preserving the attorney-client privilege require this. At times you may need outside help; for example, an accountant or other expert.

The outside investigation has different considerations.

For what might be called a pure evidence gathering investigation, your role may be pivotal and active. In the case of the Man-Made Cove, for example, counsel tracked down the numerous old deeds and patents, and charts and maps that described and depicted the area before dredging.

Other examples come to mind—gathering statistics, examining public records, compiling data on a relevant market.

In this type of investigation, you often will want to work with an expert in a particular field. An economist would be a key person on data for a relevant market, for example.

For the detective type of investigation, the "what happened and who did it" sort of thing, ask yourself if you have the time and ability to conduct the investigation. In the simple case, the answer may be that you can. In the complex case, the answer may be a professional investigator.

A good professional investigator has several advantages over a lawyer—in using pretexts in getting to see witnesses; in exploiting sources of information he has built up; in surveillance activities; in *sub rosa* investigation; in immediately following up on leads.

You must brief the investigator. Give the investigator the background so he can use his head in developing the investigation. At the same time, give him specific points you want covered.

Until you know your man, guard against these several pitfalls. Some investigators tend to color their material favorably. Others tend to lead witnesses too strongly. Still others will go off on tangents. A few, unfortunately, fill in the gaps with make-believe.

If the investigation is an on-going one, you have to guide it. In the plane crash case previously discussed, either of the two men in the front seat of the Beechcraft could have been flying the plane. Either could have been operating the radio.

The tape of the transmissions between the tower and the plane contained the expression, "Tally-ho the airport." An investigator, observing that tally-ho was a fox hunting expression, suggested looking into which of the men was a fox hunter.

Tally-ho also happens to be fighter pilot jargon. One of the men had been a fighter pilot. The main point, though, was that either man could have been operating the radio.

Counsel called the investigator off the fox hunting lead.

5.4   How to Conduct a Mass On-the-Scene Investigation

In the case of the Exploding T-2 Tanker, the ship exploded while discharging aviation gas at a tank farm. Two seamen died. One got caught in the holocaust. The other had a heart attack. The rest saved themselves by sliding down ropes over the fantail.

Counsel rushed to the scene. Getting the statements of survivors had top priority. To do it counsel followed certain time-tested rules:

—Bring enough people to conduct the interviews before the witnesses scatter. In this case, counsel for the various interests investigating the explosion pooled their efforts.

—Find out from the top man the basic facts and the key people. Here the top man was the master, as it often is in admiralty matters. The key people are those with actual knowledge of the facts.

—Establish mechanics to cover all of the witnesses. In the case of the T-2 Tanker, the men had to be assembled for advances. Counsel set up tables just beyond the paymasters. As the men came through, counsel took their statements.

—Interview the key people first. The faster counsel collects the basic facts, the more searching his later interviews.

—Get statements from everybody even if they are statements of no knowledge. At the trial if the person purports to have knowledge, counsel can impeach him.

5.5   How to Conduct an Investigation at the Office of an Institutional Client

You would not expect to get much by barging into the office of a corporate client and asking questions. You would be told politely to, "Ask the boss."

This is the key to a successful corporate investigation. You must start at the top. The boss is the man who can make decisions and open doors. By this you insure cooperation down the line.

You should also take several other preliminary steps. Get the table of organization so you know who's who. Get the names and capacities of those with knowledge of the facts. Get a contact man whom you can call upon for routine matters. Get the files assembled and preserved.

After the boss, you may then find it best to go down the corporate ladder rung by rung. More likely, you will want to hit the key people next. Frequently you will combine both techniques.

Interview the witnesses individually. The presence of a man's boss or colleague puts the damper on. The equipment case discussed in section 5.3.5 illustrates this.

5.6   How to Dovetail the Investigation and Discovery so as to Enhance the Value of Each

There are no hard-and-fast rules about how to dovetail the investigation and discovery, but there are guidelines.

Obviously you must have some idea about the case before you can use discovery. In a simple case, the client's story may be enough. In a complex case, a little more investigation might result in much more significant discovery.

By the same token, discovery can shortcut a time consuming investigation. If the other party has close to exclusive knowledge of the facts, an early deposition might be called for.

Investigation and discovery complement each other. A statement might reveal that a witness is so important you should take his deposition. The case of the Disloyal Distributor to be touched on shortly illustrates how discovery furnishes leads for investigation.

You must appreciate the strength and shortcomings of each discovery tool, and the nature of the investigative devices available in a given case. Only in this way can you decide how best to achieve what you want to achieve.

Unfettered discovery, incidentally, is something of a myth. It is much too costly. If discovery becomes oppressive, opposing counsel can apply for a protective order. The procedural rules of some states limit discovery.

Certain kinds of cases tend to fall into patterns for the use of investigation and discovery.

In a credibility case, for example, early depositions and statements can lock the other side into an unvarnished version of the facts. Interrogatories served later in the case can elicit contentions, the names and addresses of witnesses, and so forth. Inspection could be coupled with the depositions or proceed independently.

In a documentary case, on the other hand, you may want to line your case up first. Then by discovery you can spot the points your opponent will attack. Once you know this, you can set about shoring up your proof.

Take the case of a distributor; the manufacturer canceled his major exclusive license for substantial arrears. He also suspected the distributor of manufacturing and selling a competing product.

The distributor sued for breach of contract. Counsel for the manufacturer first made sure the account of the arrears was complete and accurate. He then pin-pointed plaintiff's position on each item in the account by discovery. This developed a startling fact. Several key items hinged on credibility (oral agreements, etc.). If plaintiff prevailed on them, the arrears just about evaporated.

Counsel had nothing to confront plaintiff with on the competition point. He did not want to telegraph his client's suspicions either. The bitterness between the two had reached the point that plaintiff could well have added a count for punitive damages.

Counsel and his client did not give up on this point though. They combed through plaintiff's ledger books obtained on discovery. One entry recorded an unusually large payment for plaintiff. It did not describe the merchandise but did give the seller's name and address.

The follow-up investigation hit pay dirt. The entry reflected purchase of a major component for the competing product.

At the trial plaintiff could not deny the entry or explain it away. He shattered his credibility. This carried over to the items in the account. The court found that such substantial arrears existed as to justify the cancellation.

5.7   How to Get the Whole Truth in Interviewing Witnesses

The witness should be interviewed at a time when and a place where a) he feels at ease, b) he is under no distractions, and c) he can devote his full attention to the interview.

The type of witness has a lot to do with this. For a businessman, your office might be fine. For an unsophisticated witness, at his home in the evening after dinner might be best.

Interviews at the witnesses' job can be hurried. If you have no choice about this, schedule the interview when the witness has some free time, a coffee break for example.

The interview should be held where the influence of the opposition will not be a factor. Interviewing a neutral witness in the offices of the other counsel would be a mistake.

You should take pains to interview the witness alone. You want the unfettered recollection of the witness. A spouse or relatives might warn a witness to be cautious, or not to sign a statement. The presence of a boss or colleagues just about insures that little unfavorable will be said. Witnesses interviewed together tend to agree with each other.

You should be friendly and tactful but candid and firm. Pussy-footing can make a friendly or independent witness resentful. It can reinforce the hostility of an unfriendly witness.

Make the witness see that you have a job to do, and that you need the witness's help. This is the best approach. Sometimes you can couple it with an appeal to the person's sense of civic obligation. Tread lightly on this though because you do not want to sound sanctimonious or officious.

You must be patient and even-tempered. You may have to suffer through a long-winded recitation sprinkled with banal opinions. However, to shut off a garrulous person might shut him up for good. Also in a flood of words something might come out.

You usually will have to go back and ask questions to fill in gaps. You may even have to guide the interview with questions from the outset. It all depends on the witness. A personal injury plaintiff, for example, often feels resentment at being hurt. You may have to coax him at first, and then sit through a torrent of talk.

You should not pressure or intimidate the witness. At the same time you must be tactfully firm in order to get at the truth. An erroneous story can be worse than no story at all. If the witness bristles or becomes evasive, that tells you something too.

You should have two things in mind during an interview—to get as complete and as objective an account as you can from the witness, and to get insights by which to evaluate the witness and his story. Consequently, you do not want to put words in the witness's mouth (although leading questions may be necessary to press the witness). You also want to find out as much about the witness's background and biases as you can.

You must take into account certain human tendencies to embroider extraordinary events, gloss over or forget embarrassing or unfavorable facts, and emphasize favorable facts, if not invent them.

You should not put too much reliance on behavioral traits. Not every liar turns beet red. Not every Nervous Nellie is a liar. The plausibility of the story is a more reliable test.

Soon after the interview gets under way you should take your pad and pen out. You must make it clear that you intend to take notes. A casual "You don't mind if I take notes, do you?" usually suffices.

Encourage the witness to make diagrams, identify photographs, etc. This makes for a clearer account. It also helps loosen the witness up.

5.8   How to Decide What Kind of Witness Statement Is Best Suited for Your Case

In most investigations you want to get a signed statement from the witness. The main purpose of the statement is for impeachment at the trial. A second purpose is to refresh the witness' recollection for trial. Occasionally, a statement will be used to corroborate testimony or as past recollection recorded. (Note that you should make an independent memorandum of facts not included in the statement, your impressions of the witness, etc.)

There are several forms of statement. Where a witness is friendly and the facts extensive, you might have his notes typed up and presented to the witness for review and signature. Be certain, however, that the witness will not get cold feet and refuse to sign the document.

The tape-recording of an interview has one advantage—a speedy interview. But the witness might refuse to be taped, and thus to be interviewed. Also, you may find the tape recording awkward to work with during preparation and at trial. The difficulties in laying a foundation at trial can include a) identifying the voice; b) proving that the tape has not been tampered with; c) producing the person who took the recording (which might be an insurance adjuster); d) explaining to the court's satisfaction any garbled passages.

There is one other pitfall—malfunctioning. In one case an adjuster recorded an excellent statement of the claimant in a compensation case. In a later liability suit, the statement turned out to be worthless. The recording equipment had malfunctioned.

The statement taken by a court reporter has similar problems. The witness might refuse the interview. At trial the reporter has to testify about the accuracy of his notes.

The commonest and best form of statement for use at trial is the handwritten statement. The investigator writes it out, couching it in the witness' language. He asks the witness to read and correct it, initialing the corrections. He then has the witness initial each page and sign it on the last page following the legend

"I have read the foregoing statement consisting of ____ pages, and it is true to the best of my knowledge." Some investigators purposely make mistakes so the witness will correct them. This enhances the document for impeachment.

If possible do not leave a copy of the statement with the witness. The witness might give a copy to the other side. He might read it to refresh his recollection before trial which opens it to inspection by your opponent.

6

How the Practical Lawyer
Uses Discovery
to Win Cases

6.1 How to Expand the Scope of Discovery

Rule 26(b) (1) provides that discovery may cover,

> "... any matter, not privileged, which is relevant
> to the subject matter involved in the pending
> action...."

The rule goes on to provide that this includes the existence and whereabouts of documents, tangible things, and persons with knowledge of discoverable matter. The rule then states in the last sentence,

> "It is not grounds for objection that the information will be inadmissible at the trial if the information sought appears reasonably calculated to lead to the discovery of admissible evidence."

Read literally, the rule says two things. Relevancy is the test for the scope of discovery. Inadmissibility is a ground for objection, privilege being an absolute objection, unless the person seeking discovery establishes that the inadmissible matter is reasonably calculated to lead to the discovery of admissible evidence.

Nobody reads the rule literally. The conventional interpretation is simplistic: relevancy is the test for the scope of discovery, and inadmissibility into evidence (except for privileged matter) is eliminated as a bar to discovery. This interpretation credits the words, "It is not ground for objection that the information will be inadmissible at trial . . . ." It leaves floating the words, ". . . if the information sought appears reasonably calculated to lead to the discovery of admissible evidence."

A number of courts have seized upon these free-floating words to set up a separate test for the scope of discovery. Arguably, anything with even a remote tie to the case could appear to lead to the discovery of admissible evidence. And since, as these courts say, they cannot go into the merits of the case to pass on discovery motions, they glide over the words "reasonably calculated." Consequently, for these courts, anything is discoverable that could or might lead to the discovery of admissible evidence. This has come to be known as the "Open Door" theory of discovery.

A clash over discovery of an insurance policy in the case of the drowned pilot (discussed in Chapter 2) illustrates this. The Warsaw Convention and Montreal Agreement limit recovery for death or bodily injury on scheduled international airplane flights to $75,000. To escape the limitation, counsel have started to name the pilot as well as the airline as defendants.

The pilot, who was killed in the crash, did not live in the forum state. However, an insurance company allegedly underwriting the airline did business there. The direct action statute of the forum state permitted suit against the insurer of a deceased assured if at the time of suit the estate of the deceased assured had not been probated. That had not happened here. Plaintiff named the insurance company as a defendant, alleging that the pilot was an additional assured under the policy.

The defendant moved to dismiss. Two state Supreme Court cases held the statute applied only to policies written and delivered within the state. An affidavit in support of the motion established that the policy had not been written or delivered within the state.

On the return day of the motion, plaintiff served a request to produce the policy. Defendant sought a protective order on the ground that the policy was not relevant to the subject matter of the motion. Only the place where it was written was, and plaintiff did not dispute that.

The court denied the protective order. It said, "The insurance policy might lead to the discovery of admissible evidence." It did not discuss subject matter. It did not discuss relevancy to the subject matter. It did not discuss "reasonably calculated." It did not discuss what the admissible evidence could be.

This discussion does not mean that all, or even a majority of courts, have scrapped relevancy as the test for discovery. It does mean, as the illustration shows, that courts can go far in upholding discovery. Counsel seeking or resisting discovery can be guided accordingly.

6.2   How to Predict How a Court Will Rule on a Discovery Motion

The cutting edge of discovery comes in the courts. The courts' rulings on discovery set the guidelines for your use of discovery. If you know an Open Door judge will pass on discovery motions, you can push discovery to the hilt. If you know a more conservative judge will pass on the motions, you must pay more attention by far to relevancy.

Some courts go farther than others. All courts recognize discovery as the moving force in modern procedure with three key functions to perform.

Discovery helps frame the issues by developing the facts out of which the issues arise. It supplants the pleadings in this respect.

Discovery expedites litigation by clarifying the issues and disclosing undisputed facts which can become the basis of stipulations or summary judgment.

Discovery insures trial on all the facts and guards against concealed or surprise evidence.

Because discovery plays these vital roles in the nature of things, the courts favor it. They have latitude in their approach to discovery questions. The discovery rules are broad, and do not attempt to answer many of the problems of day-to-day practice. Instead, the rules vest a wide discretion in the courts. The courts exercise this discretion to secure the purposes of discovery.

The upshot for practice is clear. If the court looks to these purposes in passing on discovery motions, you should be guided by these purposes in using discovery. Particularly you should couch arguments on discovery motions along these lines.

There are four other critical points about discovery in the courts.

The burden of persuasion rests on the party seeking to limit discovery.

Courts are busy, and sometimes tend to give discovery motions short shrift. They do not go deeply into the facts of the case to determine relevancy.

Discovery is supposed to operate extra-judicially. It has not to the extent intended. To cope with a volume of motions, some courts require counsel to certify to a *bona fide* effort to resolve their differences before the motion will be heard. The 1970 amendments to the discovery rules addressed the problem by requiring fines for "frivolous" motions.

All of these factors discourage resistance to discovery. In using discovery, you should bear them in mind and not hesitate to push the frontiers forward. In objecting to discovery, you must bear them in mind too and not fight vain battles lest you prejudice your opposition to truly objectionable discovery. When you do object, you should be specific in showing lack of relevancy, and, if the case lends itself to it, how the discovery serves no other legitimate purpose.

6.3   How to Plan a Strategy for Discovery to
        Meet the Needs of Your Case, with a
        Note on the Provisions That Enhance
        Its Use

To plan your strategy you must know the strengths and weaknesses of each discovery tool, and the mechanics of their use.

The oral deposition is the most powerful discovery tool since it can wring a topic dry. You can frame questions in light of the deponent's answers to previous questions, and you can leave and come back to a subject.

The deposition is not limited in its use to parties. Non-parties can be deposed as well.

The deposition cannot probe much beyond the personal knowledge of the deponent. Though he can be required to repeat hearsay, he does not have to guess or speculate. For this reason the deposition cannot get at technical information from unsophisticated witnesses; for example, actuarial material on damages from a widowed plaintiff in a death action.

Interrogatories do not have the flexibility of the deposition for pure fact finding. They are not altogether satisfactory for inquiring into such things, for example, as a witness's version of events. Opposing counsel will frame as antiseptic an account as he can. Also, interrogatories can only be served upon parties. But interrogatories can obtain the corporate (collective) knowledge of the party served. Under *Hickman* v. *Taylor,* 329 U.S. 495 (1947), answers to interrogatories must contain all of the information known to the party and to his agents including his attorney. Consequently, interrogatories can get at opinions and contentions, damage calculations, technical material, the existence and identity of witnesses and of documents, the compilation of data, and so forth. Answers to interrogatories can be used in evidence. However, answers to interrogatories also tend to be guarded since attorneys generally draft them.

Production and inspection gives you access to documents and things, and the power to test, sample, and enter upon land. The utility of the tool depends in good measure upon a reasonably precise identification of what you seek. You will generally use it in conjunction with other discovery tools.

The power to obtain physical or mental examinations and medical records is of paramount importance in personal injury and death actions, and occasionally in other situations. The topic is covered in Chapter 9.

The deposition upon written questions is cumbersome. It requires the drafting of questions on direct, cross, redirect, and re-cross examination, plus getting a person to administer the questions. It can be useful to get relatively indisputable evidence into form for proof at trial from friendly or neutral witness(es) located a distance away. Business records, the entries in a ship's log, a hospital chart are examples that come to mind.

Technically, the request to admit is not a discovery tool. It is a device to obtain "conclusively binding" admissions for purposes of the particular case only. It has not become popular. Conceptual problems have arisen about admissions of disputed facts, and of ultimate as distinguished from evidentiary facts. To pass on an objection to an "insufficient" answer just about requires trial on the merits. Also, interrogatories tend to elicit as many admissions as the other side will admit to anyway, though these admissions are not conclusively binding; i.e., the answering party can introduce other evidence on the point.

The discovery tools may be used in any sequence. They are complementary, not exclusive. They may be used any number of times (though opposing counsel can seek a protective order against harassment).

The parties may engage in discovery simultaneously.

Opposing counsel cannot bring discovery to a halt by selective objections. If he objects to certain interrogatories or requests to admit, he must answer the others within the prescribed time. If he instructs a witness not to answer certain questions on a deposition, the deposition can proceed pending a later court determination on those questions. A blanket objection to discovery usually fails.

Ordinarily, prior discovery need not be supplemented, but it must be supplemented in three situations—when new witnesses are discovered; when a trial expert is decided upon; when new information indicates that a prior response though correct when made is no longer true, and a failure to correct the response would amount to a knowing concealment. Some courts by local rule require supplementation routinely. A recent provision in the rules states that a party can obtain supplementation "through new requests for supplementation of prior responses." Whether this means, for example, serving a new set of interrogatories covering the same ground, or serving a simple request to supplement remains to be worked out in the courts.

Planning a strategy for discovery depends on four factors— what you want to achieve by discovery; any particular demands imposed by the case; the relationship of discovery with the *ex parte* investigation; and, in some jurisdictions, pressure from the court to close discovery early.

The scenario for a credibility case might go as follows: early depositions to lock the other side into its version of the facts; inspection under rule 34 coupled with the depositions or conducted independently; interrogatories later to pin down contentions, fill in details left open on the depositions, ascertain witnesses, get the substance of expert testimony, etc. If the case involved a personal injury, defense counsel would want the medical records early, and a physical examination timed to get the earliest possible cut-off date for maximum medical benefits.

The following tax case illustrates the planning and modification of a strategy, and the power of the deposition. Plaintiff deducted a huge fine it had paid to the government as an ordinary and necessary business expense deduction on its tax return. The Internal Revenue Service disallowed the deduction. Plaintiff paid the tax and sued for a refund.

The law was clear. If the violation giving rise to the fine had been due to inadvertence, the deduction would lie. If it had been due to negligence or wilfulness, it would not.

The violation had been of complex regulations. The penalty had been the first under the program. The suspicion existed that for its first case, the Government had been more interested by far in one where the fine would be huge and the impact dramatic than in one where the violation was egregious. To boot, plaintiff's business was complicated.

The technicalities had tested the mettle of the officials determining upon the violation. By the time of suit, most of them had scattered or could not remember any of the details. For counsel handling the case, the technicalities posed an almost impassable barrier.

Only one man still had a lively recollection, the retired manager of plaintiff's business. From the outset, he denied any violation. He had a persuasive and apparently irrefutable version of the events. He came across as a forthright witness. He obviously had been an able manager.

Defense counsel knew the retired manager would carry plaintiff's burden of proof. He knew that for practical purposes, defendant would have to prove negligence or wilfulness. He knew that to do this he would have to unearth fresh facts about an ancient event.

Counsel decided upon a strategy of exhaustive fact-finding. He interviewed every friendly and neutral witness he could find. He deposed every adverse witness still available. From neither group did he get anything solid. He examined the retired manager in detail but could find no chinks in his story. *Mene mene tekel upharsin—counsel began to see the handwriting on the wall.*

Counsel withheld discovery of plaintiff's attorney at the time of the violation until the end. He foresaw bitter battles over privilege. The deposition, in fact, took that turn. The attorney answered candidly, but volunteered nothing and knew when to pause for the objections of privilege to be made.

From answers to interrogatories, counsel knew that the attorney had prepared memoranda. On his deposition the attorney said just enough to wrap them in a cocoon of privilege and stopped. But counsel persisted. He avoided questions that touched on the contents. Instead he kept digging away at the circumstances of how the memoranda had been prepared. He would seize upon any concrete fact that crept into an answer to frame questions about that fact.

Slowly but surely, he began to draw out a picture of fact interviews by the attorney of the retired manager. A strong inference emerged that the memoranda memorialized these fact interviews.

With this ammunition, counsel modified his strategy for an all-out assault to get the memoranda. He first stripped the case to its bare bones so the court could grasp it instantly. He next canvassed his discovery and investigation to show that he had covered everything and that only the retired manager had a true recollection of the events. He then brought the memoranda in as the only other probable source of the facts.

The attack succeeded. The court inspected the memoranda. It satisfied itself that they indeed reported on the facts. It ruled that counsel had made a sufficient showing under *Hickman* v. *Taylor, supra* to obtain the attorney's work product.

The memoranda did not contain any admissions. In most respects they added little to the manager's story. But they did add a few crucial details. These details fitted in with certain other facts. Together they gave rise to an inference that struck at the root of the manager's story. Inescapably, the court found, the manager had to have had certain knowledge when he did certain things.

The defendant won the case.

6.4   How to Obtain Your Opponent's Work Product Through Discovery

The case of the Memorable Memoranda arose before, however it illustrates the amendments providing for discovery of trial preparation materials in certain situations. The rule permits discovery of:

- Documents and tangible things otherwise discoverable under rule 26(b) (1),
  - Prepared in anticipation of litigation or for trial,
  - By a party, or for a party, or for a party's representative,
- Only upon a showing of substantial need for preparation of the case and the inability to obtain the substantial equivalent by other means without undue hardship.

The court, if it orders such discovery, must protect against disclosure of mental impressions, conclusions, opinions, or legal theories.

Here are several pointers about the rule for practice.

It applies a two-pronged test of relevancy and necessity. The necessity test appears to embody the *Hickman* test.

The rule is couched affirmatively; i.e., it does not say discovery shall *not* be had *except* upon a showing. You might argue this indicates a test less strict than that in *Hickman.*

If faced with this argument, bear in mind that the first draft of the amendment only required a showing of good cause. Adding the necessity test, you can argue, really added the *Hickman* test.

The rule only applies to documents and things. In light of the admonition to protect mental impressions,could you then depose the party upon the documents?

If you are opposing discovery of work product, you cannot expect the court automatically to protect against disclosure of

mental impressions and privileged material. You must take three
steps. Identify every passage you believe should be protected. Put
them in context so that the court can see why they merit
protection. Persuade the court to examine the material *in camera*
in order to make its determination.

The rule does not mention protection of impeachment
material whether subject to ordinary discovery or discovery of
work product. Some courts have local rules providing for an *in
camera* inspection by the court. Since impeachment material is a
powerful instrument for getting the truth, you should make every
effort to protect it from discovery. You should attempt to cloak it
as work product. Short of that, you should employ the routine
suggested above with one possible addition. With an inexperienced
judge or a judge with no trial background, you should discuss the
importance of impeachment material in revealing the truth.

The rule also covers two other kinds of work product,
statements and expert testimony, that can be obtained directly.
Both will be covered later.

Interrogatories are an indirect but powerful means of obtaining work product. The answers to interrogatories must contain all
of the information known to a party or his agents including his
attorney. If an interrogatory covers a topic that opposing counsel
has spent time upon, the answer should include the fruits of this
work. An example would be an interrogatory asking for the names
and addresses of all persons with knowledge of the incident. The
answer should list the witnesses opposing counsel has developed.
The bearing this has on the timing of interrogatories has already
been discussed.

6.5   Utilizing the Rules to Get Witness State-
ments Taken by the Other Side

A party or a witness may on request obtain a copy of any
statement he has previously given concerning the action or its
subject matter. If you find out that your client has given a
statement to your opponent, you or the client should demand a
copy at once. But the rule gives you another string to your bow. If
you find out that a witness has given a statement, you can try to
persuade him to request a copy and give it to you.

A friendly witness probably would cooperate. A hostile witness probably would not. An independent witness might be persuaded to cooperate by an argument along these lines. He, the witness, has a right to and a need for the statement. If he interviews both sides, as a good citizen should, he would want to be accurate and consistent. If he testifies at trial, he would not want to be embarrassed by inconsistencies.

For these reasons he should request a copy of his statement. You offer your services to help the witness obtain it.

6.6   How to Eliminate the Need to Call a Weak Witness

You often have to prove elements of a case through a weak witness. Of course, weakness is a relative term. A witness may not be as strong as you would like but you call him to the stand anyway. Sometimes, though, a witness can be so vital yet so weak that you face a dilemma. If you call him, the witness may hurt the case badly. If you do not call him, a link in the proof may be missing.

In certain situations the deposition may solve the problem. If the witness resides more than 100 miles from the place of trial, or cannot be subpoenaed for trial, his deposition may be used at trial. If this situation exists, you could depose the witness before trial. At trial you can use the deposition, thus eliminating the need to call him as a witness.

In one case, an architect had been sued for professional liability under the long-arm statute. For personal reasons, he had left the state before suit had been brought. For the same personal reasons, he refused to return to the state for trial.

Plaintiff had problems with the case. Counsel for the architect believed defendant would be entitled to a directed verdict at the close of plaintiff's proof. However, he knew this scarcely meant that the judge hearing the case would actually direct a verdict.

To be on the safe side, counsel had to have the architect's testimony available. And ordinarily he would have insisted that defendant be present during the trial. In so serious a case, the jury might construe his absence as a lack of concern.

Counsel had one powerful countervailing consideration. The architect made people bristle. If he took the stand, as he would have to if he attended the trial, by the time he left it the jury might react against him.

The defendant's deposition solved the problem perfectly. As the trial turned out, plaintiff's case did have weaknesses. The judge reserved decision on defendant's motion for a directed verdict. Counsel used defendant's deposition to good effect. Defendant's absence from the trial never assumed any proportion because of the weak case in chief. The judge also reserved decision on the renewed motion for a directed verdict at the close of the evidence. The jury returned a verdict for defendant.

6.7   Reaping Advantages from Your Opponent's Discovery—A Checklist

The motto of the veteran trial lawyer is to make virtue of necessity. At no time does he follow this advice more than when faced with hostile discovery. The following checklist presents the more important benefits you might realize from your opponent's discovery:

• You can assess how your client and your witnesses respond under fire at a deposition.

• By careless fishing around, opposing counsel may develop material favorable to your case.

• The impact of the oath in discovery often forces your own client to reveal things he has attempted to hide.

• Interrogatories force the client to dig out the information necessary to answer them.

• Opposing counsel may perpetuate the testimony of a witness hostile to him.

• Opposing counsel may unwittingly make out a *prima facie* case or defense in deposing your client such that the deposition can be used at trial if the client happens to have died or is otherwise unavailable.

• By the way he conducts his discovery opposing counsel can reveal the trend of his thinking and the theory of his case.

• He can give tip-offs on impeachment material. The areas he digs into may be those he is weak in. The areas he avoids may be those he is strong in.

The case of the Grasping Clerk discussed in Chapter 1 illustrates the advantage of hostile discovery. Plaintiff had an air-tight case of a rear-end collision. Plaintiff served interrogatories just before trial. In preparing the answers, defendant for the first time revealed that when he put on his brakes he slid on a patch of ice. This gave defendant's counsel the defense of unavoidable accident in a case previously with no defense at all.

7

How to Realize
the Hidden Potentials of
the Oral Deposition

7.1   Beyond Discovery—How to Use the Deposition Tactically to Win Cases

You can use the deposition tactically as well as for discovery. There are no rules for this. It depends on how well you can see the tactical potential in your case. The following examples illustrate deposition tactics that paid off.

A "tough-minded tycoon," a prominent local citizen, had a finger in a number of businesses. One of them, the River Land Company, owned a 50% interest in No-Dent, Inc. National Corporation owned the other 50%.

No-Dent operated a parking lot on land leased from River Land. Another concern, U-Park-It Corp., managed the parking lot under a management agreement with No-Dent. U-Park-It was a subsidiary of National.

123

U-Park-Its management fee came off the top. The balance of the revenues after expenses went to No-Dent, which made periodic distributions to the two stockholders.

After many happy years together, trouble brewed when profits began to dwindle. U-Park-It, though, still collected its tidy management fee. The tycoon could not reach an adjustment with National. Bad went to worse. Then one day River Land moved. It ordered the U-Park-It man off the property. It took over management of the lot. It stopped paying the management fee. It deadlocked No-Dent to stop distribution. It closed the public entrance to the lot and opened one on a private way it owned. It turned a deaf ear to National's attempts to get satisfaction.

National bit the bullet and sued. But the case never came to life. It could not seem to get reached for preliminary injunction. Neither side commenced discovery. The case was not marked ready for trial.

Biting the bullet again, National put the pressure on its counsel. A grim executive told it like it was. The new lawyer put on the case knew a "must win" situation when he saw one. He started from the beginning, and worked his way through the facts, the leases and contracts, the amounts involved, the works. He studied the complaint again in light of the facts. He decided to add key counts and recast others.

Amending the complaint proved to be a turning point. At a conference with the court, opposing counsel commented, "The new complaint states a cause of action." He also intimated that perhaps defendant owed something to plaintiff. He pointed out though that he had a strong-minded client, and that the relationship between the parties could hardly be worse.

Plaintiff's counsel saw the problem as one on how to make the tycoon want to settle, and to give opposing counsel leverage with his own client. He saw the answer in the tycoon's busy schedule. Eat up large amounts of the tycoon's time.

The case lent itself to the tactic. The stakes were high. The case was complex and required discovery. The tycoon's role put him in the middle of things.

Counsel cleared his calendar for several months of depositions at weekly or bi-weekly intervals. He sent out his notices with sweeping subpoenas *duces tecum.* He commenced the depositions, and did not let up. He went over each document painstakingly. Once in awhile he examined another deponent to give the tycoon a taste of how nice it would be to have this ordeal over.

After a number of weeks, the tycoon's patience began to rub raw.

Casual talk about settlement soon blossomed into negotiations. Then all of a sudden the case settled. The tactical use of the deposition had paid off.

In a malpractice suit, plaintiff claimed a negligently administered injection had injured a nerve. The episode had occurred, she said, on a certain date at about 10:00 a.m. in the city of Central Rapids.

On that date a mass inoculation program had taken place at several clinics in the area. The doctor had been to a number of clinics on that and other dates.

At his deposition, though, the doctor said he had not gone to the Central Rapids' Clinic on the date in question. Counsel got him to reaffirm this.

Early in the trial, counsel called the doctor under the adverse witness statute. He elicited the same answer. He left the subject and then came back to it again. By the time he let the doctor go, counsel had the alibi implanted in the jury's mind.

Then counsel sprang his trap. He produced records showing that the doctor had put in a voucher for mileage to the Central Rapids Clinic on the day he had denied being there.

With one stroke, counsel had driven a dagger into the doctor's credibility. The doctor's explanations in his own case could not undo the damage. Plaintiff won.

Here, counsel had the travel vouchers from investigation. He did not anticipate that on his deposition the doctor would deny being at the Clinic. The instant the doctor did, however, counsel began to weave the web that ensnared him at trial. And if the doctor changed his testimony at trial, counsel at least could impeach him.

7.2   **How to Compel Production of Documents
and Tangible Things for Inspection and
Copying at a Deposition—The Pros and
Cons of Using a Subpoena Duces Tecum
or Request for Production**

There is only one way to compel a *non-party* to produce
documents and tangible things at his deposition—by serving him
with a subpoena *duces tecum*. This has become the standard way
to obtain production and inspection of materials in the hands of a
non-party. In other words, production of the materials, not
questioning of the witness, can be the real reason for the
deposition of a non-party.

There are two ways to compel a *party* to produce documents
and tangible things at his deposition. By serving him with a
subpoena *duces tecum*, or by accompanying the notice of deposition with a request for production, in which case the rule 34
procedures apply.

Whenever a subpoena *duces tecum* is used, the notice of
deposition must contain or have attached to it the contents of the
subpoena.

The scope of both the subpoena *duces tecum* and the request
to produce is the same (that set forth in rule 26(b)), but the
methods of attacking them differ.

The subpoena *duces tecum* can be attacked (a) by a motion
for a protective order made before the deposition, (b) by a motion
to quash made before the return date of the subpoena, or (c) by
written objections served within 10 days after service (or less, if
the return date itself is less than 10 days after service). If written
objections are served, the party serving the subpoena cannot
inspect the materials except by a court order for which he may
move before or during the deposition.

The request to produce requires the party served to provide a
written response within 30 days after service in which he agrees to
or objects to each item sought. The party serving the request may
move for an order compelling discovery of items objected to.

In the ordinary case, the subpoena *duces tecum* is superior to
the request to produce. The request to produce stretches out the
time for the deposition—30 days to serve a written response plus

possibly the time for a motion to compel. A deposition date can get lost in this length of time. The request to produce also invites objections. If a party has to serve a written response, whether he agrees or not, he might be tempted to throw objections in for size. The subpoena *duces tecum,* on the other hand, requires the party served to take the initiative to attack the subpoena.

7.3   How to Depose the Persons Within an Organization with Knowledge of the Facts and with Status to Bind the Organization

When you depose an organization, you want to examine persons with knowledge of the facts and with status (officer, director, or managing agent) to bind the organization by their testimony. If you do not know these persons, you have to name them blindly in your notices. At the depositions, you may find them disclaiming knowledge.

The relatively new procedure of rule 30(b) (6) can partially solve this problem. In the notice of deposition or in the subpoena served upon a non-party organization, you can name the organization as the deponent, and designate "with reasonable particularity" the matters you seek to examine.

The organization must then designate one or more persons to testify, setting forth if it wants to the topics each designee will testify upon. The designees may be officers, directors, or managing agents, or other persons (e.g., employees) who consent to testify on behalf of the organization.

The designees must testify as to matters known or reasonably available to the organization. The testimony binds the organization.

Use of the designation procedure does not preclude you from taking a deposition in the usual way.

The procedure looks great, but all that glitters is not gold. It has some built-in problems.

a. The organization might deliberately or carelessly misdesignate. At best, it cannot know precisely what you want.

b. As for the "known or reasonably known" provision of the rule—How far must an organization go to reasonably apprise itself of information? How far can a deponent testify about matters he does personally not know about?—He can parrot a corporate position but he does not have to guess or speculate. In this situation, examining counsel cannot very well get behind the "party line."

c. There also is a trap. You depose a number of designated deponents. You think other witnesses may have information and notice their depositions under the usual procedure. Opposing counsel seeks a protective order on the ground that the organization has produced all persons with knowledge and that it is being harassed.

The long and the short of it is that the designation procedure does not guarantee that you will get all that you need to get or all that you can get from an organization. In a simple case you probably can be reasonably precise in your designation, and be reasonably confident about the designation. In a complex case, if you use the procedure, you must be sure to probe about other persons with knowledge. When you are on a pure fishing expedition, you might prefer the usual procedure of either starting with deponents you know about or starting at the top and working your way down.

The following example illustrates how counsel makes these decisions. Several professional men had practiced together for years as a firm. One died. A bank, co-executor with the widow, largely handled the affairs of the estate. The surviving members of the firm thought they dealt openly with the executors. They bought out the stock interests in the firm held by the estate for what they thought was a fair price.

Not long afterwards the surviving members sold out to a national firm, continuing in the business as a local subsidiary. All seemed to be going well.

Then a canker developed on the rose. Apparently the widow did not realize as much from the estate as she expected. Events moved to a climax. The executors, with the widow now in the lead, sued the surviving members as insiders, charging they did not reveal the national deal when they bought out the estate.

The surviving members were incredulous. "If ever men had been open and generous. . . . " Counsel listened. He commiserated.

But more important, he saw he would have to dig out every scrap of information from the bank to show the scope of the executors' knowledge.

He first deposed the bank officers in direct charge of the estate. He got leads on topics which he followed up on. He got the names of other bank officers whose depositions he thereupon took. In all he took about 20 depositions.

He did not use the designation procedure. He could not have easily designated with reasonable particularity. And no matter what he designated, the bank probably would never have thought to designate as deponents all those he ultimately deposed.

7.4   Preparing to Take a Deposition—Litigation-Tested Techniques that Save Time Yet Guarantee a Searching Examination

You should take the following steps to prepare for the deposition:

* Re-examine the facts and the law.
* Study the pleadings and the various analyses in the trial book.
* Decide upon the purposes for taking the deposition. For example, you may have in mind pure fact-finding as in the case of the Incredulous Insiders. Or you may have a specific objective in mind such as seeking admissions of facts you know exist in order to defeat jurisdiction.
* Decide upon the subject matters to be covered and those to be avoided. For example, as counsel for defendant you will often leave an area untouched so that the deposition of an out-of-state plaintiff will not complete a *prima facie* case.
* Organize the documents to be used at the deposition, and make copies of originals for filing with the transcript of the deposition.
* Prepare an outline for questioning. The outline should include the topics and key points to be covered. It does not have to be as detailed as a witness sheet for use at trial. At most depositions you will tend to ask exploratory type questions, the

answer to one leading to the next question. When you want the
deposition to reflect definite information, the outline should
include each fact sought.

• The outline should be in the order of questioning you plan
to follow. Usually, you will want to use the chronological or
legally logical order. If you anticipate a rehearsed witness, you
might want to jump from topic to topic in order to break the links
in the chain of rote testimony. When you want to mask your own
analysis of the case, you should also use a random order of
questioning.

• Documents should be keyed into the outline at the points
of use.

• You must be flexible in using the outline. When an area
opens up you can explore it right away, and come back to the
exact place you departed from the outline. Or, you can make a
note of the new area in the margin, and come back to it at a
convenient time. (The outline, like the witness sheet, should be on
the right half of the page, with documents keyed in on the left.)

7.5   How to Conduct a Deposition for Maximum Results with Minimum Resistance, with a Note on How to Handle Obstructive Tactics

You must be firm but courteous with the witness.

Courtesy will disarm the witness; it encourages him to open
up and testify freely. The slam-bang, "police court" manner only
raises hackles. It puts the witness on his guard. It forces his
counsel to protect him. And even if the intimidation works, it
does not usually pay off. The trier of fact does not see the results.

Your courtesy must be matched by your firmness. You must
keep control of the situation. You may let the witness wander to
see what he says, but you must always bring him back to the
point. You may tolerate a string of "I don't know" or "I don't
remember" answers, but then you should hit home with questions
that expose these answers, or that require a "yes" or "no" reply.

You should not argue with the witness, nor lose your temper.

If the witness can goad you into this he has taken control of the deposition. Occasionally, you might want to simulate anger or become indignant. This must be a controlled display.

In the case of the Runaway Witness, counsel noticed the deposition of a high official of a national union. He hoped to pin the union down on the development and implementation of a certain union policy. He expected to get the jump on the union by scheduling the deposition early.

The deponent was an able man. He had not risen in the union through faintheartedness. He took the whip hand at the deposition, and kept it.

For openers, he produced next to nothing on the subpoena *duces tecum*. He philosophized. He argued with counsel. He bobbed and weaved. In short order he slipped out of the examiner's control.

The runaway witness in the example threw up roadblocks. He did not obstruct the deposition in the crude sense. The pure obstructionist refuses to answer, or obviously evades the question, or sometimes tries to disrupt the examination. If the obstructionist is the counsel for the deponent, he keeps objecting, or arguing, or instructing the witness not to answer.

As examining counsel you first must make sure you have an obstructionist on your hands. If you do, you should try the firm approach, the iron fist in the velvet glove. If after two or three attempts you fail at this, you have a decision to make. Should you continue the deposition and raise the incidents on a motion to compel afterwards? Or should you suspend the deposition and go to the court immediately for a ruling?

With few exceptions you should go to the court and not continue the deposition. You will have enough incidents for the court to get the picture. You will be able to point to your own efforts to solve the problem. By going to court early, you have a better chance for long-range success on the deposition.

Sometimes you will expect trouble from the beginning. In some jurisdictions you can take the deposition in the courthouse. This puts you in the position to make on-the-spot applications for rulings. The mere threat of a swift ruling often will turn a potential lion into a veritable lamb.

7.6   How to Safeguard the Use of Deposition at Trial by Properly Asking Questions and Handling Objections

How you frame questions at a deposition depends on why you are taking the deposition and who the deponent is. You can take the deposition for pure discovery, or to obtain impeachment material or affirmative proof for trial. The deponent can be an adverse party, a hostile witness, or a friendly witness.

To understand the problems in asking questions and handling objections, you must understand certain technical provisions in the rules.

1. The examination and cross-examination at a deposition are the same as at trial; i.e., a friendly witness must be asked direct questions, whereas an adverse party or hostile or unwilling witness can be asked leading questions. Rule 30(c). An adverse party (and by implication, an unwilling or hostile witness) can be contradicted or impeached. Rule 43(b).

2. At trial any party can use a deposition (a) to contradict or impeach the deponent as a witness, or (b) for any purpose if (in substance) the deponent is unavailable. At trial an adverse party can use the deposition of a party for any purpose. Rule 32(a).

3. The use of the deposition at trial is also subject to the rules of evidence which, however, have to be raised in certain ways. At a deposition, objections are noted and the evidence (except for privileged material) is taken subject to the objections. Rule 30(c). At trial under rule 32(b), any objections to receiving a deposition into evidence may be made subject to rule 32(d) (3). That rule provides that objections to the competency of a witness or to the competency, relevancy, or materiality of testimony are not waived if not taken unless the ground of the objection could have been removed if the objection had been taken.

The rules put the pressure on all counsel to raise and if possible correct evidentiary problems at the deposition.

To preserve your objections for trial, for practical purposes as opposing counsel you must object. Otherwise, at trial you would have to prove a negative—that had you taken the objection, counsel conducting the deposition could *not* have removed the ground for the objection.

As counsel conducting the deposition, you can risk taking the evidence subject to a ruling on the objection at trial. To be on the safe side, you should recast your questions to meet the objection.

Counsel sometimes attempt to stipulate that all objections except those to the form of the questions are preserved for the trial. By local rule many courts forbid such a stipulation.

In short, you cannot ignore the impact of these rules.

As examining counsel you should not examine a friendly witness with leading questions. You can do so of course if opposing counsel does not object. If opposing counsel does object, you must reframe your questions or risk not being able to use the deposition at the trial. Though you usually will not depose your own client or a friendly witness, sometimes you must in order to perpetuate testimony for trial. The problem more often arises with the independent witness. Unless you believe you can convince the court that the witness is hostile or unwilling, you must be careful about the form of your questions if you want to use the deposition at the trial.

By the same token, as opposing counsel you must be on your toes to object to the form of questions. This includes improperly framed questions to witnesses hostile to the examiner (double questions, unclear questions), as well as leading questions to friendly witnesses. If you do not, you waive your objection since examining counsel could have removed the ground of the objection.

Experienced trial lawyers have developed a way to have the best of both worlds. They use leading questions to dig out information. They they use direct questions to get the information they just dug out in admissible form.

When opposing counsel objects to a question on the ground of privilege, he will instruct the deponent not to answer. As examining counsel you should not let the matter drop at that. You should ask background questions to see if the objection is valid and can withstand a motion to compel.

With these technical points in mind, we can discuss the broader aspects of how to ask questions at a deposition in the next section.

7.7 How to Ask Questions on a Deposition and Certain Key Questions to Ask

It is worth repeating that how you frame questions at a deposition depends on why you are taking the deposition and who the deponent is.

In a case involving a fiduciary, for example, counsel wanted to elicit facts he knew to be true from an administrator of an estate in support of a motion to dismiss for lack of federal diversity jurisdiction. The administrator, plaintiff in a wrongful death action, alleged that he was a citizen of state X, and the defendants were citizens of the forum state.

The administrator had commenced the action between the dates of the primary and general elections in the forum state. The investigation brought out some startling facts. Plaintiff had voted in both of those elections. When he canceled his voter registration in the forum state, he filed an affidavit saying he moved to state X after the elections. The address he gave on the probate papers for his residence in state X appeared to be wrong. There was other material indicating that at the critical times he actually resided in the forum state.

If he could establish the matters uncovered by the investigation, counsel for the main defendant believed he had a good chance of destroying the basis for diversity jurisdiction. However, he had to get some of the information from the administrator himself in his deposition. He had strong leverage with the voting records and affidavit.

At the deposition, counsel bored in with leading questions requiring yes or no answers. If the deponent answered yes, he made an admission. If he answered no, he could be contradicted by matters of record.

Following the deposition, defendants successfully moved to dismiss for lack of diversity jurisdiction.

In the average deposition, you will be deposing an adverse party or a hostile witness, and will have three aims in mind: to get information; to pin the deponent down to his story; to obtain admissions.

This means that you want clear and unequivocal answers. To get this kind of answer, you must ask clear and unequivocal questions. However, you must gear your questions to the deponent. The less sophisticated the deponent, the simpler the questions, although you never can go wrong with simple questions to any deponent.

On this kind of deposition, you want the witness to talk; to tell his own story in his own words. When a witness talks, he may reveal things. When he tells a story in his own words, he cannot walk away from it.

You can achieve this by starting out with general questions on a given topic. This makes the witness cover all the points on that topic. As the witness testifies you note things you want to follow up on. When the witness begins to flag, you ask questions to get him going again.

When the witness more or less has finished up on the topic, you can go back over the topic with specific questions to nail the topic down. To do this you may use direct questions or leading questions.

Besides going over the topic with the deponent, you should routinely have him:

• identify all other witnesses (persons present at a conversation or event, etc.);
• identify and explain the content, including any changes and notations, on the original and copies of documents;
• identify and explain all photographs;
• make diagrams in appropriate instances;
• identify and produce for inspection all materials he used to refresh his recollection in preparation for the deposition.

There are two general rules about questioning on a deposition.

When you get a favorable answer or admission, move on. Do not give the witness time to realize what he has said, or a chance to explain his testimony either in answer to another question on the same topic or by volunteering during a pause in the questioning. This is why you should not get into the habit of repeating the answer as his next question.

You should not correct answers you know are incorrect unless you have a good reason. An incorrect answer may turn out to be good impeachment material at the trial.

When you believe you have exhausted a topic, ask several "wrap-up" questions before you move on. "Is that all?" "You're sure now that there's nothing more?" "I take it then that Exhibits 1 through 10 are all the correspondence between the parties?" If the witness tries to add to his testimony at trial he can be effectively impeached.

Sometimes you must go beyond general wrap-up questions. When you have had to squeeze facts from a reluctant witness often the record is not altogether clear. You can use the summary technique to make it clear. You summarize the deponent's testimony on a point and ask him if that is his testimony.

Make sure that you couch your wrap-up and summary questions as leading questions in order to prevent the witness from explaining his previous answers. Do not ask these questions if they might jeopardize an admission.

7.8   When as Opposing Counsel You Should Ask Questions at a Deposition and When You Should Not

As opposing counsel you should not question your own client or a friendly witness at his deposition. You only add more information and run the risk of opening up new areas for questioning.

There are two exceptions to this rule—to correct mistakes or clear up obscure points that might be used for impeachment at the trial; to get testimony for use at the trial if the deponent might not be available for trial.

As opposing counsel you have two reasons for questioning a neutral witness at a deposition—pure discovery, and to get testimony for use at the trial if the deponent might not be available for trial.

In deposing a witness, do not get carried away by your own knowledge of the facts or a subject. In one case, examining counsel began to slip into long questions that displayed his knowledge of a subject. After a bit, another lawyer quipped, "I have a suggestion, Charlie. Why don't you testify and let the witness ask the questions."

**7.9   The Pros and Cons of Submitting the
           Deposition to the Deponent for Reading
           and Signature**

Counsel usually waive the reading and signing of the deposition, and try to persuade the deponent to agree to this.

As examining counsel, however, you must consider the double impeachment argument for not waiving reading and signature. If the witness does change his trial testimony from his deposition testimony, you can say that he twice affirmed his deposition testimony—when he gave it, and when he did not change it when he read it over.

However, you must also realize that giving the deposition to the witness lets him think his testimony over. He might change favorable testimony.

When the deposition covers technical points or complicated figures, have the deponent examine it for errors. Mistakes in this kind of deposition can be costly to everybody.

**7.10   How to Unlock the Benefits of the Depo-
           sition—A Note on Indexing and Abstract-
           ing**

The mineral in a rock cannot be used until the ore is smelted. The information in a deposition cannot be used until the transcript is indexed. For a short deposition, notes on a sheet of paper might do. For a longer deposition, or a series of depositions, a formal index is necessary.

The first step is to list every single item to be indexed. The test is usefulness—what information in the deposition will you need to have access to. If there is any doubt about an item of information, include it. Examples of items would be names of people, witnesses, and organizations; issues; sub-issues; fact incidents; key points; etc. Each main item must be broken down into sub-items, the details or logical sub-parts of the main item.

The items and sub-items must be worded so that they can be found in the index. The question to ask is where in the index would the reader look for the item? What word would he look it up under? Each item should be identified by one or more key words. It should be indexed under each such key word.

For example, in the following case, on a training flight a student pilot and his instructor planned to execute a missed instrument approach for landing in actual instrument flying conditions. The exercise consisted of following the glide slope beam down, and, at a point variously called decision height or minimum altitude, pull the plane up. Something happened and the plane crashed. Here, "decision height" and "minimum altitude" would be key words for indexing. Since other altitudes figured in the case (at the outer marker, at the middle marker), "altitude, minimum" properly could be a key word for indexing, too.

The steps in indexing are to enter each item and sub-item with page numbers on a separate card, arrange the cards alphabetically, edit the cards, and then prepare the index from the cards as edited and arranged.

Where there are sub-topics, the cards would look like this in indexing the topic of Altitude in (say) the instructor's deposition:

"Altitude,
    (at) Middle Marker   p.   "
"Altitude,
    Minimum (see Decision
            Height)   p.   "
"Altitude,
    (at) Outer Marker   p.   "

The cards would be edited and the final index would be typed to read like this:

"Altitude,
    (at) Middle Marker   p.
        Minimum (see Decision
                Height)   p.
    (at) Outer Marker   p.   "

Note the cross-index here to Decision Height (there conceivably could be cross-indexes to Middle Marker and Outer Marker as well). Under "Decision Height" there could be sub-items that need not be repeated in the Altitude entry in the index, e.g.

"Decision Height   p.
   feet above ground   p.
   feet from point of impact   p.
   feet from wreckage   p.   "

The index paves the way for an abstract. An abstract gives you instant access to the gist of information on a given topic in one or more depositions, or of the gist of all the material covered in one deposition. The material is boiled down and typed onto a sheet into separate short paragraphs with page references to the deposition(s).

7.11   How to Take a Videotape Deposition

A videotape is a motion picture with sound electronically recorded on a magnetic tape. It comes in black and white or color. Since the electronic impulses are invisible, a videotape can only be seen and heard by projection on a television screen. The picture and the sound can be played separately which allows for editing.

Videotape equipment consists of a videotape recorder, a videotape camera, microphones, and a receiver monitor or screen. The equipment is portable and easy to use. You can buy or rent the equipment. Or better yet, you can hire a videotaping service which avoids any problem about an impartial operator. Either way, the cost usually runs less than a court reporter.

The videotape deposition outclasses the manual deposition as a courtroom tool.

The jury sees and hears how the witness testifies. This demeanor evidence helps the jury pass upon credibility.

The jury absorbs and remembers a videotape deposition better. Reading a deposition soon bores a jury. A bored jury is an inattentive jury.

A witness can refer to visual aids, work with models, and perform experiments on a videotape deposition. This opens the door to demonstrative evidence that otherwise could not be brought into the courtroom live. It also opens the door to effective testimony of experts who cannot be available for trial, or whom a party could not afford for trial. For example, you could retain a nationally known expert and videotape his testimony with demonstrations. Or, to take another example, if it looks like the court will force you to trial when an expert such as a treating physician cannot make it, you can videotape his deposition.

When the jury sees and hears a witness on videotape contradict himself on the stand, you have impeached him far better than you ever could by a dry recitation of transcribed deposition testimony.

To illustrate the use of a videotaped deposition combined with a demonstration, plaintiff lost part of his hand while operating a steel press in defendant's machine shop. Defendant moved to take plaintiff's deposition in the machine shop to demonstrate how he had operated the machine.

Plaintiff objected that the events could not be recreated but only staged to his disadvantage.

The court permitted the videotape deposition for the purpose of showing how plaintiff approached and operated the press with the qualification that plaintiff did not have to operate the press but could use a pointer instead.

A party must obtain court permission to take a videotape deposition. On motion under rule 34 (b)(4) a court may order a non-stenographic recording of a deposition. (The rule thus covers purely audio recordings as well.) The order must designate the manner of recording, preserving, and filing the deposition. The order may include other provisions to assure accuracy and trustworthiness. In the case of the Apprehensive Amputee, for example, the court provided that the videotape operators swear to record accurately in a trustworthy manner.

If the court grants permission to videotape a deposition, any other party can have it stenographically transcribed at his own expense. For that matter, the sound track of a videotape can be transcribed.

The parties can also stipulate to a videotape deposition.

The rules do not literally require that the witness examine, read, and sign the deposition. The power of the court to insure accuracy and trustworthiness supports this close reading of the rule. In the case of the Apprehensive Amputee, for example, the court required the operators to certify the correctness and completeness of the recording in the same way a court reporter would certify a typed transcript, and then immediately file an original. The court did not mention submitting the recording to the witness.

You will find taking a videotape deposition simplicity itself if you bear these points in mind.

—Take the deposition in a room away from noises and electronic disturbances.

—Place the witness in normal light at an uncluttered desk or table without distracting bric-a-brac, and with space for the use of visual aids and models.

—Place the examining attorney so that he appears in the picture, too. Do so also for other counsel who will actively participate, as, for example, on a deposition for use at trial where you can foresee a number of objections. A second camera may be necessary.

—Provide each speaker with a microphone. Use the playback feature of videotape to check the setting and make any adjustments.

—Set ground rules for the use of the zoom lens. The camera is usually placed about the same distance from the witness as the witness stand in a courtroom is from the jury box. At a trial the witness would not suddenly be projected in front of the jury to emphasize testimony. At a deposition a zoom shot to emphasize testimony might be objectionable. On the other hand, a zoom shot to better display a visual aid or manipulation of a model probably would not be objectionable. Keep up the viewers' interest. Occasionally, vary the angle of the camera. Have the witness move or do things.

—Start the deposition at the beginning with the swearing of the witness. To keep a flow, minimize off-the-record conferences and visual and auditory distractions. Record all pertinent events such as stipulations, objections, argument, and colloquy. Close with a statement indicating the deposition is over.

—Prepare your questions and the scenario for the deposition beforehand so that the videotape will flow. This will be relatively easy for a friendly witness who can be horse-shedded. It will be more difficult for a hostile witness whose answers you cannot predict.

—Pin-point the nature and location on the tape of all objections and exhibits. If possible, get the court to rule on admissibility before the trial. At the trial, flash the tape by sustained objections and inadmissible exhibits.

—If the court does not rule beforehand, at the trial stop the tape at the appropriate spots so the court can rule.

—Do not edit out any objections (sustained or over-ruled) because they must be preserved for appeal.

—Set up one or more screens for normal television viewing, the number depending on how best to accommodate the jury, court, and counsel.

—To let the jury inspect exhibits, stop the screening at the point they were marked.

8

How to Get the Most
Out of Interrogatories,
Production and Inspection,
and Requests to Admit

8.1 Interrogatories Can Boomerang! Some Tips on When to Serve Them, and When Not to

You should have a purpose for serving interrogatories. Purposeless interrogatories can do more harm than good. For example, if your opponent is not prepared, your interrogatories may force him to dig up material for the answers and organize his case for trial. Sometimes the result can be fatal.

In the personal injury case discussed in Chapter 1, plaintiff's car had been hit in the rear by defendant's car. Plaintiff claimed he suffered a whiplash injury to his back.

The defendant's insurance company tried to settle the case without suit. The plaintiff demanded much more than the company thought the medical reports justified. As the case progressed, though, the company slowly kept upping the offer.

On the basis of the insured's statement taken by the adjuster, there was no defense, not even any extenuating circumstances to argue to the jury.

Plaintiff had to know that defendant had no defense. There had been months of candid discussions about the case. The offer had kept creeping up. The offer, in fact, was high for the type of case.

Then plaintiff served interrogatories. This injected defense counsel into an active role for the first time. To get the information to answer the interrogatories, he had to interview the defendant. To counsel's surprise and delight, the defendant said that when he put on his brakes his car slid on a patch of ice.

From nothing, all of a sudden counsel had something, the defense of unavoidable accident. This stiffened the insurance company's resolve not to offer a penny more. At the trial, as was brought out before, the jury apparently believed the plaintiff exaggerated his condition and was malingering. They reacted against him and found for the defendant.

The defense of unavoidable accident gave the jury something to peg its verdict on. If the court granted a new trial, defendant had a powerful point on appeal. If defendant lost an appeal from a new trial ruling, plaintiff still had to retry the case with the same infirmities.

The case settled for a modest amount.

Plaintiff had no need to obtain collective knowledge. He had no need to discover damage calculations (obviously), the existence of documents, the explanation of technical matters. In short, he did not need most of the things interrogatories are best suited to get.

It might be said that plaintiff wanted defendant's account of the accident since it had become clear that the case would be tried. If so, with a deposition he could have followed up on the icy patch story then and there. As it was, defense counsel had a chance to work it into an artful defense.

The dangers of interrogatories forcing the other party to prepare his case can take subtler forms. Most cases for example have an inherent dynamic. At certain points in the course of the case the chances for settlement are higher. One of these points typically comes after the case has been pending awhile. The parties have had a taste of combat. Each had shown the flag. Neither as yet had run up too much expense, or had been personally bothered, in preparation. But the reckoning of expense and time in working the case up for trial soon has to be paid. At this point economic realities can prevail to effect a settlement.

Interrogatories can be a catalyst releasing the economic realities to do this job. On the other hand, interrogatories either ill-timed or coupled with a hard attitude can shatter this possibility for settlement. Once he has spent the money to prepare the case, a party has incurred the expense and often finds he can negotiate from greater strength. The case of an "impetuous dealer" illustrates this.

The defendant corporation had been an exclusive dealer of the plaintiff manufacturer for years. The dealership had prospered to the mutual benefit of both parties. Then the principal of the dealer died. Management passed to a relative. Prosperity gave way to hard times. After a few years the dealership needed an infusion of capital. The manufacturer lent the dealer a substantial amount of money.

The loan helped keep the dealership afloat but did not stop it from slowly sinking. Then the manufacturer had a personnel shake-up. The new management took a long, hard look at the dealership. It began to demand better performance.

The new head of the dealership did not take to the pressure. The manufacturer stuck to its guns. One day, out of the blue, the dealer canceled the franchise. This rash step took the burden of cancellation off of the manufacturer. It opened the door for a suit by the manufacturer for the large amount owing to it. It stripped the dealer of such classic defenses to a cancellation by the manufacturer as unfair cancellation and anti-trust violations.

The manufacturer's claim was made up of dozens of different items. For practical purposes each item was a distinct lawsuit with its own set of facts. Most of these items were complex. The manufacturer had a reasonably accurate idea of the total claim. To work up each claim would have been a major job. In short, the manufacturer had a good enough grasp of its total claim to be able to seek a settlement with the dealer that had little by way of assets, and with the principal (on a personal guarantee) whose assets were tightly tied up. The manufacturer wanted to get the best settlement it could without throwing good money after bad. This meant the manufacturer was prepared to discount its claim substantially.

The dealer's counsel knew this. He knew his leverage lay in the time and expense the manufacturer would be put to in order to prove each of its many claims. He too, as well as the manufacturer and its counsel, was willing to cut the Gordian knot by arriving at a figure. But not so the defendant. He wanted the manufacturer to establish each claim to the penny. He insisted on threshing out to the last detail contested positions on each item.

The defendant finally forced his counsel into serving interrogatories. This forced the manufacturer to go through the protracted exercise it had hoped to avoid. By the time it had finished the answers, it had organized and prepared its case for trial. Its position on settlement hardened. It, not the dealer, now had the leverage. As the trial approached, the pressure on the dealer increased daily. He held out, stubborn as he had been impetuous. But he finally caved in under the pressure. He had to agree to a settlement.

Consider another illustration of how interrogatories plus a little flexibility can force a settlement at the propitious time. Here the manufacturer had to cancel a distributorship for a failure to perform. The dealer, a small town big-shot, insisted they "can't do this to me." He rushed off to his lawyer who commenced the boilerplate anti-trust suit.

From the outset the case had a cost of defense settlement value. Depositions and requests to produce verified the thin liability and flimsy damages. But plaintiff only expressed outrage at the nominal settlement offer.

Then defendant fired a salvo of intricate and detailed interrogatories. Plaintiff staggered under the impact. Defendant then sweetened the offer, not by much, but by just enough so that plaintiff could save face. Plaintiff swallowed his pique and accepted the offer.

These examples illustrate that you have to have a purpose in serving interrogatories, and that you have to evaluate whether and when to serve them in the context of the case. The examples do not illustrate hard-and-fast rules.

One final point on this subject. You have to draw a line between an opponent who is not, and probably will never be prepared, and one who has not yet attended to preparation. In the case of the Impetuous Dealer, counsel for the manufacturer ultimately would have engaged in the same preparation that the dealer's interrogatories precipitated. The mistake there was one of timing and attitude. In the wrongful death case discussed in Chapter 3, defendant's counsel knew his opponent had virtually completed his investigation of the accident. In both instances counsel prepared their cases very well indeed. The different circumstances of the two cases dictated when counsel had to work his case up.

The rule specifically permits interrogatories that ask for opinions or contentions that relate to fact or to the application of fact to law. This kind of interrogatory can be valuable in pinning the other party down to what he really contends.

In the case of the Man's Good Name, for example, an investigator looked into the person's background, habits, associates, and the like, at the request of a client. The investigator rendered a report. Whether on the basis of the report or otherwise, the client took steps which the subject deemed adverse. The subject sued the client on a variety of grounds, and he sued the investigator for slander, invasion of privacy, and violation of the Fair Credit Reporting statute. This ambiguous statute uses the concepts of consumer reports, and consumer investigative reports.

The investigator's counsel knew plaintiff's counsel prepared a thorough case. The complaint reflected an understanding of the concepts underlying each count. Counsel did not hesitate to serve interrogatories asking in what respects the investigator's report was libelous or invaded plaintiff's privacy, and more important, in what respects it constituted as a consumer report, or a consumer investigative report under the statute.

The use of interrogatories to obtain the substance of the testimony of trial experts will be considered in Chapter 10.

8.2   How to Frame Evasion-Proof Interrogatories

The important thing to remember about interrogatories is that a lawyer probably will prepare the answers. In propounding the interrogatories, you cannot expect him to do your work for you. Unless he has some purpose of his own to serve, he will interpret questions literally, construe ambiguities in his own favor, and not volunteer the information that would have been elicited by an unasked question. For example, if the interrogatory asks, "What doctors treated plaintiff?", the answer will give the names but not the addresses or specialties of the doctors, much less the dates and nature of treatment.

There are seven key points to framing a good set of interrogatories.

First, you have to get a clear picture in your own mind about what you want to accomplish by the interrogatories. You then have to analyze just how far the interrogatories will in fact accomplish these purposes. Finally, you have to weigh what realistically you think you will get against any disadvantages or dangers in serving the interrogatories.

In a wrongful death case, for example, defendant's counsel had several principal objectives in serving interrogatories—to get plaintiff's damage calculations; to get the names and addresses of witnesses; to identify any expert witnesses and the substance of their testimony; to pin down legal contentions.

Second, you have to block out the areas of inquiry in a logical and systematic way. Then within each area of inquiry you have to list each point to be covered. Liability, for example, would be a typical area in every case. Each aspect of the *prima facie* case and the defenses would be points within that area. Damages, documents, witnesses, expert testimony are other examples of typical areas. In large cases, you might serve several sets of interrogatories on different areas of inquiry. The set of interrogatories in the last section of this chapter illustrates a thorough set of interrogatories in a simple case.

Third, you must ask clear, concise, and precise questions. To get unequivocal answers, to avoid mere yes or no answers, and to forestall objections, you must ask unequivocal questions. In framing questions, you have to keep in mind that words have connotations as well as denotations. If a question begins to get complicated, you should break it down into its component parts or into sub-questions. Too many sub-questions though and sub-sub-questions can become confusing.

When you are asking questions in crucial areas of the case, or if you anticipate an objection or an evasive answer to a question on a crucial point, you should frame several questions covering the point. Answering counsel might be hard put to sustain objections or evade them all.

Fourth, you should use the services of your expert in framing questions on technical points. In the case of the Vanishing Damages discussed in Chapter 1, defendant's theory of the case was that plaintiff itself had changed the embossing roll some time after defendant had manufactured and shipped it to plaintiff.

The roll, which resembled a giant rolling pin, had failed in operation. An inflammable coolant had spewed causing a fire. The failure involved a weld that helped hold and seal the journal to the head. Plaintiff claimed it had ordered a roll with a one-piece construction of the head and journal.

Defendant's expert, a metallurgical engineer, helped frame a set of searching interrogatories covering a number of technical points. One of these technical interrogatories asked about the nature of the cooling system used in the embossing process at the time of the incident.

The answer revealed that it was a flow-through system; that is, the coolant went in through the journal at one end of the embossing roll and went out through the journal at the other end. At the trial, defendant produced expert testimony that plaintiff's blueprint for the roll called for a system whereby the coolant went in (through an inner pipe) and out the same end of the journal. Only an expert would have known the right questions to ask on the interrogatories that set up this powerful defense.

Fifth, you should avoid interrogatories that will invite objections, especially those to which objections probably will be sustained. This includes asking for too much, more than you need, which opens the door to a charge of harassment or oppression. It also includes ambiguous and overly broad questions which are the chief offenders. Most courts, for example, sustain objections to questions asking for "each and every fact relevant to...." You can get the full answer by a series of narrower but specific questions, one following the other.

Sixth, you should automatically ask several tag questions. After a series of questions on a topic, you should ask:

"Is there any other information that the respondent has on the topic covered in interrogatories blank to blank not included in the answers to those interrogatories, and if so state it."

At the end of the interrogatories, you should ask:

"In preparing the answers to these interrogatories, have you inquired of all persons within your control who have or who might have information to answer them?

"If the answer to the preceding interrogatory is 'no,' state the names, addresses, and capacities of the persons not so consulted, and as to each, state the reason why that person was not consulted.

"List the names, and addresses, and capacities of all persons consulted in obtaining information to answer these interrogatories, and as to each, indicate each answer to which they contributed information."

The purpose of these tag interrogatories is to prevent the responding party or one of its witnesses from slipping out from underneath the answers at the trial. An answer to an interrogatory is not conclusively binding on the responding party and does not limit his proof. The responding party can introduce rebuttal or other evidence at the trial on the point. These interrogatories, therefore, can be invaluable for impeaching such additional evidence.

The spread of loan receipts and Mary Carter type agreements has caused defense counsel to routinely ask another tag question.

"Has the plaintiff entered into any settlement or arrangement with any party to the suit or with any person potentially liable to the plaintiff, and if so, as to each such arrangement, state the particulars and identify by a sufficient description all documents pertaining to it."

Seventh, to insure clearness and preciseness at the beginning of complicated interrogatories, you should include a set of definitions and rules to follow in answering the interrogatories. Some counsel also refer to the rule in *Hickman* v. *Taylor*, 329 U.S.

495 (1947), that the answers must include information known to the agents of the party, including his attorney, as well as the party himself.

The case of the Omitted Interrogatory illustrates the care that must be put into the planning and execution of a set of interrogatories. The case involved the economic and social impact of a particular statute. The proof in the case consisted mainly of economic and statistical data. The data came from government and state agencies, foundation studies, and so forth. The interpretation of the data lie entirely with experts.

One of the parties served interrogatories designed to get the information the other party relied upon to support its position on the economic and social issues involved. When the interrogatories were served, the responding party had not yet been able to obtain any of the data.

Later, the responding party got the data. Its expert came up with a relevant analysis, and inferences on the economic and social issues. But the responding party never had to disgorge the findings of its expert. The interrogating party neglected to ask specifically about the identity of trial experts, and the subject matter and substance of the experts' testimony. The failure to ask this question relieved the responding party from the duty of supplementing its answers.

8.3   How to Frame Requests for Admission That Elicit Binding Responses

There are four key features about requests for admission.

Any matter admitted is conclusively established for the pending case and cannot be withdrawn or amended unless the court finds that to do so is necessary to preserve trial on the merits and will not prejudice the requesting party.

A request may seek the admission of any matter within the scope of rule 26(b) that relates to statements or opinions of fact or of the application of law to fact including the genuineness of documents.

Denials, qualifications, and objections to requests must be specific and the responding party has the duty to make a reasonable inquiry for information to answer.

On a motion to test the sufficiency of an answer or objection, the court has power to deem a matter admitted or postpone answering until before trial as well as to sustain or over-rule an objection and require an amended answer.

These features give rise to a general rule about requests to admit that can be expressed negatively. The court will be reluctant to enforce speculative, vague, or ambiguous requests because to do so would expose the answering party to the drastic remedy of a conclusively binding admission as to something less than true and accurate.

Consequently, you as a requesting party want to serve unequivocal requests with as much evidence as possible to back up the truth of the requests. This will help to insure three things—that you get unequivocal answers; that the answering party cannot object to or deny the request, or qualify his answer; that if he does, you can more readily get the court to enforce the request.

This means that besides being backed up by the truth, requests must be unequivocal. There are seven rules for framing unequivocal requests.

Each matter sought to be admitted must be set forth separately in a single sentence.

A complicated matter must be broken up into its component parts, each separate part being set forth successively in a single sentence.

As a corollary, each request should be complete in itself without incorporation by reference.

Each request must be clear, concise, and precise.

Documents for which admissions of genuineness are sought should be attached to the requests.

You have to keep two things in mind when you decide to use requests for admission. You have to be clear about what you want to accomplish by serving the requests. You have to time the requests properly.

It is sometimes said that requests for admission can eliminate the need to investigate and assemble proof on entire issues, or on specific elements within an issue. This statement is true so long as you do not forget that often a considerable amount of investigation on a point may be necessary before you are in the position to serve requests on that point. On the other hand, the requests may be and often are about matters in your own case that you know are true and do not have to investigate to any appreciable degree. In the case of the Taciturn Trucker, to be discussed in the next section, the plaintiff consignee requested the defendant trucker to admit the genuineness of the clean on-board bill of lading the trucker issued when he picked up the shipment from the consignor for delivery to the consignee. Here, counsel did no investigating except to double-check with his client, the consignee, that this was the original bill of lading issued by the trucker for the shipment in question. This case also illustrates use of requests to facilitate proof on a simple point.

Counsel may even request to eliminate an entire issue. This has become much more feasible because the rule now permits requests on the application of law to facts.

For example, plaintiff's decedent had been the employee of a subcontractor. He had been killed in an accident on the job site. Plaintiff sued a number of defendants including the general contractor.

The general contractor asked the plaintiff to admit that the following statement was true:

"At the time of the accident sued upon, the premises on which the accident occurred were occupied or under the control of the defendant general contractor."

At first, plaintiff tried to fudge the answer. Finally, plaintiff had to admit the request. Under the applicable state law the general contractor therefore became the statutory employer of the decedent and immune from common lawsuit. The court so ruled.

Both of these examples could illustrate another point. You might want to eliminate the need to prove a fact at trial not merely to speed things up but because the witness you would have to use might be weak or vulnerable in other areas.

The question of when you should serve requests has a theoretical answer and a practical answer. The theoretical answer is, as early as you can in order to minimize trial preparation. This neglects several realities of litigation.

First, as mentioned already, you have to be on sure grounds for your requests. To put yourself in this solid position may require considerable investigation.

Second, you must also evaluate whether your case is as

crystallized as it will be later on. This sounds like saying the same thing, but it is not. Perhaps perspective is a better word. As more material develops, the exact framing of issues and their relationship to each other may be sharpened and defined. You want admissions on facts or issues precisely as they relate to the case.

Third, your opponent might not yet be able to answer. If you brought on the sufficiency of an "I don't know" answer, the court could postpone his obligation to respond until just before trial. This could force you to assemble the very proof you hoped to avoid putting together because you cannot risk that the court might go along with an unsatisfactory response or objection.

The practical answer lies in timing requests to the nature of the admissions sought, and the circumstances of the case, and in the realization that more than one set of requests can be served. The two examples illustrate this. There was no reason why the plaintiff could not, if he wanted, have served a request for the Tactiturn Trucker to admit the genuineness of the bill of lading at the outset of the case. On the other hand, in the case of the Vicarious Employee, the defendant contractor hardly could expect an admission on the central issue in the case except as it careened toward its conclusion.

8.4   How to Answer Interrogatories and Requests to Admit Without Giving Your Case Away—a Checklist

You have a number of alternatives when you are served with a set of interrogatories or requests for admission. The following table sets them out schematically:

Interrogatories	*Requests for Admission*
1. Answer.	1. Admit, or deny or qualify, in whole or in part.*

---

*A response must differentiate those parts denied or qualified from those parts admitted. For denial, use the word "deny." Some courts have held phrases like "refuses to admit" do not constitute denials. A request is deemed admitted if not responded to.

2. "Do not know," but subject to duty of reasonable inquiry.

2. a. Neither admit nor deny, stating reasons.

   b. Statement of lack of information or knowledge sufficient to admit or deny but that party has made a reasonable inquiry.

3. Object with reasons spelled out (e.g., privilege, not relevant, work product, too broad, vague, burdensome and oppressive, seeks material from nontrial expert, question of law unrelated to fact, etc.).

3. Object with reasons spelled out (e.g., privilege, vague, or otherwise improperly framed, etc.).

4. Object or move that answer to interrogatory seeking application of law to fact should be deferred until pre-trial.

4. Object that answer be deferred until pre-trial.

5. Seek a protective order under rule 26(c).

5. Seek a protective order under rule 26(c).

6. Specify and offer the records from which the answer can be ascertained if the burden of ascertaining would be substantially the same for the serving party as for the answering party.

Because you can object does not mean you should object. You should avoid making captious objections or evasive answers.

If you do, you might end up worse off than if you had answered forthrightly. The reason for care lies not only in your duty as an officer of the court but in the court's power to compel discovery and penalize evasions. The discovering party can move to test objections or the sufficiency of answers. The court can not only compel discovery, but also it can order that a matter is admitted, and impose costs in obtaining the order including attorney's fees.

Formerly, the discovering party could not move to determine the sufficiency of answers. It is true that at the trial the court might hold that a defective answer constituted an admission. The trouble is that the discovering party could not gamble on getting such a ruling; he had to prepare his proof. Now the rule lets the discovering party test the sufficiency of an answer. If the answer does not comply with the rule, the court can order an amended answer or that the matter is admitted.

The case of the Taciturn Trucker which arose before the rule change illustrates the importance of the change. A carrier had issued a clean bill of lading for shipment of an exothermic generator from the manufacturer in Rhode Island to a consignee in Montauk, Long Island. The generator arrived damaged. The consignee sued the manufacturer and the carrier.

The consignee struck out on three different sets of requests for admission. The consignee first asked the carrier to admit the genuineness of the bill of lading issued by the carrier. The carrier denied the request. The consignee then asked the carrier to admit, among other things, that the manufacturer had delivered a generator for shipment to the consignee in Long Island. The carrier denied this request stating that the generator was not sufficiently described. The consignee attempted to solve this by asking the carrier to admit that the manufacturer had delivered goods to the carrier for shipment to the consignee in Long Island. The consignee denied this request also on the grounds that the goods were not sufficiently described.

A transparent evasion? Of course. How many exothermic generators are shipped to Montauk. But the consignee still had to prepare its proof. It could not risk whether the court would rule the matter admitted at trial.

The trucker's tactic was as transparent as its evasive answer. The trucker knew it was a subrogated case and that the insurance company, the real party in interest, would be reluctant to incur expenses for bringing witnesses up to the trial. By answering evasively, the trucker sought this leverage. Under the new provisions, the trucker could not have gotten away with this for a minute.

The best approach to answering interrogatories and requests for admission is the open approach. This does not mean that you must knuckle under to improper interrogatories and requests, or give your case away in answering them.

The following checklist gives the 15 steps you should take to protect your client's interests and yet answer responsively:

1. Analyze the interrogatory or statement for its exact meaning, and keep an eye out for double or loaded questions or statements.

2. Weigh the words and phrases for ambiguities.

3. Determine if any privilege or other grounds for objection or postponement of answers lie, and if so, whether they should be asserted.

4. Determine if documents can be offered under rule 33(c) in answer to interrogatories.

5. Answer the exact question asked.

6. Answer clearly, precisely, and concisely; i.e., be short, sweet, and to the point.

7. The answer to a request for admission must clearly differentiate those parts denied or qualified from those parts admitted.

8. Do not guess or volunteer.

9. Identify those answers or parts of answers based upon hearsay.

10. If you answer an ambiguous interrogatory or request, state the interpretation upon which you base the answer.

11. Consult with experts on answers involving their expertise.

12. Answer each interrogatory or request separately.

13. If outside materials are referred to in the answer, identify the reference.

14. You as counsel have the responsibility of drafting the answers into final form.

15. You as counsel should not sign answers to interrogatories since they must be sworn to under oath, and possibly you could be examined upon them at trial.

An "outside director" case illustrates the importance of answering the exact question. A defeated tender offeror sued a target corporation and its directors for damages measured by the difference between the value of the minority stock position it bought into and the majority stock position it claimed it would have had but for the allegedly wrongful actions of the defendants.

Top management and the inside directors had managed the defense for the target corporation. The outside directors had participated only at special meetings of the board of directors convened to pass on certain matters.

Plaintiff served a set of sweeping and identical interrogatories upon all of the defendants. Defendants' counsel prepared a master set of answers on behalf of the target corporation. The target corporation would be charged with the knowledge of all of its officers and directors. Directors' counsel prepared answers many of which incorporated answers of the target corporation by reference.

One of the outside directors, a top-drawer lawyer, refused to go along with this blanket incorporation by reference. He pointed out that he had no knowledge of much of the information in the answers of the target corporation. At the trial he did not want to be examined or impeached by answers incorporating information he knew nothing about. He drafted and served answers based upon his knowledge, and his knowledge alone.

The reaction of plaintiff's counsel was interesting. He moved to compel responsive answers from the other directors who incorporated the answers of the target corporation by reference. He argued that they had not answered about what they personally knew. He referred to the answers of the one director as the proper way to answer.

The wrongful death case previously discussed points up the pitfalls of a less than precise incorporation by reference. Plaintiff sued for a maritime death under a state wrongful death statute. That statute did not apply. The general maritime law governed the case. The statute measured damages by loss to the decedent's estate, the general maritime law by loss to beneficiaries.

Defendant served interrogatories asking for the calculations and facts for each and every element in the damage formula. Plaintiff answered by attaching a copy of her economist's report. She did not identify sections of the report as applicable to any given interrogatory, which was bad enough. To compound matters, the report had been prepared on the basis of the state statute and not the general maritime law.

The court granted defendant's motion for more responsive answers.

8.5 How the Option to Produce Business Records in Answer to Interrogatories Can Avoid Costly and Disruptive File Searches

The rule 33(c) option to produce business records in answer to interrogatories has become so important that it requires separate discussion. The provision meets an abuse. Some attorneys would serve scores of intricate interrogatories knowing that to answer them would require a costly and disruptive file search. Counsel served them more to grind his opponent into a settlement than to gather information for trial. The responding party either had to prepare answers or try his luck with a protective order. (That the option became necessary indicates how unresponsive the courts were to motions for protective orders.)

Now, however, if the answer can be derived from business records and the burden of deriving the information would be the same for the interrogating party as for the answering party, the latter may "specify" such records and offer them to the former for inspection and copying.

The answering party has the duty to find out whether the information sought can be derived from a given batch of records.

In other words, he must designate concretely the records from which the information can be derived. He cannot respond that a given batch of records may or may not contain the information sought.

The case involving a distributor—discussed in Chapter 2—illustrates this device. The distributor had a so-called dual franchise. He handled automobiles made by Mammoth Motor Works and specialty vehicles made by defendant. Defendant also manufactured its own line of automobiles.

Defendant canceled the distributorship for non-performance and awarded the franchise to one of its own high-performance automobile dealers in the area.

The distributor sued the defendant manufacturer and the new franchisee and unknown others for an attempt to monopolize the market for specialty vehicles. The distributor claimed the defendants conspired to cancel specialty vehicle franchises held by Mammoth Motors dealers in order to award them to franchised distributors of defendant manufacturer's cars.

Plaintiff dumped a set of intricate interrogatories on the defendant manufacturer. A number of them inquired about the pattern of distributorships over a five-year period; the number of dual franchises at the beginning of the period; the changes by year; the reasons for termination; the number of the defendant manufacturer's dealers handling both lines; and so forth.

The information such as existed lay in thousands of index cards for current and terminated franchises. Availing itself of rule 33(c), the defendant manufacturer proffered the records to the distributor.

8.6   Using Production and Inspection of Documents and Things to Win Cases

A good argument can be made that production and inspection is the most powerful discovery tool. The reason for this is that it gives you access to documents and all manner of recorded material, and the right to test and sample tangible things, and to enter upon land. Documents, testing a product, measuring and photographing land can be crucial in certain kinds of cases. The result may give you the solid, virtually irrefutable evidence that the jury will latch onto as dispositive.

Going back to the tax case discussed in Chapter 6, it illustrates not only how certain memoranda provided the key to victory but how a resourceful pursuit obtained their production and inspection. In an earlier suit, the government had sued a company for violation of price control regulations. The suit had culminated in imposition of a substantial penalty. The second suit was by the company to take the penalty as a tax deductible, ordinary and necessary business expense.

The tax case involved the same facts as the penalty case. The deduction would lie if the underlying violation had been the result of inadvertence, but not if the result of negligence or wilfulness.

During depositions in the tax case, government counsel found out that the company's attorney in the penalty case had recorded his interviews with the company's general manager about the facts. These memoranda were the only contemporaneous version of events which had happened over a decade before.

Government counsel saw a big obstacle to getting the memoranda. Arguably, they were attorney's work product, and the general manager not only was still available but had been deposed. Showing the impracticability of getting the information elsewhere, the *Hickman* v. *Taylor* test for discovery of work product, would be difficult.

But counsel saw a possible way around the obstacle. The work product was the work product of a prior and different case. Also a sort of inherent necessity existed. The memory of the general manager had to be far more fallible 10 years later, and he had an interest in justifying his actions.

Counsel took three steps to bolster his motion for production. He first completed the balance of his discovery and investigation. He thus enabled himself to show that nothing else afforded the type of information the memoranda contained. He worked up his presentation of the facts so that the court instantly would see the pivotal role played by the general manager. He emphasized the unique value of contemporaneous information to the just disposition of a suit arising over 10 years later. Counsel urged that the court examine the memoranda.

Counsel's approach paid off. The court did examine the memoranda. Because counsel had put the memoranda into context and had pointed out the type of things to look for, the court granted the motion.

The memoranda provided important links in the chain of evidence that convinced the court that the underlying violation had not been due to mere inadvertence.

There are two limitations to production and inspection. It only lies against parties to an action. It only lies as to materials

within their possession, custody, or control. Control is the operative concept. In the case of the Dominant Parent, for example, a
parent corporation which was a party to the action had to produce
records of a subsidiary which was not a party. In the case of the
Uncooperative Assured, on the other hand, an insurance carrier
which was a party sued under a direct action statute, did not have
to produce a propellor blade under the control of the airplane
manufacturer, which was not a party to the suit and which refused
to relinquish it to the carrier.

The secret to the successful use of production and inspection
is knowing what you want and describing what you want with as
much preciseness as you can. The rule requires that the material
sought be set forth by item or category, and that the item or
category be described with "reasonable particularity." This is an
elastic concept depending on the circumstances and the judge.
You should ask yourself two questions: How much do I as the
inquiring party know about what I want so as to be able to
designate it? How specific does the particular judge tend to think
designations should be? Some judges think that rule 34 discovery
should be able to proceed independently of other discovery. Other
judges think that if necessary, a party should get a description of
materials through interrogatories or the depositions of such persons as records custodians.

Even with a liberal judge, the more precise you can be the
better. Specificity does not give your opponent the loophole of
arguing that he cannot tell what is sought and that he is being
asked to decide at his peril. It also facilitates the court's determination about whether an objection has any foundation, or
whether a request has been properly complied with.

The following case illustrates the value of precision. Plaintiff's counsel requested production of the instrument panel of a
plane that had crashed. Defendant's counsel took the request
literally. He produced a thin metal panel with many holes in it but
with nary an instrument. Plaintiff's counsel fulminated. Defendant's counsel blandly produced the parts book describing this
object as the instrument panel. Plaintiff's counsel moved to
compel, which gave the court the opportunity to splutter. The
court ordered the instruments reinserted and produced but could

not gainsay that counsel had produced precisely what plaintiff had asked for.

There are two reasons for not leaping into production and inspection until you have a good idea of what you want. You must be sure that you ask for enough. The reason is obvious. But you also must be careful not to ask for too much. If you ask for too much, your opponent can either object with a fair chance of success, or worse yet, he can flood you with more material than you can cope with.

The request to produce should ask that all documents withheld on a claim of privilege be identified and segregated. This facilitates court review if you decide to make a motion to test the privilege.

You can only resolve questions about the thoroughness of compliance by depositions. Who you depose will depend on the circumstances. Logical choices are the persons conducting the file search, the records custodian (who presumably could testify about the party's document destruction policy), correspondents or memo writers of letters or memos referred to in other material but not themselves produced, and so forth.

When you are served with a request to produce, you have several simultaneous jobs. Study the request to see precisely what it seeks. Ascertain if any objections can be taken, and decide whether to take them or not. See if any of the material sought is privileged, or involved trade secrets (for which a protective order as to use can be sought). Estimate the time and cost and hazards of production. Organize the file search. Acquaint yourself with the material to be produced and material not to be produced. (You should make memoranda of the reasons why materials are not included so you can refresh yourself if the non-production is questioned.) Index and copy all material to be produced. Decide upon the best way to produce the material; e.g., only sorted into the broad categories in the request or carefully classified as to issues and cross-indexed. The former way puts a big burden on the discovering party. The latter way may let you shape how your opponent will view the documents, and furnish a basis for discussion of the documents with him.

8.7   A Model Set of Important Interrogatories in a Negligence Case

The use of forms in litigation can be a boon or a curse. This is especially true of interrogatories. There are common elements to virtually every type of case. If you have well-drafted interrogatories on one or more elements of a type of case, there is no reason why you should not use them in another case of the same type. There are three provisos to this.

Keep the questions up-dated on changes in the law. Tighten the draftsmanship when you see areas for improvement. Make sure that the form questions in fact fit the case. If some of the standard questions miss the mark even slightly, they should be reworded to hit the mark. If the standard set of interrogatories does not cover all features of the case, you must draft additional interrogatories to cover.

The following model set of basic interrogatories illustrates a number of the points made in the preceding sections:

STATE OF THE UNION
ANY COUNTY, Sc.   SUPERIOR COURT

)
) C. A. No.
)
) *DEFENDANT'S INTERROGATORIES*
) *PROPOUNDED TO PLAINTIFF*
)
)
)

Instructions

The answers to these interrogatories must include all information known to you, your agents including your attorney, and all persons acting on your behalf or under your control. If you do not have information to answer an interrogatory you are under a duty to make a reasonable effort to obtain such information.

As used in these interrogatories:

The phrase "practitioner of the healing arts" includes all doctors, physicians, surgeons, nurses, thereapists, psychologists, and other persons who treat mental or physical conditions.

The word "person" includes all natural persons, corporations, partnerships, associations, foundations, governmental or private agencies, and any and all other organizations.

(1) State your full name, any other names you have been known by (if married, your maiden name), date of birth, marital status, home address, occupation or business, name of employer or business, business address, and social security number.

(2) Give a particular description of the injuries alleged to have been suffered by you, designating those which were temporary and those which are permanent, and, as to the latter, state how they manifest themselves.

(3) State the names and addresses and specialties of all practitioners of the healing arts and hospitals and institutions from whom or where you received treatment, examination, or consultation for the injuries alleged to have been suffered by you, specifying as to each the dates and nature thereof.

(4) Identify by a sufficient description all medical reports, hospital records, x-ray reports, laboratory tests, and other records or reports bearing on the injuries alleged to have been suffered by you and the treatment for them, and state the names and addresses of the person or institution having possession or custody of each item.

(5) List and describe each item of special damages incurred by you as a result of the incident sued upon, including but not limited to, hospital charges, medical charges, x-ray charges, laboratory fees, the cost of medicines, the expenses of special nurses or helpers, charges for substitute help, charges for special appliances, lost wages, loss of services or consortium, property damages, etc., giving the name and address of the person or organization to whom each item of expense has been paid or is payable and the dates such expenses were incurred.

(6) State the nature in which and the extent to which your earning capacity has been impaired and set forth the

calculations by which you arrived at your claim for impaired earning capacity.

(7) If you had any injuries, diseases, disabilities, physical defects, or abnormalities of a nature similar to the injuries claimed to have been suffered by you in the incident sued upon, state as to each for the five-year period prior to that incident and for the period since that incident,

(a) the nature and date,

(b) the names and addresses of all practitioners of the healing arts and hospitals and institutions from whom or where you received treatment or examination or consultation, and the dates of the same, and

(c) the names and addresses of all persons against whom any claim was made or action commenced and the name and location of any court or commission in which an action was brought, and the result of such claim (indicating the amount of any settlement or award).

(8) If you have made any claim or received any money or both, including but not limited to workman's compensation benefits, occasioned by the incident sued upon, as to each such claim or payment of money, state the date, the amount and nature, and the name and address of the person or organization to whom made or from whom received.

(9) For the two-year period preceding, and for the period since the incident sued upon, state the names and addresses of each person by whom you were employed (including self-employment), and as to each, state

(a) the capacity in which you were employed

(b) the nature of the duties you performed,

(c) the dates you worked for each person (indicating the dates after the incident sued upon that you were unable to work and the dates that you first resumed part of and then all of your usual duties), and

(d) the average weekly wage, salary, earnings, or profits you were receiving.

(10) State fully how the incident sued upon took place.

(11) State in what respects you contend the defendant is negligent or breached a duty owing to you.

(12) If you have ever been convicted of or pleaded guilty or no contest to any crime, as to each, state the date and nature and disposition thereof and the court or tribunal which heard it.

(13) If you claim that any further medical attention is necessary, as a result of the incident sued upon, state the nature thereof, when such attention will be given, the name and address and specialty of the doctor or person recommending the same, and the estimated cost thereof.

(14) State the name and address and telephone number of each person known to you, your attorney or any person acting on your behalf having any knowledge concerning the incident sued upon, and indicate how they came by such knowledge (eyewitness, passenger, etc.).

(15) As to each oral or written statement, report, or memorandum obtained with respect to the incident sued upon and as to each visual representation (photograph, motion picture, diagram, etc.) of the vehicles or objects involved in or near the scene of that incident, state the names and addresses of the persons making and/or taking it, the date thereof, if a statement, report, or memorandum, whether it was recorded in writing or on tape, and the name and address of the person having custody or possession of it.

(16) State the time, place, and substance of any conversations you had with the defendant about how the incident sued upon happened and the damages, indicating the name and address of all persons present at the conversation.

(17) State whether or not you have been involved in any accident prior to the date you answer this interrogatory in which you received personal injuries for which a claim was made against anyone, giving the names and addresses of each person(s) or organization(s) against whom claim was made, the date of each such accident, and if suit was brought or claim made before a court or commission, state the name and location of each court or commission in which suit was brought or claim made and the disposition thereof.

(18) With respect to each witness you intend to call as an expert witness at trial, state

(a) the name and address and area of expertise, and

(b) the substance of the facts and opinions to which he is expected to testify, and

(c) a summary of the grounds for each opinion.

(19) Is there any other information that the respondent has on the topic covered in interrogatories blank to blank not included in the answers to those interrogatories? If so, state it.

(20) In preparing the answers to these interrogatories, have you inquired of all persons within your control who have or might have information to answer them?

(21) If the answer to the preceding interrogatory is "no," state the names, addresses, and capacities of the persons not so consulted, and as to each, state the reason why that person was not consulted.

(22) List the names, and addresses, and capacities of all persons consulted in obtaining information to answer these interrogatories, and as to each indicate each answer to which they contributed information.

(23) Has the plaintiff entered into any settlement or arrangement with any party to the suit or with any person potentially liable to the plaintiff, and if so, as to each such arrangement, state the particulars and identify by a sufficient description all documents pertaining to it.

( ) If this is a motor vehicle accident case, state:

(a) How far in feet from each other and from the point of the accident were the various vehicles involved in the accident when you first saw the defendant's vehicle.

(b) The initial directions and speed and the changes in course and speed of the various vehicles in the accident from the time you saw the defendant to the instant of the accident.

(c) The points of contact between the various vehicles in the accident and their relative position to each other when they came to rest.

(d)What actions, if any, did you or the driver of the car in which you were a passenger, make to avoid the accident.

(e)The weather, road, and visual (any obstructions, etc.) conditions at the time of the accident.

(f)Whether the vehicle in which you were a passenger was equipped with seat belts, and, if so, what seats were so equipped, in what seat were you seated, and were you wearing a seat belt at the time of the accident.

(g)The amount of damage to the vehicle in which you were riding and the parts of it that were damaged, and the name and address of the concern making the estimate or repairs.

(h)The length of each skid mark left by any vehicle involved in the accident.

(i) If you were the driver of a vehicle involved in the accident, state whether your operator's license had ever been revoked, suspended or restricted, and, if so, the nature thereof, and the date, place, and name of the entity imposing the same.

( ) If this is a fall case, state:

(a)If actual notice is claimed, the name and address of each person so giving it, and the name and address of each person to whom given, the date or dates thereof, and the substance thereof (identifying by a sufficient description any pertinent documents).

(b)If constructive notice is claimed, the nature thereof and when it is claimed the defendant had such constructive notice.

(c)The exact way in which you fell, indicating the parts of your body that you landed on.

(d)The exact location where you fell (identifying the spot in relation to nearby objects).

(e)The nature of any substance you fell on, and, if you know, how that substance got there and/or the nature of any defect or condition you claim caused your fall.

(f) How did you happen to be on the premises, and what was your purpose in being on the premises leading up to and at the time of the incident sued upon, indicating the names and addresses of any person whom you were to see or had seen and/or who had caused you to be on the premises.

(g) What were the lighting conditions at the time of the incident sued upon.

Dated:

                              Attorneys for Defendant
                              [address]

TO:

                    [Certificate of Service]

9

Using Medical Proof
Imaginatively
to Win Cases

9.1   How Medical Proof in Unexpected Areas
Pays Dividends

"**M**edical proof is hard to define but you know it when you see it."

At best, this statement is only half true. It is true that you must put on your thinking cap to come up with a workable definition of medical proof. It is not true that you necessarily will know medical proof when you see it, especially in the other-than-conventional areas where it can play a vital role.

Medical proof is that kind of evidence respecting the physical or mental conditions of human beings, or their behavior. This is broader than the dictionary definitions of medical and medicine. Those definitions center on the prevention and cure of disease. Self-evidently, medical proof goes well beyond that.

A checklist on the types and areas of medical proof would fall short of being complete. The subject is too diverse. But examples can be used. The following examples will range from the conventional to the other than conventional. They are designed to give you insights into how to think creatively about medical proof. The imaginative use of medical proof can win cases for you.

Medical proof may be necessary to prove a duty or a breach of duty. For example, a substance causes an allergic reaction. The issue in the case likely will be whether the risk of harm was foreseeable such as to create a duty to warn, or to make tests, or to eliminate an ingredient. The physiology of plaintiff in particular and human beings in general are central to proof on this issue. In a medical malpractice action, medical proof through an expert or text establishes the standard of care. Attitudinal surveys may be used some day in court as proof bearing on what constitutes reasonable behavior in unusual circumstances.

Medical evidence has been used to prove or disprove liability in a variety of cases. Attitudinal surveys have been introduced on the issue of confusion in trademark and passing-off cases. In the case of the Badgered Bus Driver, which will be discussed later, a party sought to have the driver of a bus examined to show that he was physically and mentally unfit for the job.

Another case illustrates how counsel recognized the potential in an eight-word medical entry and built the liability case on it: A serviceman became seriously ill mentally. He was admitted to an army hospital, then to a veterans' hospital. The time came when the government psychiatrists believed he could be discharged from the hospital. He was.

Out on his own, he began to pursue an interest in physics. As he progressed in his studies he developed theories. In time he became convinced that the electron did not exist. He wrote a paper on the subject which he submitted to a prestigious scientific society.

The society rejected the paper. Whereupon, the veteran acquired a pistol, proceeded to the offices of the society, and shot dead the first person he saw, the young woman receptionist.

The District Attorney swiftly obtained an indictment for first degree murder.

At his arraignment the veteran pled not guilty by reason of insanity. The court appointed a panel of experts to examine him.

The court also asked the government to furnish the veteran's medical records. The government did so after extracting the court's promise to keep them confidential.

The experts reported that the veteran was insane. The court accepted the plea and committed the veteran to a mental hospital.

On these facts, the girl's estate had a slim case against the government for negligently releasing the veteran. Psychiatric opinion recognizes that mental patients can and should be released from institutions, but that it is a matter of professional judgment whether to do so.

But one further fact came out. When it committed the veteran, the court released a statement quoting a psychiatrist's opinion in the veteran's medical record that, "The prognosis is bleak and fraught with danger."

The estate sued, claiming that the government psychiatrist admitted the veteran should not be released.

Plaintiff did not win. Too much else in the record vindicated the judgment to release the veteran. But the point still remains that plaintiff almost rode the statement to victory.

In the area of causation, the need for expert medical testimony in medical malpractice actions comes to mind immediately. The case of the Sensitive Suicide illustrates an imaginative use of psychiatric testimony. An insurance company refused to pay the proceeds of a life insurance policy claiming that the insured had committed suicide. He had been found in his car in his garage, the motor still idling, dead of carbon monoxide. The company contended he had been having marital difficulties which had culminated in an emotional exchange with his wife just before his death. The company obtained expert testimony as evidence of a suicidal profile in suicide conducive circumstances.

The use of medical proof on damages ties in closely with the use of medical proof on causation. Much of this chapter will be devoted to techniques in the more conventional areas of damages. To mention a newer area as part of these examples, psychiatrists or psychologists could testify about the nature of psychic injury, as for example, when a mother sees her child mangled in an accident.

The various tests of competency and capacity invite the use of medical proof. One test centers on an understanding of the nature and significance of a transaction. Another test stresses knowing the nature and extent of one's property and the natural objects of one's bounty. Still another test measures one's ability to manage a business or property. A fourth test deals with one's judgment or emotional control. A fifth test concentrates on the accuracy of one's senses.

A person may be competent for one purpose but not for another. In the case involving the epileptic discussed in Chapter 1, for example, defendant saw the bomb-shell in an innocent entry in the medical record. It indicated that plaintiff had tunnel vision. The case hinged on whether plaintiff or defendant had edged across the center line of the highway. Defendant produced expert testimony that with tunnel vision plaintiff could not have judged whether she had driven over the center line.

The defendant attacked plaintiff's reliability as a witness in the area of capacity or competency, not veracity. This same plaintiff had perfect capacity to make a will. The tests vary. The case of the Unsisterly Sibling illustrates the imaginative marshalling of many items of medical evidence in a suit involving testamentary capacity.

The testatrix had been raised from infancy by her aunt and uncle. Her mother and father lived in the same town and raised her brothers and sisters.

Though she lived a long life, she never became close to any of them. She never married. For many years she kept house and served as a companion for a bachelor uncle.

She and her uncle both accumulated an estate. When he died, he left all he had to her outright.

Over the years she had made three wills. In none had she left anything to her siblings. In each, she had left everything to strangers to the blood.

Within a year of her uncle's death she became ill and was hospitalized. During the hospitalization, she changed her will for the fourth time. She still did not leave a sou to her brothers and sisters.

They contested the will on the ground that she lacked testamentary capacity and did not know the natural objects of her bounty. They argued that the bulk of the estate came from their mutual uncle who would be incredulous if he could know she had left it to strangers. They characterized the beneficiaries of the will as mere casual acquaintances such as her hairdresser. They contended that drugs during her final illness affected her. They alluded to a reputation for eccentricity.

Counsel for the proponents knew he had a strong case. He also knew he could not take the contestants' arguments for granted. He decided to put in a bare *prima facie* case in the probate court (the subscribing witnesses' testimony that the testatrix had been of sound mind) with enough proof lined up in case he needed it for rebuttal. He figured that the contestants would save their ammunition for the trial *de novo* in the Superior Court on appeal from the admission of the will to probate.

For the Superior Court proceeding, he decided to be prepared to prove in rebuttal that the testatrix had been competent and that her sisters and brothers were not the natural objects of her bounty.

He lined up the following proof:

• The testimony of her lawyer that she detected an error in the last will which had to be changed before she executed it.

• The hospital record establishing that she had not been given any drugs prior to or at the time she executed her will.

• The testimony of the treating physician that any possible effects of previous drugs had worn off by the time she executed her will.

• The testimony of the treating physician and specialists and nurses that she was lucid up to and well beyond the time she executed her will.

• Lay testimony about her upbringing, her competency in the affairs of life, the lack of relationships with her brothers and sisters, her personality, etc.

• The three prior wills excluding her siblings.

• Expert opinion testimony of a psychiatrist based upon this profile that she had understanding and was not mentally infirm.

The probate court admitted the will to probate. The contestants appealed. Both sides pulled out all stops on discovery. The contestants finally caved in under the sheer weight of the proponents' medical proof. The case settled reasonably for the proponents.

9.2   For the Plaintiff—How to Present Medical
        Evidence so as to Enhance Damages

Your efforts to enhance the award of damages should start at
the beginning of trial, the selection of the jury, and the opening
statement. Your efforts should continue throughout the trial to
and including the damage evidence proper, rebuttal, and the
closing statement.

You have two general objectives and several specific ones.

First, you should design the liability phase of the case to turn
the jury "off," on the defendant, and "on" for the plaintiff.
Over-stating the point, you should paint the defendant as thought-
less, unfeeling, and reckless, and the plaintiff as innocent, careful,
and prudent. Of course, you must work with the facts you have.
And even if the facts warrant a dramatic contrast, you should let
the facts speak for themselves. In other words, do not over-play it.
And do not take this as suggesting that you appeal to sympathy,
passion, and prejudice. Do take it as emphasizing the fact of life
that sympathy for one party and antipathy for another plays a
vital role in damage awards.

Second, you must tie plaintiff's damages to defendant's
negligence with unmistakable and unshakable testimony of
proximate cause. To do this, you have to remember several things
about causation in law and in medicine.

Proximate cause is a legal concept. A doctor usually only
goes into cause insofar as it helps in diagnosis or treatment.
Furthermore, medicine is not an exact science, and in many
instances medical cause may be unclear.

For this reason, the law requires that the doctor need
only testify to "*a* competent producing cause" and this only to a
"reasonable *medical* certainty."

Explain this to the doctor. He will be firm on causation if he
sees that he can be, without compromising his professional
integrity. Understand this yourself so you do not automatically
look for an unequivocal medical cause, and so that in complex
cases you will expect contradictory testimony on medical cause.

Accident suits have given rise to a class of "trauma induced"
condition. Plaintiff has an accident and a trauma, and tries to tie

his condition following the accident to the trauma—that the trauma caused the condition, or aggravated a pre-existing condition, or precipitated a latent condition. The case of the Traumatic Epileptic discussed in Chapter 1 illustrates this kind of case.

To turn now to specific objectives. There are perils in the proof of pain. The jury does not like a whiner. They do not like a person who dwells on his injuries. They do not like to be exposed to disfiguring disabilities. They frown upon the plaintiff who exaggerates his injuries and ailments.

The problem is that you must have the plaintiff testify about his injuries, his pain and suffering, and his residual disabilities. The problem is compounded because you must get the true dimensions of these facts across to the jury.

You will find the solution to the problem in dovetailing several trial techniques.

First, when plaintiff testifies, he should under-play his injuries. He will not avoid the dangers just mentioned. If anything, he should gain ground because the jury likes people who bear up under adversity.

Second, you should use objective proof to prove subjective suffering. Your top card here is the testimony of the treating physician. You must prepare him to give a thorough and vivid recounting of plaintiff's treatment and condition. You should key his testimony to significant entries in the hospital record. You must have him explain in lay language such things as how readings and tests (pulse, blood pressure, EKG, etc.) are taken, and what they mean, and how they help a doctor make a diagnosis and prescribe a treatment.

You should also make the hospital record speak about pain. Have the doctor or nurse go over for the jury the drugs listed on the nurse's notes to indicate how often they were given. If, as they sometimes do, the nurse's notes contain comments about pain and discomfort, have the nurse read and amplify these to the jury.

Third, you should dramatize the residuals through lay witnesses. Line up selected friends and relatives to describe in the context of daily life how plaintiff has had to curtail his activities and perhaps still gives evidence of pain.

Fourth, you should judiciously use demonstrative evidence to help the jury understand the testimony. The key word is judiciously because this kind of evidence tends to dramatize the injuries too. And here you must be careful. Such things as pictures of a gruesome injury may make the jury think you are embarrassing the plaintiff. This negative reaction to you could rub off on plaintiff's case.

Take the following case illustrating several of these points: One morning mid-week, plaintiff and her daughter went supermarket shopping. It was still early so they were the only customers. They saw one clerk, at the check-out counter. Three-quarters of the way down an aisle, plaintiff slipped and fell on a pool of syrup. A bottle had broken and spilled.

Plaintiff was taken to the hospital. She had a torn meniscus in her right knee. Though she was old, she responded well to treatment. She performed her therapy faithfully. But she still had a rather severe permanency.

At the trial, plaintiff developed that a clerk had been shelving in the area of the fall. Counsel came up with the theory that the bottle had fallen during this shelving, that the clerk had gone to get a bucket and a mop, but took time out in the back for a cup of coffee.

The theory smacked of sheer speculation. It might well have remained just that but for the shelving clerk. He denied the theory all right, but he slouched on the stand; he looked no one in the eye, not the jury, or the judge, or the counsel; he hemmed and he hawed; he gave the impression that he did not care what had happened to the plaintiff; worst of all, he fell into inconsistencies in his timing of events.

Plaintiff, on the other hand, came on as a strong, self-reliant person. She under-played her injuries. She barely mentioned pain. Every day, though, she gamely came into court with her cane. The daughter with whom she lived described her mother's quadriceps exercises, her sleepless nights, her medications. Another daughter told how her mother used to bowl regularly and would work part-time, but that she could not do these things anymore. The attending physician conveyed his admiration for the plaintiff as he went through the medical record describing her hospitalization and out-patient treatment, and the extent of her disability.

It was a toss-up whether the jury's antipathy for the clerk or their sympathy for the plaintiff affected them the most. The combination of the two proved more than they could handle. They returned a large verdict for the plaintiff, so much so that the court ordered a remittitur.

9.3 For the Defendant—How to Present Medical Evidence so as to Hold the Line on Damages

Your efforts as defense counsel to hold the line on damages start at the same time your opponent's start, at the beginning of the case. Like his, they should continue throughout the trial.

As a rule-of-thumb, if you can, you want to do just the opposite of the things the plaintiff does. Thus, overall, you want to turn the jury "off" on the plaintiff and "on" for the defendant. One trial-tested technique is to get the plaintiff to exaggerate his injuries and condition. Then you show that the hard medical evidence, the testimony of plaintiff's doctors, and his medical record, do not support the plaintiff. In extreme cases, he can come across as a monster of greed to the point that a jury will even find against him on liability.

But even short of that happy eventuality, this vivid contrast creates doubt that clouds all aspects of plaintiff's case, from liability to damages. Whether this doubt leads the jury to discount the damages as such or to increase the plaintiff's contributory negligence, or to compromise the verdict, the result is the same, lower damages.

You cannot use this technique in every case. If the plaintiff does not exaggerate or if the medical facts support him, you probably would reinforce damages by trying to lead him down a garden path that did not exist. But the principle of creating doubt is still true. You must turn to other methods.

Another major method is to attack proximate cause with all you have. You want to loosen if not unravel the direct tie plaintiff tries to make between negligence and damage. You can do this in either or both of two ways. One is to counter plaintiff's proof with negative proof. The other and better way is not only to negative that proof but also to come up with alternative causes unrelated to defendant's alleged negligence. With the test of medico-legal causation being such a wavery thing, you often can do this quite readily. In short, you want a sharp clash on causation and indeed on all major medical issues.

In any important case, you must strongly consider producing a top-flight forensic physician as an expert. You want a man whose credentials awe a jury and whose testimonial ability impresses them. If plaintiff has an expert like this lined up, you must get one of your own. You cannot avoid the challenge. The Tietzse Syndrome case illustrates why.

On a wintery day several years before the trial, plaintiff had been riding in the rear seat of her parent's car. Defendant's car skidded on icy slush across the center line into plaintiff's car. Plaintiff pitched forward, hitting her chest against the back of the front seat. Plaintiff and her driver denied icy conditions, and said defendant was speeding.

Her doctor diagnosed a sprain of several right ribs. He treated her with diathermy. A few months later plaintiff moved and came under the care of an orthopedist, as skilled on the witness stand as he was in the surgery.

Plaintiff opened the damage phase of the trial with him. And for good reason. He dominated the courtroom. He had a physically and intellectually commanding presence. He charmed as well as awed. He knew his calling. Above all, he knew how to deliver the goods.

He testified that plaintiff had Tietzse Syndrome or traumatic chrondritis. He said the condition was permanent, and that she would have pain for the rest of her life. In time, he said she would have to start using her left hand. He doubted if she could play tennis or ski.

As he testified the doctor almost assuredly sensed that he had the court and jury in the palm of his hand. He went on to say that if plaintiff became pregnant, the weight of the baby would cause her pain. He described pain-relieving injections into her breast. He gravely opined that because of the condition plaintiff might have difficulty in sexual intercourse.

This expert's testimony had a terrific impact. Plaintiff thought so much of it that she moved to more than triple her demand for judgment.

Plaintiff called the first treating physician second. After "Dr. Dynamite," plaintiff only put him on for the formality. He had only diagnosed a sprain but did testify that he knew about Tietzse Syndrome.

Defendant's counsel knew before trial that he had a forensic doctor on his hands. He checked and found out how formidable the foe would be. He did the only thing he could do, hire a top-flight forensic doctor of his own. The defense doctor stated flatly that plaintiff did not have Tietzse Syndrome, but only a sprain.

The pity is that the shoot-out at high noon never took place. Plaintiff suddenly came down from the sky in her settlement demands, and the case settled. There were three apparent reasons for this. First, plaintiff had told defendant's examining physician that she had pain in her left not her right ribs. Second, defendant produced police reports of two other skidding accidents on the same curve within minutes of this accident because of icy conditions. Third, with two flat contradictions in the record already, plaintiff did not dare face defendant's forensic expert, straining to clash with "Dr. Dynamite" on every material point.

A clash in medical testimony means a clash on substantive medical points. It does not mean producing witnesses ostensibly but not substantively adverse to plaintiff. Thus do not call the defense examining physician if he will only bear out plaintiff's medical proof. You are better off to suffer comments in plaintiff's summations about the failure to call him. The best solution is to call him for limited purposes, such as establishing an earlier date than plaintiff gives for maximum medical benefits and a lower degree than plaintiff claims of disability. These two points are central to your effort to hold the line on damages whether or not you can attack causation.

The rule about not re-enforcing plaintiff's damages especially applies in cross-examination. Unless you have the horses do not cross-examine plaintiff's medical experts, or only conduct a careful peripheral examination for the sake of show. More of this in the chapter on expert witnesses.

Any discussion about how to hold the line on damages has to emphasize and re-emphasize one point. You must comb the medical records for facts. Section 9.6 discusses medical records and gives several pertinent examples. One additional case should be given here, because an item in the medical record undercut proximate cause and cut damages to the bone.

A longshoreman in his sixties mangled a finger while guiding a pallet of cargo being off-loaded from the ship. After many weeks on compensation, he commuted his claim. He received a high degree of disability and never returned to work.

As was inevitable, he sued the ship claiming an unseaworthy winch, and that the injury had incapacitated him from any future longshore work.

The ship did not credit either claim. Counsel assembled proof that the stevedore had taken over full control of the ship, and that the winch was not defective. Through a neighborhood check, he established that plaintiff had voluntarily retired from work.

And he made a point to get plaintiff's complete medical record, not just that for the accident. He hit the jackpot with that from plaintiff's personal physician. Plaintiff had long suffered from emphysema. Just a few weeks after the accident, many weeks before he went off comp, his doctor told him that he was permanently unfit for work because of this condition.

9.4   Why You Must Become a Medical Expert, and How to Become One in Seven Easy Steps

Why must you become an expert on the medical points in the case? So you can do your job right. This becomes self-evident when you consider what you have to do in lining up the medical aspects of the case:

• Seeing to it that the doctors accurately translate medical terminology into terms laymen can understand.

• Preparing the doctor for cross-examination by spotting any weak areas in the testimony.

• Deciding whether and how to cross-examine the opposing doctors.

• Couching the questions and answers in discovery in precise medical terms, and being able to evaluate the answers to your discovery.

• Programming the entire medical presentation for maximum impact on the jury.

• Choosing medical texts for use at the trial.
• Planning effective demonstrative evidence.

The easy way to become a medical expert is the systematic, step-by-step way.

First, go over all the medical records with reasonable thoroughness in order to get a working knowledge of the medical facts.

Second, ground yourself in the nature of the injury or condition from the basic texts and standard periodicals. Your expert can recommend these materials, or they can be found in medical association libraries.

Third, go over the medical records again in order to fill in your working knowledge in light of your basic study of the texts.

Fourth, consult with your expert. Ask him questions about the injury or condition in general and the patient in particular. Ask him what other material you can study.

Fifth, do the follow-up work your expert suggests.

Sixth, somewhere along the line obtain and study everything the opposing experts have written on the subject.

Seventh, keep consulting with your experts and studying the medical records until you have mastered the subject and the records.

9.5 How to Interview the Client for Medical Facts—With a Checklist

People approach their injuries in different ways. Some play them up. Some play them down. Some forget unpleasant things. Some are reluctant to talk about them. Some do not have the ability to describe them.

However, you need an accurate and complete picture from the client. The question is how do you go about getting it. The sympathetic but firm approach is best. You need to show concern to get the client's confidence. You need this confidence for the client to speak freely. You also need it to pose the probing questions you must ask to get accurate facts. You need it when you must be firm in insisting on answers, and in keeping the client on the track.

Using a checklist in interviewing the client insures that you cover everything. You must be flexible in using it. Sometimes you must let the client tell the story in his own words first. You can go back, using the checklist, to fill in details. You also have to be alert for special questions suggested by what the client tells you.

You can have the client fill out a questionnaire based on the checklist before the interview. This saves time. You can study it before discussing the case with the client. If you use a questionnaire though, you must make sure the answers are accurate and complete by at least touching on them at the interview.

MEDICAL CHECKLIST

Identifying Material

Name. All other names ever known by. Maiden name.
Date and place of birth.
Social Security number. Military serial number.
Marital status. Names, addresses, and ages of spouse and children. Prior marriages.
Residences for past five years. Telephone number.
Schools attended.

Work Record

All employers. Dates. Type of work. Position. Reasons for leaving. Earnings.
Time missed from job. Loss of earnings or profits. Ability to return to same work. Attempts to return to work. Loss of earning capacity. Cost of substitutes or help at home.
Compensation or loss of work benefits.
Tax returns.

Previous Health Record

All injuries, disabilities, and diseases (including childhood diseases).
Hearing and eyesight.
Dates and addresses of all treatments and hospitalizations, and nature of treatment.
Names and addresses of all treating and consulting doctors.

General health and specific impairments and conditions before accident in suit.

Physical examinations (such as those incident to employment and applications for life insurance).

Applications which ask questions about health (e.g., life insurance, operator's licenses, etc.).

Claims and Driving Record

All prior accidents, claims, and lawsuits.
When and where licensed. Limitations.
License suspensions.

Description of Accident and Trauma

How accident took place with the emphasis on the specific impact and trauma.

Factual description of pain and injuries. Mental and physical condition after accident.

Res gestae. If unconscious, how long. Activity at scene. First aid. Statements about accident or condition. Ambulance or rescue wagon. Condition and treatment on way to hospital. Names and addresses of witnesses.

Police accident report description of injuries.

Hospitalization and Confinement

Name and address of hospital or nursing home.

Name and address of doctors, nurses, attendants, and other patients.

Description of stay in hospital: arrival, history given, complaints, duration and degree of pain, medications, treatment, surgery, therapy, x-rays, tests, casts, examinations, exercises, when ambulatory, visits and consultations with attending physicians, consultants and nurses, braces, crutches, etc., any unusual events, general description of conditions from arrival to discharge.

Description of stay in nursing home (see above).

Confinement at home: exercises, degree of pain, complaints, degree of activity, how long in bed, when ambulatory, nurses or help, pick-up of tempo of activities, medications, exercises, doctors' visits, etc.

Psychic problems.

Follow-up visits to doctors, therapeutic or out-patient facilities. Names, addresses, and details.

Dates of discharge from all treatments for accident.

Residuals

Description of pain (how often, degree, where, what it feels like, etc.).

Description of permanent conditions, impairments, and injuries (how handicapped, what it feels like, crutches, braces, etc.).

The degree of aggravation of a pre-existing condition.

Scars, disfigurements, visible marks.

Life Activities Before and After Accident

Sports. Prowess. How often played.

Hobbies.

Handyman or housewifery.

General picture of life activities before accident.

What handicaps to such activities after accident.

Medical Expenses

Doctors' bills. Hospital bills. Nurses' and nursing home bills.

Bills for physiotherapy, diathermy, etc.

Cost of special appliances (walkers, crutches, collars, etc.).

Pharmacy bills.

Estimated future expenses for drugs, treatments, therapy, corrective surgery, appliances, nursing, hospitalization.

Collateral Source Payments, Liens, and Subrogated Claims

Blue Cross, Blue Shield, Med-Pay, Major Medical.

Liens for hospital and doctors' bills.

Compensation payments and agreements to reimburse employer.

9.6   Tips on Getting Medical Records and What to Look for in Them

You need signed and acknowledged authorizations from the patient to get medical records from a doctor or hospital. You should get the authorizations and records early in the case. If you are defending the case, serve a request to produce or take depositions whenever plaintiff stalls in giving you authorization. If you are defending the case, you need the records for use at the plaintiff's medical examination by your doctor. Get enough authorizations for each doctor and facility. (Some attorneys have the authorization recite that reproduced copies of the authorization are valid; using duplicate originals of the authorization is better). Try to have the authorizations permit you to discuss the matter with the doctor.

The following is an authorization designed for general use. The covering letter can give such data as the dates and reason for treatment.

"To Whom It May Concern:

I authorize you to permit the bearer to inspect and copy all hospital, medical, and other records, including x-rays, tests, and examinations, of any and all treatment I had at your facility, or received from you, and to discuss any matters relating to them with you or any medical or other personnel involved.

(Signature)

(Name Typed, Social Security Worker)"

You should get the complete medical record for the injury or condition in suit. The complete medical record consists of four categories—the collated hospital record; the records of departments in the hospital that do not become part of the collated hospital record; the office records of the treating and consulting physicians; the records of any outside facility the patient has been sent to.

In most cases, plaintiff will have some sort of prior medical record. Whether you represent the plaintiff or defendant, you have to decide how much of that prior record to get. If any part of the prior record concerns the same injury or condition in suit, you should get that much of the prior record. If you think you might pick up some useful information, you should get the complete prior record. The case of the Long-Suffering Longshoreman just discussed illustrates the benefits that can come from thoroughness. If you have no special reason but want to at least get some idea about the prior record, you can get an abstract or summary of prior hospital records.

The usual parts of the medical record are: fact sheet or abstract, admission sheet with history, emergency room record, ambulance note, physical examination, progress reports, order sheets, temperature charts, laboratory tests, consultants' reports, consents, operative note, anesthesia note, nurses' notes, x-ray reports, transfusion records, physical therapy notes, electro-encephalogram, out-patient clinic record. Sometimes a hospital will not include the emergency room record, physical therapy notes, out-patient clinic record etc. in the collated hospital record. You have to check about this.

The hospital record can prove the dates of confinement, the diagnosis, prognosis, and treatment. Sometimes it can establish causation where, for example, the diagnosis states the cause. The materials in the record that were used in examination, diagnosis, and treatment are admissible into evidence under the business entry exception to the hearsay rule. The history of the accident, complaints of pain, and the like technically are not admissible unless used in examination, diagnosis, and treatment. An admission against interest by the plaintiff in giving the history is admissible. The modern trend is for the courts to let the entire record into evidence. However, local law and practice governs this. You can always call the person making the entry.

The medical record, the hospital record especially, becomes vitally important because it has a stamp of truth. An injured or sick person wants to be cured, and to insure that he is, tells it like it is. Busy doctors and nurses usually are factual and terse. Tests to be useful must be accurate.

This is the theory. By and large, the facts support it. But there are exceptions. For example, nurses can get dramatic or editorialize in their notes. You will recall that in the case of the mentally ill serviceman, a psychiatrist lapsed into purple prose, "The prognosis is bleak, and fraught with danger." In malpractice situations, false or incomplete entries have been made.

You should look for items such as the following in the medical records:

• The emergency room notes for a graphic description of the injury.

• The nature and frequency of medications as bearing on pain and suffering.

• The nurses' notes which reflect the patient's distress and course of recovery.

• The operative note and order sheets to serve as a corroborating peg for the doctors' or surgeons' testimony at the trial.

• The patient's past medical history, his version of the accident, and biographical data. For the reasons mentioned, this probably will be unvarnished and may be revealing.

• Omissions—things that should be in the chart but are not.

A malpractice action illustrates how combing the medical record forced the defendant doctor into a favorable settlement. This took place in that bygone era when doctors and their carriers did not settle malpractice actions and plaintiffs won very few of them.

The doctor was old. He had a severe and progressively crippling arthritic condition of his hands. He had had it for a relatively long time. He still kept up his practice though. He still had privileges at the hospital. He still had at least one surgeon who continued to use him in surgery.

This surgeon engaged defendant to give the anesthetic for a routine operation. The defendant decided to use a spinal anesthetic. Now a spinal injection must be administered in an exact spot. It must be administered with a sure hand. It must be administered deftly. If it is not administered this way, the hypodermic needle can injure the nerves inside the spinal column.

Defendant gave the spinal. The patient came out of the

operation with a permanent foot drop. He sued the anesthesiologist for malpractice, claiming an improper injection.

The defendant could not deny the foot drop since the records of post-operative care verified it. Instead, he insisted that this was an unusual but not necessarily negligent complication following a spinal.

Plaintiff's counsel had found out too much about the defendant's background to accept this. He still had to face up to the defense though. And given the situation, he anticipated an especially tight conspiracy of silence.

He cracked the case because of an omission in the medical record. As he read and re-read the various reports, the dawn came. The operative note cryptically stated "no complications" on the spinal anesthetic. There had been, self-evidently. Counsel also knew that the doctor had tried twice unsuccessfully before the ill-fated shot to administer the injection, and that the patient had cried in pain. Armed with these bits of information, he got off-the-record corroboration from sympathetic operating room personnel.

A jury could easily believe the operative note had been deliberately falsified. This, combined with the spectre of defendant sitting in court with hands twisted by arthritis caused the defense to collapse.

9.7   Pitfalls in Obtaining a Physical Examination, and How to Avoid Them

The field of physical and mental examinations is strewn with pitfalls.

First, unlike other discovery, you do not have a right to an examination. You either must get your opponent to agree or get permission of the court "for good cause shown."

Second, in moving for permission, you must show more than the fact that the physical or mental condition is "in controversy" as the rule provides. You must show that a party has *affirmatively* put his condition into controversy. In other words, you must show more than mere relevance. This is the rule laid down in the case of the Badgered Bus Driver [*Schlagenhauf* v. *Holder,* 379 U.S. 104 (1964)].

A bus collided with a truck. The passengers sued the bus driver and the owners of the bus and truck. The defendants cross-claimed. The truck owner contended the accident happened because the bus driver was not competent, and sought his physical and mental examinations. The district court ordered the examinations. The court of appeals denied mandamus.

The Supreme Court granted certiorari and reversed. It held that examinations cannot be routinely ordered where a party has not put his own physical or mental condition into issue, merely because negligence has been claimed.

Third, the rule provides for the exchange of reports. Unless the agreement provides otherwise, the exchange provisions apply to examinations by agreement as well as to those by order.

In a nutshell these provisions are:

(a) The party examined can request and obtain from the examining party the report of that examination and of all prior examinations for the same condition.

(b) By doing this, or by deposing the examiner, he gives the examining party the right to reports of, and he waives any testimonial privilege respecting, all prior and subsequent examinations for the same condition.

(c) There is no time limit set upon requesting the report.

(d) The rule permits discovery of the examination report by other discovery devices.

There are too many variables to lay down any hard-and-fast rules for practice. However, there are some rules-of-thumb.

If you have no prior reports, or if they are harmless, and your client's condition has stabilized, and you must or are willing to waive the privilege, request the report. This is one extreme.

If you have harmful prior reports, or if you fear future harmful reports, and your client's condition has not stabilized, and you are unwilling to waive the privilege, do not request the report. This is the other extreme.

Most cases fall between these two extremes. You should find the two extremes useful in analyzing whether or not to request a report in your case.

There also are loopholes.

If the examining party intends to use the examiner as an expert witness at trial, you can get the substance of his facts and opinions by interrogatories under rule 26(b) (4) (A).

Since there is no time limit on requesting reports, you can hold off until you see what develops; e.g., if your discovery ploy works.

If you represent the examining party, you will be hard-pressed to counter these ploys. You could argue the case authority that rule 35 is preemptive. Or, if you can honestly do so, you could withhold decision whether to call the examiner as a trial expert. He then would become an expert under rule 26(b) (4) (B) and expressly not subject to discovery. If later you decide to use the examiner as a trial expert, the rule about supplementing answers to interrogatories requires that you then answer.

There are *seven key points* about the physical examination itself.

First let's consider the plaintiff's standpoint.

1. Agree to the examination and do not quibble about the examiner. In a personal injury suit, the court almost invariably will grant defendant an examination. Settlement will be easier if the carrier has a report from a doctor of its choice, not some stranger. There is an exception. If you expect a trial, and defendant picks a slick forensic expert, you might be able to persuade the court that he should not be used as an examiner.

2. If you agree to the examination, work out the exchange provisions beforehand.

3. Brief the plaintiff shortly before the examination. Prepare him to describe the injuries, how they happened, the period of disability, the nature and duration of the pain, and his present complaints. Warn him not to answer questions the doctor might ask that are unrelated to the examination.

4. Have plaintiff keep track of exactly how long the doctor took in examining him. You can profitably compare the opinion of your treating physician based on extended care with that of the defendant's examiner based on a brief, one-shot examination.

Now let's consider the defendant's standpoint.

5. Choose an examiner with these four qualifications—standing in his profession; credentials to impress a jury; ability as a witness; objectivity in his findings.

The first three points are obvious. You need objectivity, the fourth point, so you know what you have to face and can prepare for it. Put yourself in the shoes of counsel in the case of the Flip-Flopping Physician. He had the doctor examine plaintiff. He got a report that practically put plaintiff in the grave. He called up the doctor about this.

"Oh," the doctor said, "I got mixed up. I thought you represented plaintiff. I'll send you another report."

The doctor did just that. A week or so later, he sent counsel a report that put plaintiff in the pink.

6. Brief the doctor about the case before the examination. Since the doctor will be cross-examined, he needs all the medical facts as a foundaton for his opinion. The briefing usually can be accomplished in a letter with enclosure, and includes:

- Pertinent biographcial data about the plaintiff.
- How the injuries occurred.
- The complete medical records.
- The injuries, complaints, and disabilities as claimed by plaintiff, especially as set forth in answers to interrogatories.
- Any special points on which an opinion is sought.
- Other pertinent information. (For example, that surveillance detected the plaintiff with a bad back hefting his wife's laundry basket.)

7. Schedule the examination intelligently. You will know about plaintiff's condition from the medical records. From the standard texts you can get some idea about the usual recuperative periods. With this information, schedule the examination (a) to verify or refute plaintiff's claims, (b) to establish when he has reached maximum medical benefits, (c) to establish when he can go back to work, and (d) to verify the degree of disability.

9.8   How to Prepare the Medical Brief

The medical brief is part of the trial brief which was discussed in Chapter 4. In a simple case it may be a few notes. In a complicated case it may be a dossier.

A well-drafted medical brief collates and summarizes the important medical information with page references to the source documents.

To set up the medical brief, use the same format as the other parts of the brief (brief paragraphs, wide margin for notes, cross-references, etc.). Let the nature of material determine the subdivisions, and organize them chronologically. Typical subdivisions are: summary of hospital records; summary of doctors' reports; summaries of experts' reports; summaries of special tests, therapy, etc.; summaries of pertinent prior medical history; references to and excerpts from medical texts.

This last category is the repository of your medical research. At the top of a page put the title of the text or article, the author's name, and the biographical material that establishes him as an expert. Quote the pertinent portions of the text or reproduce and insert it. If the references are extensive, summarize the points with page references to the text.

10

Expert Testimony—

How to Maximize Its Value

and Minimize Its Dangers

10.1 How Expert Witnesses Win Cases, and Sometimes Lose Them

You should memorize the following schema about the use of expert testimony.

1. The basic rule is that a witness must testify to facts based upon his perceptions and not to inferences (opinions and conclusions) based upon these facts.

There are two broad exceptions to this rule.

2. Where a witness cannot adequately testify to facts based upon his perceptions except by inferences, he may do so. Examples would include the speed of a vehicle, matters of taste or smell, the genuineness of handwriting, etc. Some of these fall under the so-called "shorthand expression" exception.

3. Where the subject is of a scientific, technical, or other specialized nature, not within the common knowledge of lay persons of average intelligence, and testimony on the subject is either essential to the proof of the issues or will aid the jury in understanding the issues, expert testimony will be allowed.

There are two kinds of expert testimony.

4. Where the expert testifies only to expert facts and the jury draws inferences from, or otherwise uses such facts.

5. Where the expert draws inferences (i.e., gives his conclusions in the form of an opinion) from facts in evidence. These facts may be (a) expert facts to which the expert or other experts testified to, or (b) observational facts observed and testified to by the expert himself or by other witnesses, or both, or (c) a combination of both.

Rule 703 of the Federal Rules of Evidence, broadening these rules, allows an expert to draw inferences from facts made known to him before the hearing, and also upon facts not admissible in evidence if such facts are of a type conventionally relied upon by experts in the field.

6. As a rule-of-thumb, where the inferences to be drawn from the facts require a specialized knowledge, an expert will be allowed to draw those inferences. Where the inferences to be drawn from the facts lie within the knowledge of laymen of average intelligence, an expert will not be allowed to draw those inferences.

7. An expert must give an opinion to a "reasonable certainty." However, the testimony and opinion of an expert is not conclusive. The weight, credibility, and sufficiency to be given the expert testimony, including the opinion, are for the jury.

8. Whether a witness qualifies as an expert lies within the discretion of the court.

The typical medical malpractice action illustrates two of these points—the kind of case where expert testimony is essential to proof of the issues; the two kinds of expert testimony. An expert must establish the standard of proficiency in the community. These are expert facts. He must also state his opinion that the defendant physician breached this standard, and that this breach caused plaintiff's injuries. These are inferences the expert draws from the facts.

In the case of the Forgetful Physician, plaintiff claimed that the defendant had negligently administered an injection causing a nerve injury. The defendant had been using a hypo-spray gun at a mass inoculation clinic. This gun, one of the wonders of medical science, inoculates with lightning rapidity. It "shoots" the serum through the skin. No needle pierces the flesh. Hence, the gun can inoculate at almost any part of the body without harm.

The conventional hypodermic injection with a needle must be administered in a meaty portion of the body. The upper arm and buttocks are the usual choices.

Plaintiff's nerve injury occurred in the lower, non-meaty part of the upper arm. She naturally testified that this was the place defendant had inoculated her. This also was the place where a neuro-surgeon had operated on the nerve injury.

The surgeon knew nothing about the properties of the hypo-spray gun. He did not know that a hypo-spray injection did not have to be in a meaty area. He did not know the standards for mass inoculation programs. He did not know that physiologically the hypo-spray gun could not cause the injury plaintiff claimed.

On a voir dire at trial about his qualifications as an expert, the surgeon admitted all of these things. However, he had previously stated that he thought the hypo-spray injection had caused the injury. The court held the surgeon qualified as an expert. The surgeon, locked in by his previous opinion, reaffirmed it at trial. And once locked into this, he also had to testify to the expert fact that the "proper" place to inoculate was the upper meaty part of the arm, not where plaintiff said defendant had given it.

Thin—still the magic words had been uttered by an expert. On both points, standard and causation, the testimony established plaintiff's *prima facie* case.

The use of an expert to establish expert facts has a number of fine points as the following illustrations show.

In a case involving a fiduciary, the expert facts as facts, not as a basis for inferences, served to support the court's ruling in a trust deviation case.

A prosperous industrialist had settled an intervivos trust several decades before. To constitute the corpus, he conveyed the entire outstanding stock in a holding company that in turn held controlling interests in a number of operating companies that made up his business empire. He provided fixed yearly stipends in varying amounts to the various life tenants, the members of his family, in order to contribute to their "comfortable maintenance and support." He presumably did not adopt the usual device of giving a percentage of net income to the life tenants because the trustees needed a free hand with the net income to manage the operating companies.

Over the years the value of the corpus had increased tenfold, whereas inflation and taxes had ravaged the value of the fixed stipends. The toll had been particularly severe in the period preceding the last interim accounting.

At that accounting, the life tenants asked the court to approve an agreement they had reached with the trustees to increase the annual fixed stipends due to the drastic change in economic circumstances. The erosion of value, they contended, violated the settlor's intention that the stipends contribute to their comfortable maintenance and support, such as to require a deviation from the literal language respecting the amounts.

To illustrate and support their position, the life tenants produced a leading economist to testify as to economic facts—the rate of inflation since the turn of the century; the value of the dollar now compared with the value at the time of settlement; the growth in government spending; his opinion that the upward trend of inflation would continue; and so forth.

The facts about economic history were indisputable. Most, if not all, economists would have agreed with the opinion about the future; it, too, became a fact. The facts furnished the context in which the court had to decide the case. It so happened the facts had to be supplied by an expert.

At times, an expert fact as we have used the term is in form an inference (opinion). In turn, the trier of fact uses this expert fact, this opinion, as the basis for inferences it draws as to the ultimate issues in the case. This is to be distinguished from the instances where the inference (opinion) drawn by the expert embraces the ultimate issues; for example, in a medical malpractice action where plaintiff's expert testifies that in his opinion the defendant doctor did not meet the standard of care in the community.

To further illustrate these points: Late one night a sedan and a truck crashed head-on. The driver and passenger in the car, and the truck driver all died. The wreckage indicated a high-speed accident. It did not indicate whether one or both vehicles were speeding, or which had crossed the center line. To boot, both occupants of the sedan had been thrown free. It was impossible to tell who had been driving, and who riding.

Each estate sued the other. The estates of the two sedan occupants had a common interest in proving that the truck had crossed over the line. They had adverse interests as to which of the two occupants was the passenger. The estate of the truck driver hoped to prove the sedan had crossed over, but did not care which of the two occupants was the driver. Obviously, only the estate of the sedan passenger, whoever he was, had a guaranteed full recovery.

One estate retained an accident reconstruction expert. He took measurements, analyzed the positions of objects, tested samples of metal, estimated velocities and directions, performed computations.

When he had finished, in a manner of speaking he ran the motion picture of the accident backwards. He testified that in his opinion, the decedent of the estate he represented had been the passenger. This was an expert fact, at least in the sense that it was an opinion not embracing the ultimate issues. (It might be argued that it did embrace an ultimate issue, lack of contributory negligence.)

He also said that in his opinion, the truck had crossed over the center line. This opinion embraced the ultimate issue of negligence. If believed, the opinion proved negligence even though the expert did not say in so many words, "The truck driver was negligent."

You should not use expert testimony lightly. The expert witness can easily blow up on you. When he does he might blow up the whole case with himself. All too often you cannot know how expert the expert really is, how well he has prepared, or how he will do on the stand.

For example, in a wrongful death action, plaintiff looked excellent on liability and damages. The decedent had been killed in a rear-end collision. He had been 28 years old with a well-paying job in a steady industry.

Then plaintiff's economist took the stand. He computed the decedent's earnings from age 28 to age 110! He had a theory to back this up. The trouble was he could not fit the theory into the statute or explain it to the jury. The jury thought he said that the decedent had a life expectance of 110. Naturally, they rejected this as nonsense. In a clear liability case, they gave the plaintiff a minimum in damages.

10.2   Four Guidelines for Using Expert Witnesses

1. Ascertain if you need expert testimony as a matter of law. Absent a compelling need, expert testimony is not legally indispensable. [*Salem* v. *United States Lines,* 370 U.S. 31 (1962).]

2. Determine whether you want or need expert testimony as a practical matter. Some of the reasons would include:

a. To stampede the jury by a top-drawer expert with an impressive grasp of his subject or a commanding presence, or both.

b. To create a clash of expert testimony.

c. To explain and simplify technical subjects.

d. To start or defend against a battle of experts.

3. Do not use an expert witness unless you have carefully thought through whether or not you need one.

4. Do not use more than one expert on a given subject. If you do, your opponent may develop a conflict between them.

10.3   The Ideal Expert Witness and How to Find Him

The ideal expert witness should possess the following traits:

—*True Expertise.* He must be able to explain the subject thoroughly and be able to withstand cross-examination.

—*Outstanding Credentials.* He must be able to impress the court and the jury with his experience and accomplishments.

—*Objectivity.* He must tell you and testify to things "as they are," and not slant them.

—*Commanding Personality.* If he can dominate the courtroom with his personality, and can combine this with other qualities, he will stamp "credibility" on everything he says.

—*Ability as a Witness.* He must be able to testify in terms the layman can grasp. He must be firm so that he projects conviction. He must be forthright, admitting damaging facts or acknowledging that he does not know, rather than hedging. He must be responsive, answering the questions asked fully but without getting lost in his explanations.

—*Temperament.* He must not get angry when counsel attacks him. He must not obstinately cling to a position when it begins to crumble beneath him. He has to resist becoming a "know it all," a partisan expert on all phases of every subject.

—*Willingness to Work with Counsel.* He must be willing to help you prepare the case and recognize that you have the final say on trial matters.

No expert will score a hundred percent on these points. But use them to pick an expert that scores high. If you do not, you may have the headaches plaintiff's counsel had in a case with a "headstrong surveyor."

A yacht burnt to the waterline at defendant's marina. The yacht had been insured several years before under a stated value policy. The yacht had been new then. The stated value reflected its value as new.

The carrier paid the stated value as the loss. It sued the marina as a bailee for that amount. However, though the carrier paid that amount, the marina would only be liable for the fair market value of the yacht at the time of the fire.

Plaintiff called a marine surveyor as an expert on damages. He had good credentials. He had seen the yacht after the fire. He had been involved in the sale of yachts. He looked good on paper.

He did not look as good on the stand. He testified that the yacht had a fair market value at the time of the fire equal to its stated value in the policy. And he clung to this position. He acknowledged that the yacht was new when the stated value was set. He refused to acknowledge that the yacht, or yachts in general, depreciated in value over the years. He conceded that he used the industry *Blue Book* listing the average values of used yachts. He refused to concede that the Blue Book value for the yacht applied at all.

When the expert finished testifying, plaintiff settled for approximately one-tenth of the original demand, which had been the stated value.

There are four steps in getting an expert—pin-pointing the area of expertise; tracking down the candidates; checking the candidates; retaining the candidate you choose.

To pin-point the expertise, the first step, you must analyze the matter to be proven. Usually this will be enough to let you decide. If it is not, you will at least know the general field and can consult somebody in that general field to help you narrow the field.

To track the candidates down, the second step, you have to ask questions and make inquiries. The following list suggests possible sources: attorneys who have handled similar cases, specialized lawyers' associations, university faculties, testing laboratories (*Thomas' Register* publishes a list by specialties), professional societies, trade associations, *Who's Who* publications, *The Journal of Forensic Sciences, The Directory of Medical Specialists,* the public library, the yellow pages.

To check on the candidates, the third step, you should speak to lawyers who have used them. If you do this before you get in touch with the candidates, you can screen out unlikely candidates. Ask the candidates for references as well as for their resume. Then, of course, you must interview the candidates. In talking to other lawyers and interviewing the candidates, use the checklist for the ideal expert at the beginning of this section.

To retain the candidate you choose, the fourth step, make the arrangements clear at the beginning. Retain him on a time basis. He will cooperate more in preparation than if he is on a fixed stipend. Pay him irrespective of the result. Your opponent will not be able to impeach him by showing that he has an interest in the outcome of the case.

10.4   How to Prepare Your Expert for a "Cross-Examination Proof" Direct Examination, with a Note on the Technical Brief

To prepare your expert to testify, you must educate yourself.

Immediately upon retaining the expert, you should brief him on the facts and give him the pertinent materials. Even at this early stage you should make a point of getting feedback—his tentative thoughts, leads that occur to him, any ideas he has about tactics, and so forth. The educational process has begun.

You should rely heavily upon him in preparing the case—for example, in preparing technical interrogatories and answering and evaluating the answers to technical interrogatories; in seeking to develop facts along lines he suggests; in working up demonstrative evidence. The education process continues.

A point comes when you and the expert have to pull the technical aspects of the case together. The objective is to insure that you thoroughly understand the technical aspects of the case, wrap up loose ends, and make final decisions about trial.

At or about this time, you should be putting the finishing touches on the technical brief, the section of the trial book covering the technical points. The contents and format are substantially the same as for the medical brief. Besides the excerpts and quotations from authorities, the brief should contain an explanation of the technical points, in as much detail as necessary, so that you can refresh your understanding of these points.

At or about this time too you should prepare your expert for his direct examination. Easing off here can spell trouble. You cannot just discuss his testimony with the expert and let him prepare it. You must prepare it with him, and put it down in black and white on a witness sheet.

The consequences of poor preparation can be disastrous. For example, an accountant had been retained by defendant in a net worth tax case. The Government tried to show that the cost of defendant's style of living exceeded the income he reported on his tax returns. The defendant naturally took the position that he could live as he did on his reported income. To support defendant's case, counsel had the accountant analyze defendant's records for the years in question. The accountant meticulously reconstructed defendant's costs and expenditures.

At the trial, the accountant testified that defendant and his wife indeed could have lived as they did on his reported income. He used his written analysis in a convincing point-by-point presentation. When he had finished, counsel put the analysis into evidence.

Government counsel took the document. He examined it. He compared it with his notes. He then rose and asked the accountant,

You didn't include any figure for food and drink for the defendant and his wife during this period?"

The following steps are essential to prepare the expert properly for his direct testimony:

1. Review the facts to which he will testify.
2. Review the facts upon which he will base inferences.

3. Review the inferences to which he will testify, and the reasons for them. The reasons must be clear and convincing, because the expert's reasons, not his naked conclusions, are what persuade the jury.

4. Prepare the hypothetical question in writing for inclusion in the expert's witness sheet. You may have to modify the hypothetical question at trial but should do the major work on it beforehand.

5. Make sure that he will testify in language the jury can understand. Try to eliminate technical terms. Too many of them can turn a jury off. When he must use a technical term, see to it that he has an explanation about what it means.

6. Program the testimony for maximum impact. Great globs of expert testimony can lose a jury's attention. Plan questions to punctuate it.

7. Key the demonstrative evidence into his testimony for maximum impact. For example, an actual demonstration in court could usually be the high point of an expert's testimony. Also, work out mechanical problems about how to use the testimony.

8. Prepare the expert to qualify himself. You should insist on a complete resume. You have to know everything about him to present his qualifications best. Since the jury will pass on the weight of his testimony, you want to impress them with his credentials. For this reason in most cases you should not accept your opponent's concession that your expert is an expert. Occasionally, you will want to avoid having the expert appear immodest when he gives his credentials. You can do this by having him cover general points and you ask questions to fill in details.

"And are you not also, Dr. Jones, the author of the most widely used textbook in the field of industrial relations?"

9. Explain how he should testify and conduct himself on the stand. This includes the usual instructions for witnesses and those points discussed earlier dealing specially with experts.

10. Go into the types of cross-examination he may have to face. Do not pull any punches on this. In the case of the Instrumentless Engineer, for example, an expert had been called in

to inspect a piece of industrial equipment that had failed. He took certain measurements involving small dimensions and curved surfaces. At the trial he testified to these measurements as the basis for crucial conclusions he drew. On cross-examination, counsel brought out the fact that he had taken the measurements with a small wooden ruler and a piece of string. He had left his tools in the trunk of his car.

11. Carefully go over his direct and cross-examination. You want to check on the completeness and clearness of his direct testimony. You want to make sure he does not stumble on cross-examination. You can often rehabilitate a fact witness who does. You will find it hard to rehabilitate the expert who does.

10.5   The Hypothetical Question—How to
Decide Whether you Need One, and How
to Frame One if You Do

The hypothetical question lays a foundation for inferences (opinions and conclusions) to be drawn by an expert from facts.

The newer view, that in the Federal Rules of Evidence for example, is that the hypothetical question is not necessary. The older view, with many variations depending upon the jurisdiction, is that a hypothetical question is necessary.

The gist of the older view is as follows:

To the extent that an expert bases an inference upon facts testified to by other witnesses, the question must indicate the hypothetical nature of the inference and the specific facts upon which it rests. The theory is that the jury must be put in the position to accept or reject the inference, depending on whether they accept or reject the specific facts upon which it rests.

An expert can base an inference upon facts he personally observed and testified to or upon an object shown to the jury. For inferences so based, there is no need for a hypothetical question. An expert can base an inference upon a mix of hypothetical and observed facts. He can base an inference upon an inference testified to by another expert.

The facts upon which an expert can base an inference need

not be undisputed facts, but they cannot be such that a jury could well find them not to be true.

The facts must be made clear to the jury. For this reason the courts do not allow omnibus questions such as, "On all the testimony in the case. . . ."

In short, the facts must be made specific, something easier said than done. Generally, the hypothetical question need not include all the facts on the subject in the questioner's case. If it did and the facts were extensive, the jury might be swamped and come away with an overall impression without remembering or evaluating the basis for the inference. On the other hand, selecting less than all the facts opens the door to the culling of facts. This can take the form of picking facts from the testimony of one witness alone in order to credit or discredit his testimony. Or it can take the form of only picking favorable facts with the danger of misleading the jury. The court should monitor this, but you have to be aware of the possibilities and dangers.

To sum up, there are three key points in framing a hypothetical question.

Be on the inclusive side as to facts. You cannot tell what facts in your case the jury will accept or reject, or what facts your opponent will prove.

Do not leave out any critical fact which, if your opponent asks about it on cross-examination, will cause your expert to change his opinion.

Select and organize the facts so that the hypothetical question itself becomes an instrument of persuasion. Lawyers use it as a free summation.

There are several steps in handling the hypothetical question at trial.

Ask the expert, "Assume the following facts." Check the cases about how strict your courts are about shorthand assumptions; e.g., "Assume the truth of the testimony of witnesses, Jones, Doe, and Smith."

Ask the expert "Based on those facts, do you have an opinion to a reasonable certainty whether"—and here ask the question, e.g. "An inherent defect in the vaporizer caused it to explode?" If the expert's opinion will be based in whole or in part on facts he observed, check whether they have to be included in the hypothetical question.

The expert answers "yes" or "no" to the "Do you have an opinion. . ." question.

If he answers "yes" (the usual response), ask him "What is your opinion?"

The expert gives his opinion; e.g., "The vaporizer had an inherent defect which caused it to explode."

Ask him the reasons for his opinion.

After this, if he has a report you might want to introduce it.

Now for a look at the newer view.

Unless the court requires otherwise, under rule 705 of the Federal Rules of Evidence, you do not need to ask a hypothetical question. An expert may draw an inference and give his reasons "without prior disclosure of the underlying facts of data." Opposing counsel, however, may go into these on cross-examination.

Rule 703 of the Federal Rules of Evidence deals with the bases for opinion testimony by experts. The rule provides that if facts are of a type an expert in a particular field uses in drawing inferences, such facts need not be admissible in evidence. In other words an expert need no longer base his inference on facts in evidence as required at common law. He can rely on hearsay. For example, a treating doctor bases his diagnosis of plaintiff on blood tests, E.E.G., and other tests. Counsel would not have to introduce those tests into evidence as foundation for asking the doctor about his diagnosis.

Rule 703 does not set up any mechanism for opposing counsel to check whether an expert properly relied upon off-the-record facts. Indeed, since rule 705 requires no foundation at all, opposing counsel cannot tell what the expert relies upon at all, off the record or on the record. Thus rule 705, giving opposing counsel the right to cross-examine the expert, is an invitation to walk into a mine field. At best, he brings out the foundation facts that enhance the expert's testimony. At worst he may trigger a mine that his opponent deliberately planted—a fact relied upon by the expert which will dramatically enhance the expert's testimony if brought out on cross-examination.

These dangers pave the way for a finesse—examining counsel

presents an expert with strong opinions and self-evident experience as a forensic witness but without solid grounds to support the opinions, trusting that opposing counsel will not risk cross-examining on the grounds at all.

The Federal Rules of Evidence give you a range of options. You can use a hypothetical question exploiting its tactical advantages. You can forgo the hypothetical question exploiting a different set of tactical advantages.

If you will be facing an expert called by the other side, the Federal Rules of Evidence made it imperative that you discover experts fully under discover rule 26(b) (4).

There is one last but important point. Can an expert testify to an inference that embraces the ultimate issue to be decided by the trier of fact? At common law the answer depends on the topic, and on fine distinctions drawn in different jurisdictions. Under rule 704 of the Federal Rules of Evidence, the answer is "yes." How far the federal courts will go in this area remains to be seen.

To illustrate the nature of the problem, the parents of an infant placed a vaporizer near the crib. The vaporizer exploded, scalding the baby. The parents sued for strict liability in tort.

Under that doctrine, the plaintiff must prove an inherent defect in an instrumentality that makes it "unreasonably dangerous," and that proximately caused the damages. "Unreasonably dangerous" is an ultimate issue for the jury.

At common law the expert could give his opinion on the nature of the inherent defect, why it made the vaporizer dangerous in everyday use, how the accident happened, and so forth. He could not testify that in his opinion the vaporizer was inherently dangerous. Of course the expert's testimony by nature excluded any contrary facts and opinions, and if believed required the ultimate inference. Still it was not "to" the ultimate issue. (At common law there are limited exceptions; e.g., a subscribing witness can give an opinion about the testator's testamentary capacity.)

What happened in the case was this. Plaintiff had an exceptional expert, an engineer with impeccable credentials whose candor and ability had won the jury over completely. Counsel naturally sought to take advantage of this. He asked the expert,

"Do you have an opinion whether the vaporizer is inherently dangerous?"

"Objection."

"Overruled."

"Yes."

"What is your opinion?"

"Objection."

"Overruled!"

"The vaporizer is inherently dangerous."

This would have been error under the common law. Under the Federal Rules of Evidence it probably would be proper. Apart from all else, the question let an expert who had charmed a jury certify a crucial point. You should expect more and more of this under the Federal Rules of Evidence.

There is an amusing footnote to the case. Defense counsel called an expert. He got to the point where he asked his expert the same question. Plaintiff's counsel objected. The court sustained the objection!

Defense counsel flatly refused to accept the ruling. He finally convinced the court. The court overruled the objection. The defense expert answered the question, but to no visible effect since he had been outclassed by the other expert.

10.6   How to Benefit from Your Opponent's Expert Through Discovery

Traditionally you could not discover your opponent's expert. You would go to trial guessing but not knowing the inferences the expert would draw, the facts he based them on, and the reasons for them. At trial you might thrash around using cross-examination for discovery. More likely, to avoid the risk you would not try to cross-examine on the merits.

Yet modern litigation increasingly hinged upon expert testimony—patent, condemnation, product liability, medical malpractice, etc. The courts struggled with how to permit discovery of experts. The result was a hodge-podge of theories and conflicting results.

Rule 26(b) (4) solves the problem by permitting discovery of certain kinds of information from two types of experts upon specified conditions.

The rule has three subsections, each subject to a twofold prefatory requirement that the facts and opinions sought, (a) are "otherwise discoverable" under rule 26(b) (1), and (b) have been "acquired or developed in anticipation of litigation or for trial."

Subsection (A) (i), the most important provision, permits discovery of right of trial experts. By interrogatories you can ascertain (a) the identity of each expert the other party will call at trial, (b) the substance of the facts and opinions each will testify to, and (c) a summary of the grounds for each opinion.

A party cannot escape this discovery by holding off on getting a trial expert until after he receives interrogatories. Rule 26(e) requires that answers to interrogatories about trial experts be seasonably supplemented.

Under subsection (A) (ii) the court on motion can order discovery of trial experts by other means but subject to the same restrictions as to scope in (A) (i) and to the provisions about expenses and fees in subsection C. The rule does not define other means or set up any test. Probably the courts will come to allow depositions and production when the answers to the interrogatories must be amplified to fulfill the purposes of the rule.

Subsection (B) deals with the expert "retained or specially employed . . . in anticipation of litigation or preparation for trial and who is not expected to be called as a witness at trial. . ."

Such an expert may be discovered (subject to payment of fees and expenses) in two instances—under rule 35(b) dealing with doctors; by order of the court "upon a showing of exceptional circumstances under which it is impracticable . . . to obtain facts or opinions on the same subject by other means."

Subsection (B) does not cover two other kinds of expert. A general employee of a party not specially employed on the case; e.g., the defendant's R & D men in a products liability case. An expert informally consulted in preparation for trial but not specially retained or employed.

Subsection (B) does not provide how initially to discover whether the other party has retained or specially employed an expert. If you think your opponent has such an expert, and that you fall in the exceptional circumstances category, you should

serve interrogatories asking about such an expert. If your opponent answers that he has one, you can then make a motion. If he
objects to the interrogatory, you can ventilate the subject with the
court. An abstract interrogatory without regard to need in your
regular interrogatories would be objectionable. Even if your opponent answered no, he would not have to supplement the answer.

Subsection C covers fees and expenses for discovery of
experts other than of trial experts by interrogatories. If you
contemplate or are faced with this discovery, you should carefully
consult it. The costs could run high.

One last point. Rule 26(b) (4) does not deal with the expert
to the extent that he acquired information as an actor or viewer of
the events giving rise to the lawsuit. He can be discovered as an
ordinary witness.

For example, a doctor sees an accident and rushes to help the
victim. He can be discovered on what he saw. He can also be
discovered on the physical condition of the victim even though
this involves his expertise; he cannot have helped without using his
expert medical skills.

For another example, an architect designs a greenhouse for a
rich man's estate. A general contractor builds it according to the
design. The greenhouse gives trouble. The owner sues the general
contractor for poor construction. The general contractor could
discover the architect as an ordinary witness on expert points
about design.

For still another example, the general contractor sues the
architect as a third party defendant for indemnity. He can discover
the architect on expert matters as a party. An expert who is a
party and whose expertise is involved as the subject matter of the
suit can be discovered without recourse to rule 26(b) (4).

10.7   Should You Cross-Examine Your Oppo-
nent's Expert? If You Do, How to Cross-
Examine Him so That You Help Your
Own Case, Not Jeopardize It

The final decision whether to cross-examine must be made at
trial. However, you must think through your options on cross-
examination and prepare to meet them before trial.

You should not cross-examine a witness unless you can answer four questions:

Has the testimony on direct examination hurt my case?
If it has, can I impeach the testimony on direct examination?
Can I obtain testimony helpful to my case?
Do the probable benefits of cross-examination outweigh the possible dangers of cross-examination by a big enough margin to justify the risks of cross-examination?

The second and third questions state the two main purposes of cross-examination.

The main points about getting testimony helpful to your case are clear. Cross-examination is limited to the scope of the direct examination. If you try to get information beyond the scope of the direct examination, you may be precluded altogether or may make the witness your own witness, in which case you can no longer ask leading questions. You should be clear about what information you want to get. You have a much better chance of getting helpful testimony from an impartial witness than from a partisan or hostile witness. Almost invariably the expert is a partisan witness.

Helpful testimony can take several forms: An admission against interest. Testimony corroborating that of the cross-examiner's witnesses. Testimony generally supportive of the cross-examiner's case. Specific helpful facts.

Impeachment is more complicated. The word brings to mind a slashing cross-examination marked by personal insinuations. Actually, impeachment is the process of introducing evidence tending to discredit the direct testimony of a witness. Wigmore says that "devaluation" expresses the actual process.

This definition makes two important points for practice. You can impeach by introducing extrinsic evidence as well as by cross-examination. You can impeach by a cross-examination that neutralizes the direct testimony as well as by one that destroys it.

There are three distinct modes of impeachment. Mark these distinctions well in conducting impeachment. You can impeach direct testimony by showing that:

1. The witness has moral reasons to be less than truthful.

Conduct of the witness bearing on veracity. Conviction of a crime involving veracity. Corruption, e.g. subornation of perjury in the case. Bias, sympathy for or hostility against a party. Interest to favor one party or to disfavor another.

2. The witness has a testimonial defect. Temporary or permanent physical or mental incapacity to observe, understand, recollect, or communicate. Inexpertness in an expert.

3. The witness is in error on a specific fact (contradiction) or that he has acted or spoken inconsistently on prior occasions (self-contradiction). Note that the error or inconsistency can be for a moral reason or due to a testimonial defect. A witness, for example, can be a deliberate liar, or honestly mistaken, or simply confused.

The general rules governing cross-examination for impeachment are that:

a. You can go beyond the scope of the direct examination.

b. You can go into collateral matters (evidence not independently relevant to issues in the case).

c. To impeach by a prior inconsistent statement, you must lay a foundation by bringing it to the attention of the witness.

d. You cannot use a prior inconsistent statement as proof of the matter stated.

e. You cannot impeach your own witness.

In the newer codes, the Federal Rules of Evidence for instance, the opposite of the last three rules is generally true.

The risks of cross-examination are great. The witness may enlarge upon his direct testimony. He may get a chance to tell his story a second time. He may best counsel in a battle of wits. He may bring out things he could not bring out on direct examination. If he withstands an impeachment, he enhances his creditability.

These risks make the decision whether to cross-examine crucial. You must ask yourself:

Did the direct examination really hurt my case?
If it did, realistically can I do anything about it?
How strong was the witness?

Do I have anything concrete to impeach him with?

Can I devalue the direct testimony by other proof?

Is the judge the sort of person who will cut off or interrupt the cross-examination?

Do I have other ways to get in helpful testimony I had planned on getting from this witness?

If you do decide to cross-examine, you can do much to guarantee its success by observing the following rules:

—Ask for and inspect any documents the witness has used on the stand or refreshed his recollection with.

—Be fair. Don't be arrogant, sarcastic, or abusive. The jury sympathizes with the witness, and may react against you.

—Be firm. Don't let the witness divert your cross-examination. Bring him back to the point and insist upon a responsive answer. Be particularly firm with seasoned expert witnesses.

—Don't ask a question you don't know the answer to.

—Ask precise questions. Broad questions let the witness reinforce his direct testimony. Your opponent may have alerted the witness to watch for such openings. Seasoned expert witnesses instinctively spot and exploit them.

—Move the cross-examination along crisply. A hesitant cross-examination gives the witness time to figure out the drift of the questioning, think about how he will answer, and interject explanations. You occasionally may make an exception to this rule for the witness who volunteers.

—Don't ask the witness to explain. Save the point for summation. Don't give the witness a chance to explain. When you get a good answer, move right on to another topic. Don't ask one question too many.

—Don't ask why. This lets the witness make a speech because it asks for his motivation.

—When you get a bad answer, act as if nothing had happened. The jury may have missed the point, or under-estimated it. If you react or move to strike, you draw their attention to it, and underscore it.

—Don't impeach a woman. Male jurors have a protective attitude toward women.

—When you impeach, strike for the jugular, and strike right away. At the beginning of cross-examination, the jury is attentive and the witness apprehensive.

—When you have impeached a witness, stop. Don't give him the chance to redeem himself. Don't blur the sharp impression you have made on the jury. In summation you can argue nothing the witness said can be believed.

—Be brief. A long-winded cross-examination loses the jury.

—End on a high note. You want the jury to think you prevailed in the passage with the witness. A close trial can turn on an accumulation of psychological plusses.

—Be flexible. Break the rules when you have to. But first know the rules so that you know when to break them.

The dangers of cross-examining an expert are acute. He is a partisan. If he has forensic experience he will exploit openings to help his side. Consequently, it is hard to get helpful information from him. If he is worth his salt he will have a command of his subject that you cannot match, no matter how much you study. Consequently, he usually will get the better of you in a cross-examination in the area of expertise.

For these reasons the rebuttable presumption should be that you will not cross-examine an expert at all. Sometimes, though, you will decide that you should, even if only not to let the jury think the expert was so strong that you were afraid to cross-examine him. When you do cross-examine the expert, certain trial-tested techniques reduce the risk. They do so by focusing the cross-examination in areas not involving the expert's expertise, or where his expertise is neutralized.

The damages case discussed in Chapter 1 illustrates the dangers of locking horns with an expert in his area of expertise. To briefly repeat the facts: The shrink fit and weld securing the journal to the head of an embossing roll failed. The flammable coolant sprayed out and ignited. The degree of shrink fit and the size of the weld depended upon the pressures and temperatures the roll had to withstand in use. Plaintiff proved that defendant had manufactured the roll without checking on the operating data.

Defendant's chief engineer testified that flammable coolants were not customarily used in the industry. For this reason he said defendant could not have foreseen that plaintiff would have used such a coolant. Consequently, defendant argued the use of the flammable coolant constituted an intervening cause relieving it of liability.

Defendant's expert testified that flammable coolants were not used in the industry.

In rebuttal, plaintiff called an expert. He had an impressive record of years of experience in the industry. He had worked his way up from being a common mill hand. He soon established a self-evident rapport with the jury. He knew how to handle himself on the stand. Last but not least, he knew his subject.

The expert testified that flammable coolants were commonly used in the industry.

The direct examination ended. Defendant's counsel tried to undercut this testimony.

He could not. The expert had testified to an expert fact. He based it on years of experience and observation. For practical purposes, he testified to the result of a survey. Counsel could not shake this. He could not expect the expert to say that he, the expert, had not in fact observed what he had just testified to on direct examination. Counsel had nothing to contradict the expert with. All counsel did, therefore, was open the door for the expert to relate the many instances he had observed the use of flammable coolants.

The jury returned a specific finding in plaintiff's favor on this point.

Although you may not take the expert on in his area of expertise, you still must become versed in the field and prepare an adequate technical brief in the trial book. Before trial you cannot tell what your decision at trial will be. At trial you do not have time to become versed. Yet you must be versed, even for so basic a job as monitoring the expert's testimony for exaggerations or errors.

You also need a thorough grasp of the expert's subject matter to use a first set of techniques for the cross-examination of experts. These techniques go somewhat into the area of expertise. The use of precise questions and the nature of the techniques minimize the dangers of doing this.

The first technique is contradiction through facts or opinions by recognized authorities in the field. The older rule is that to do this the expert had to recognize the text or source as authoritative. The newer rule dispenses with this requirement. If the expert does not recognize the authority, the court can determine the authoritativeness on a *voir dire* outside the presence of the jury.

This technique can put the expert in a bind if he admits the text is authoritative or the court rules that it is. If he denies the points you cite, he casts doubt on his own testimony. If he admits the points you cite, he has to change his testimony or try to explain the points away. Even if there is a stand-off on this, he has to admit the existence of reputable authority against him.

When the expert agrees with the contrary authority you cite, you may have elicited facts helpful to your case as well as having impeached the expert.

You can also impeach effectively, and perhaps also obtain helpful information, by forcing contradiction or agreement between experts appearing for the same side on the same subject.

In the damages case just discussed, the plans for the embossing roll plaintiff had ordered called for a head and journal to be made out of one piece. Without telling plaintiff or consulting with plaintiff about operating data, defendant changed the design and manufactured the roll with a two-piece head and journal secured by a shrink fit and weld. The shrink fit and weld failed, the flammable coolant sprayed out and ignited.

Defendant's chief engineer admitted on cross-examination that the degree of shrink fit and size of weld were an element of design. He also admitted that knowledge of the operating data was important in designing a shrink fit.

Defendant also called an expert witness. A first-rate engineer, he impressed the jury with his knowledge and candor. Plaintiff's counsel approached him gingerly on cross-examination. But at a pre-planned point of the cross-examination, after counsel had gotten the expert's disagreement on a minor point or two, he asked him the key questions. Were the degree of shrink fit and the size of the weld elements of design? The expert said "Yes." With this answer, counsel asked if proper engineering practice required that the operating data be known in making the design. The expert said, "Yes."

The testimony struck like a thunderbolt. The jury specifically found against plaintiff on the issues of strict liability and negligence in manufacture. However, the jury specifically found for plaintiff on the issue of design negligence. The jury based these findings on the testimony of defendant's expert. By adroitly using the principles of contradiction, plaintiff forced the helpful testimony that obtained the jury finding.

The second technique is self-contradiction. If the opposing expert has published, you should comb his writings for points to be used against him. If he has testified in similar cases, you should try to examine transcripts of his testimony for impeachment material.

The third technique is known as the "agree-agree" technique. The tack here is to neutralize the expert's testimony by making it appear that he agrees with your position. Often a jury will not really understand the technical points the respective experts testify to. The jury will, however, understand and remember what seems to be agreement between experts. This is similar to the way they often will credit one expert instead of another for manner and not for content. The "agree-agree" technique requires a series of points to which the expert must agree and as to which you can ask precise questions. Nonetheless, you should not undertake it lightly since it obviously has its hazards. You must have authority to back up the facts you seek agreement on.

A fourth but dangerous technique is to vary the hypothetical question. For this technique to work, you must pin-point crucial omissions in the hypothetical question. You then ask the expert whether or not in adding these facts he would change his opinion. A seasoned expert will have a handy explanation why he would not. You plan that the facts you supplied will strike the jury as salient and the expert's explanation weak. Usually, you also plan to follow up on the technique by testimony from your own expert.

The danger in the technique lies in reinforcing the expert's direct testimony. In the case of the Rolling Hypothetical, the court appointed a non-partisan expert in a medical malpractice action. On direct examination, plaintiff's counsel asked him a hypothetical question embodying all of the essential facts in the medical record, especially the operative note of the procedure the defendant had performed.

The expert answered the question to the effect that defendant had not malpracticed.

Stung by the answer, plaintiff's counsel began to pile hypothetical question on hypothetical question. Each added or subtracted one fact or another taken from the medical record.

To none did the expert budge. None had a chance of prevailing because the initial hypothetical question had not omitted any essential fact. The series of hypothetical questions only reinforced the expert's opinion.

A second set of techniques for cross-examining an expert center on the principle for cross-examining an expert center on the principle of peripheral attack. You try to impeach the expert but entirely avoid his area of expertise.

Thus the fifth technique is a moral attack to expose partisanship. You ask the expert about his fee. You bring out how many times he has testified as an expert. You get him to admit that with few exceptions he testifies for the plaintiff or the defendant. You force him to acknowledge the many times he consults for insurance companies on losses. You reveal that he is on the list of witnesses for hire published by plaintiff groups.

For a successful attack on partisanship, you must find out as much about the expert as you can.

A sixth technique is a moral attack to expose personal defects. By exposing traits that downgrade the expert you downgrade his testimony. On direct or cross-examination you may spot and play up an expert's arrogance, know-it-all attitude, bullheadedness, proneness to anger, and the like. In the case of the Headstrong Surveyor discussed in this chapter, counsel hammered on the expert's refusal to acknowledge the universally accepted *Blue Book* of used yacht values. The more obstinate the expert became the worse he looked.

The case of the Forgetful Physician discussed in Chapter 7 also illustrates the point. At his deposition the defendant doctor in a malpractice action denied being at the clinic at which plaintiff claimed he gave her an injection. At the trial, counsel first called the plaintiff. He then called the doctor under the adverse witness statute. The doctor confirmed the testimony he had given on deposition. Counsel then called a witness with travel vouchers the defendant had put in for a trip to the clinic in question on the day in question.

Counsel shattered the doctor's credibility.

A seventh technique embodies the principles of ridicule. This can take a variety of forms. It can be an attack on the expert's own behavior. In the case of the Instrumentless Engineer discussed earlier in this chapter, the expert made certain crucial and allegedly precise measurements with a pencil-box ruler and a piece of string. He had left his instruments in the trunk of his car. The cross-examiner harped on making precise measurements with a piece of string. The attack can be much more subtle. In personal injury actions, plaintiffs' counsel often will compare the few minutes defendant's examining physician spent with the plaintiff with the weeks spent by the treating physician.

You should not try to make an expert or any witness an object of fun. The jury sympathizes with the witness. They will resent an attack that does not come off. In most cases, you will be better off simply to bring out the points, let them speak for themselves, and use them on summation.

11

Preparing
Demonstrative Evidence
That Will Convince Jurors

**11.1   How to Realize the Benefits of Non-
Verbal Persuasion Without Formal Proof
in Four Key Trial Situations**

Evidence can by-pass oral testimony and be
addressed directly to the senses. This type of evidence is called
demonstrative evidence.

Sight is the most important sense. Approximately 85 percent
of what we learn and remember comes through sight, about 10
percent through hearing, and only 5 percent through touch, taste,
and smell combined. Consequently, most demonstrative evidence
is addressed to sight. The term itself is sometimes used narrowly to
mean visual evidence.

However, demonstrative evidence is not the only means of
non-verbal communication at the trial. There are other direct

appeals to the senses that do not involve formal evidence. These appeals can be as important as demonstrative evidence.

Four principal situations should be reviewed for their own sake. They also serve as an introduction into the dynamics of demonstrative evidence itself:

First. How a witness testifies often is as important as what he testifies to. You want your witness to approach the stand confidently; to take the oath with hand raised high; to stand erect in the witness box; to look the jury in the eye; to testify in a firm voice; to step down with chin high.

You want your witness to act like he has told the truth, and that he expects the jury to believe him.

The slip-and-fall case, discussed in Chapter 9, illustrates the point. The supermarket clerk slouched, looked nobody in the eye, hemmed and hawed—in short, testified as if he did not even believe himself. No matter what he said, the jury would have been hard-pressed to believe him.

The core of the concept here is demeanor. There are psychological tell-tales the jury can use to evaluate the truth of the testimony. But the concept is broader. In another case, a youth had been arrested in a narcotics raid. If involved in the trafficking at all, he had only been on the periphery. His parents retained a leading criminal defense lawyer. Counsel had hopes of getting the defendant off. However, the boy had shoulder length hair before it had become commonplace. Counsel told the boy to cut his hair. The boy steadfastly refused. "It is all that I have," he said. Counsel did not get the result he had thought he could get.

In the trial of cases, the medium has not yet become the message. Yet trial lawyers probably have no single greater concern than the overall impression their witnesses will make.

Second. An object may be exhibited to the jury, and often introduced into evidence. The object may help explain a fact in issue. The existence and condition of the object may be relevant. The object may be an inanimate thing. It may be a person or a part of a person's body. The display may take the form of a demonstration—how the object works, the effect of an injury, etc.

The showing of things or of persons is sometimes called real evidence. It is subject to certain exclusionary rules: that it is relevant; that it will help elucidate the case; that it will not be prejudicial; that it is in substantially the same condition as before; that no privilege bars it.

These matters lie within the discretion of the court.

The Jacob's Ladder case illustrates why the thing itself is such powerful and important evidence.

In a distinguished career on the bench an appellate judge had become an authority on admiralty law. He had written many opinions in the field. In some of them he had laid down principles that shaped the growth of the law. In others he dealt with narrower problems. In the latter group, he had written a number of opinions over the years that dealt with Jacob's ladders in one way or another. A careful reading of those opinions raised a disturbing question. How close was the judge's notion of Jacob's ladders to the reality.

A case came up on appeal in which a Jacob's ladder had been introduced into evidence. At the argument counsel displayed it to the court. The judge leaned forward. He looked at it carefully. Finally he said, "So that's what a Jacob's ladder looks like."

Third. The view is a form of real evidence. When an object or place cannot be produced in court, the court may permit the jury to go see it. The court applies the same considerations as in producing objects. The view technically is not evidence. Evidence is not received at a view. The practice is for counsel or some other person merely to point out pertinent features.

Self-evidently, however, the view becomes a source of belief for the jury. You must take it seriously. You should always visit the scene before the trial to decide whether you want a view or want to oppose a view. If you are sponsoring the view, you should plan how to conduct it. You want to know what features to point out, why you want to point them out, and the sequence in which to point them out. If your opponent is sponsoring the view, you should decide what features you want to make sure are pointed out in the view. If you oppose a view you should plot your opposition in advance.

Fourth. "Dumb show" in the courtroom can be the most powerful non-verbal persuader of all. A thousand things go on in the courtroom that affect the result. Many of these things just happened. Some are contrived. Spontaneous or contrived, you must appreciate the importance of dumb show in order to cope with it. Dumb show falls into three broad groups.

To start with, there is the general setting. In certain kinds of cases, for example, you will not want other counsel with you at the counsel table. You want to give the impression of being a lone champion doing battle for your client against a phalanx of lawyers arrayed against you at the other counsel table. In virtually every case you will want your client with you. You do not want the jury to think your client has no interest in the case, or is above it all.

In a case involving a "stern employer," a wealthy woman upbraided a maid. The maid quit or was fired depending on your point of view. The maid sued claiming an assault during the flare-up.

The trial convened in a large city. The defendant attended court faithfully. During the noon recesses, she often went shopping. The case finally began to wind up. The evidence closed on a particular morning. The judge set arguments for two that afternoon. Two p.m. arrived. The bailiff locked the doors of the courtroom. Defense counsel began his summation.

Five minutes later the defendant arrived in the hall outside of the locked doors. She remained outside until the bailiff had taken the jury out to deliberate, and unlocked the doors.

The jury returned a verdict for the plaintiff. On motion some weeks later, the court ordered a new trial unless plaintiff agreed to a remittitur. In the circumstances perhaps the result would have been the same—a rich defendant; a working girl plaintiff; a polygot urban jury. But the defendant did have a case on the facts. She did well on the stand. She did not help her case by missing the summations.

Next, there is the contrived setting. Counsel deliberately sets about to influence the jury by dumb show. The classic example is the wrongful death plaintiff in her neat but modest widow's weeds patiently sitting in the courtroom, a brood of freshly scrubbed children clinging to her skirts. If, to lady jurors, the children are adorable, so much the better.

In the Sister-in-Black case, a teen-age girl had been involved in an automobile accident. She had not been at fault. The insurance carrier for the other driver settled her claim early. Her insurance company, however, would not meet the high settlement demand of the other driver.

The case of the other driver reached trial several years later. In the meantime, the teen-age girl had matured into a young woman. She also had taken orders. She attended trial and testified in her nun's habit. She won.

Then there can be the dramatic dumb show.

For example, in another case, counsel asked for a bench conference just before he intended to call the decedent's mother as a witness in a wrongful death action. He suggested that she might need an interpreter since she had immigrated after World War II. The defendants objected. The judge overruled the objection.

The question then arose about who would be the interpreter. Someone on plaintiff's side suggested the daughter and sister. Defendants objected strenuously. The judge again overruled the objection.

The bailiff placed a chair next to the witness box. The sister sat in it facing the jury and out of sight of the judge.

Counsel began his examination. The mother understood and answered perfectly. The examination continued perfectly. The daughter did not have to interpret a word. But as counsel began to ask the mother about the boy, the sister's lip began to quiver. She soon was stifling sobs.

Defense counsel repeatedly objected. Finally, the judge sustained the objections. He commented that it seemed the mother did not need an interpreter and asked the sister to step aside.

The episode had been a master stroke. The sister had testified previously. She had barely been able to control her emotions then. Having to think and talk about her brother unnerved her. As for the mother, she did not need an interpreter any more than a professor of English. In fact, she had a responsible position in which she dealt with the public.

An episode in the plane crash case discussed in Chapter 1 illustrates dumb show and how hard it may be to draw the line between it and bona fide demonstrative evidence.

In that case, a Beechcraft Baron and a Cessna 150 had collided on approach to an airport. The Cessna interests claimed that the Beechcraft had improperly banked right and flown into the rear of the Cessna. From the wreckage, the impact had taken place when the left wing of the Beechcraft hit the cabin of the

Cessna from the rear. The Beechcraft interests said that the Cessna had flown into the path of the Beechcraft.

The Cessna interests obtained scale models of both airplanes. Each model had a stand. Counsel used the models during the examination of various witnesses. Their expert used them extensively.

When the models were not in use, they rested in direct view of the jury on the counsel table. It seemed like every time counsel for the Beechcraft interests looked over, the Beechcraft was positioned so that it was banking right, flying into the rear of the Cessna.

Where do you draw the line? The expert's use of the models to demonstrate the rear-end collision did not disturb the other side. Counsel's placing of the models on the counsel table to demonstrate the same thing disturbed them very much indeed.

In conclusion, there are two points. First, direct appeals to the senses can take many forms. Some of these forms constitute formal demonstrative evidence. Others do not. The principles behind both are the same.

Second, as demonstrative evidence has become necessary, it has become popular. It is the "in thing" in litigation. Do not let this popularity make you forget the other and older non-verbal ways to persuade the jury.

11.2   How to Insure That Your Demonstrative Evidence Gets Admitted into Evidence

There are five general rules for the admissibility of demonstrative evidence:

- That it will help the trier of fact understand the evidence.
- That it will not prejudice, confuse, or mislead the trier of fact.
- That it is relevant and material to the issues in the case.
- That it is not barred by an exclusionary rule of evidence.
- That it is a fair and accurate representation of what it purports to represent.

The last rule deals with the foundation that must be laid for the introduction of demonstrative evidence. Although the broad principle is the same, the exact requirements for the foundation that must be laid will vary. One variable is the type of demonstrative evidence. Another variable is the nature of the case. A third variable is the state of the law of evidence in a given jurisdiction.

To take the third point first, as the courts become accustomed to different types of demonstrative evidence, they come to see that precautions required for a foundation in earlier cases often are not necessary, and hence will not be required in later cases. Needless to say, enlightenment reaches different courts at different times.

As for the other two points, compare a still photograph with a motion picture.

Generally, any witness who has viewed a scene personally can testify that a still photograph of the scene is a true and accurate representation of the scene. With a motion picture, however, consider these two cases. One film depicts the site of a vacant plant taken by eminent domain. Presumably any witness who had viewed the scene could authenticate the film.

The other film is a surveillance film showing a personal injury plaintiff claiming a limp on a brisk constitutional with his dog tugging on a leash. The person who shot the film might have to testify that he ran the camera at the standard rate for reproducing the natural speed of a person (16 frames per second on 16 mm film), that he was projecting it in the courtroom at the same proper speed, and the like. This testimony, note, is in addition to swearing that the film was a fair and accurate representation of what he saw when he shot it.

To be fair and accurate representation, an item of demonstrative evidence need not be a literal representation or exact replica. The degree of similarity will depend on the circumstances and the type of demonstrative evidence. A model, for example, usually does not have to be full size. That it be to scale may suffice. If it is a working model, it may omit many details of the original. That it fairly and accurately shows the operating principles may suffice. On the other hand, a photograph of the scene of an accident when crucial conditions had changed might not be admissible.

Whether an item of demonstrative evidence will confuse, or

mislead the trier of fact often is the opposite part of whether it is fair and accurate. That is, fulfilling the test of fairness and accuracy fulfills the test of non-confusion and not misleading. The test of non-prejudice frequently centers on gruesome or shocking objects or pictures that will inflame the jury.

The admissibility of demonstrative evidence lies within the discretion of the court. One exception would be where the demonstrative evidence would not be admissible under an exclusionary rule. For example, the privilege might exclude an otherwise admissible tape recording of a conversation between a husband and wife. The court would have no discretion but would have to exclude it.

Demonstrative evidence may be used to help illustrate the testimony of a witness. In the fiduciary case discussed in the previous chapter, graphs prepared by the expert economist illustrated the curves for the consumer price index and for output per man hour, to which he testified.

Or demonstrative evidence may be a silent witness. Case in Point: A photograph taken at the time depicted a facial feature that was the heart of the controversy.

In these and in virtually every instance, the demonstrative evidence requires the testimony of a witness standing behind it. The witness must tie the demonstrative evidence into the case. He must lay the foundation. He often must establish the relevancy.

These highlights of the evidentiary rules will help you generally in planning the use of demonstrative evidence. However, once you have decided on a particular type of demonstrative evidence, you should steep yourself in the evidentiary rules in your jurisdiction governing its use. With common types of demonstrative evidence such as still photographs or diagrams, you may already know the rules by heart. Even so, you should check on the latest decisions. With less common types of demonstrative evidence, such as motion pictures and videotapes, you should research the evidentiary rules and analyze their application to your case.

11.3   Six Guidelines on When to Use Demonstrative Evidence

This section deals with the principal circumstances where you should use demonstrative evidence. The sections following this section will deal with the advantages and disadvantages of the major types of demonstrative evidence.

But first you must start thinking in terms of demonstrative evidence. You must cultivate' the habit of mind of looking for the possibilities of using demonstrative evidence in every case. You start with the premise that if you can use it appropriately, you want to use it because it can be so powerful.

You then let your imagination go to work on the possibilities.

You have two working tools in this analysis. A knowledge of the principal circumstances for using demonstrative evidence, the guidelines covered in this section. A knowledge of the major types of demonstrative evidence is covered in the following sections.

The guidelines help you analyze the case for the potentialities of demonstrative evidence. The familiarity with the types of demonstrative evidence helps you pick the most effective type of demonstrative evidence for the case. Together, the two working tools help you decide how most effectively to use the demonstrative evidence you have selected in the case.

One other word before turning to the six guidelines. Use demonstrative evidence appropriately. Do not trivialize it by use on unimportant points. Do not use it for overkill because the jury might react adversely if it thinks you are trying to prejudice the case.

11.3.1 Helping the Jury Understand Technical or Complex Facts That Cannot Readily Be Grasped Through Oral Testimony

The ability to assimilate and evaluate oral evidence requires imagination and a capacity to think abstractly. The ability to see in the mind's eye a scene described orally requires a gift of visualization. The ability to understand oral testimony on a technical matter requires a high order of intelligence for a person not trained in that area.

The average juryman does not have these abilities or this intelligence. If your case has facts that would be hard to understand presented orally alone, you must turn to demonstrative evidence.

The use of demonstrative evidence to elucidate technical or scientific facts comes to mind immediately. You do not face a question of whether to use it but of what type to use. In deciding on the type to use, you must think in terms of the central point you are trying to get across. For example, if you wanted to explain why a piece of equipment did or did not function properly, you might use a working model. The limiting factor would be whether the operational principles could be fairly and accurately simplified. On the other hand, if you wanted to show that a safety guard on a machine did not do the job adequately, you might take a motion or videotape picture of the machine in operation.

A more extended example, a case involving Teflon-coated razor blades, illustrates how you must analyze your case in terms of the central point you are trying to get across. Some years ago, a major razor blade manufacturer burst on the scene with Teflon-coated razor blades. They gave a smoother shave, lasted longer, and nicked less than conventional razor blades. Backed by a massive advertising campaign, they captured the market.

Others rushed to develop the process. In time the competitive production of Teflon-coated blades began to reach the market. A large retailer contracted for a continuing supply of the Teflon-coated razor blades for sale under a house name. The first shipments came in. The retailer began to sell them immediately. It soon began to get customer complaints. It withdrew the merchandise and took up the problem of quality with the supplier.

The supplier contended the blades met standards. The supplier suggested that the retailer had over-reacted to a few complaints, which may not have been justified, in order to protect the house brand. The supplier offered to continue production. It found nothing wrong with the manufacturing process. This did not satisfy the retailer. The matter wound up in litigation.

The manufacturer had to get across the key point of a quality Teflon coating. However, the judge said he would not himself try the razor blades. He would not let the men on the jury do so either. Because the retailer had withdrawn the product, the number of complaints and the amount of sales did not prove anything. The naked eye looking at the blade could tell nothing.

Gingerly running a finger told nothing either. No test could simulate the blades in use.

To prove the quality of the coating the supplier took photographs of the Teflon-coated edges through a microscope. Greatly enlarged, the photographs dipicted how the coating looked on the edges of properly treated blades and on poorly treated blades. The coating on the former appeared smooth and evenly laid on. The coating on the latter appeared uneven with porosities indicating spots not covered.

The expert described these conditions and comparisons. The enlarged photographs showed them clearly.

11.3.2   Drawing Together and Crystalizing a Mass of Evidentiary Facts

A witness must describe a scene or event sequentially. He must mention each feature or happening one by one. Modern psychology tells us that we actually perceive scenes and events in groupings. Thus, a picture or a model intrinsically comes closer to the way we actually perceive a great mass of things than does oral testimony.

Many types of demonstrative evidence by their nature tend to draw together and crystalize a number of facts. This principle lies behind the conscious use of demonstrative evidence for this purpose. The Man-Made Cove case discussed in Chapter 4 illustrates this.

The owner of a large part of the land underlying a man-made cove brought a suit against a boatman for trespass upon the cove.

The cove had been in its present state for a number of years. Before the upsurge in boating after World War II, the cove had been a tranquil place enjoyed by the abutting owners and yachtsmen who used it in entirely manageable numbers. With that upsurge in boating, on the weekends the cove became a busy anchorage. Often more than 100 boats would moor. Vandalism and dangerous boating began to get out of hand. The plaintiff hired a policeman to patrol the cove and keep order.

One boatman would not recognize the owner's right to do

this. He contended that the waters were navigable in law and in fact so that the public had a right to use them without interference.

The case turned on the nature of the cove. If artificially made, the public easement of navigation did not attach to the waters; if naturally made, the easement did.

Plaintiff assembled an impressive collection of patents, deeds, maps, and charts going back to earliest colonial times. They described and depicted the area of the cove as a salt marsh with a creek meandering through it with an outlet to the Sound. From time to time, the mouth of the creek opening on the Sound changed locations.

Plaintiff's expert, an eminent geologist, explained how storms, winds, and tides caused this migration of the mouth of the creek.

Plaintiff also assembled later materials, deeds, and charts and the eye-witness testimony of a nonagenarian, establishing how the salt marsh had become a cove. At the turn of the century, the area had been dredged for sand used in building a New York City subway system. Intermittent dredging had taken place after that.

The evidence and the testimony proved the man-made nature of the cove. But each piece was a fragment.

The geologist had a rare ability to explain how the written descriptions and pictorial representations led to the present state of the cove. But even his conclusions and reasons came across as fragmentary. The wealth of detail necessary to make the reasoning meaningful buried the subject. The evidence could not be marshalled effectively in oral form.

The expert and counsel tackled the problem. How to depict the evolution of the cove tieing in the foundation evidence. They decided on maps. The expert prepared four. One depicted the cove in early times. Another depicted the cove at the time of suit. The other two depicted the cove at pivotal stages in its history.

The maps in color succeeded brilliantly. They drew together and crystalized the mass of evidence in four graphic and artistic exhibits. From them, even without testimony about dredging, the conclusion was inevitable that the cove had been formed by artificial means. The exhibits became the centerpiece of the case at trial and on appeal.

11.3.3 Stamping Crucial Facts into the Jury's Mind so That the Jury Understands Them When Introduced and Remembers Them Through and Until the End of Trial

The losing lawyer often complains the jury missed something.

He complains the jury did not remember something. If he is right, he has no one to blame but himself. In his planning, he did not isolate the crucial points and take the necessary steps to stamp them into the jury's consciousness.

As the saying goes, counsel had his "emphasis" in the wrong place, or he might not have had any emphasis at all. He may have swamped the jury with a mass of unrelieved detail. Either way, he let the jury come away with a blurred or misplaced impression on a crucial issue, or perhaps with no impression at all.

You can emphasize points in a number of ways. You can do so by repetition. In the case of the Spry Septuagenarian discussed in Chapter 9, counsel emphasized the plaintiff's fortitude and pain and suffering by her testimony and that of her two daughters, and her attending physician. (In a way the example proves too much. Better courts do not allow cumulative testimony because of prejudicial emphasis.)

You also can achieve emphasis by properly highlighting points in the oral testimony of a strong personality. In the Tietzse Syndrome case, also discussed in Chapter 9, plaintiff produced "Dr. Dynamite," an impressive forensic medical expert. He gravely told how he gave the female plaintiff injections through her breast to relieve her pain. The jury winced as he described this, and never forgot it.

You can achieve emphasis in a remarkable number of ways with demonstrative evidence. To start with, demonstrative evidence by its nature furnishes emphasis. If the demonstrative evidence is in any way elaborate, the very process of setting up for it and eliciting it adds to the emphasis. If it can be combined with the testimony of a strong witness, it can become lethal in its emphasis. If in addition it has been programmed into the case for maximum impact, it can become the whole case. This surely is the ultimate in emphasis.

In the case of the Migrating Plane Crash discussed in Chapter 1, the demonstration by the Cessna interests stamped their version of the facts indelibly into the jury's mind. After the demonstration, the trial theory of the Beechcraft seemed fanciful.

Two light planes, a Beechcraft Baron and a Cessna 150, collided in mid-air on approach for landing at an uncontrolled airport. At uncontrolled airports all turns must be to the left.

The eyewitness produced by the Cessna interests testified that the Cessna was flying South on final approach for landing, descending and heading straight for the runway which ran almost due North and South. The Beechcraft, they said, came in fast from the Northwest in a shallow right bank to line up with the runway. They added that it smashed into the rear of the Cessna at a point about 100 yards from the end of the runway and on a direct line with it.

Experts for both sides as well as for the National Transportation Safety Board examined the wreckage. There was no dispute that the leading edge of the outer part of the left wing of the Beechcraft smashed into the rear part of the cabin of the Cessna on the right side. About 8 feet of the Beechcraft wing sheared off embedding itself in the Cessna.

The Beechcraft interests went to trial on the following four-pronged theory: That the Beechcraft had come in from the Northwest and banked right to enter a pattern of flight paralleling the runway to the West by approximately 100 yards. That the Cessna being flown by a student pilot had mistakenly flown approximately 100 yards past the point where it should have banked left for a straight-in approach. That, however, it then banked left and began to angle back left toward the runway. That as a result, it flew into the Beechcraft's line of flight from the right.

The Beechcraft interests had an expert ready to testify that technically the Cessna could have executed an unusual and complicated maneuver that would have taken it into the Beechcraft's line of flight in an attitude that would account for the points of impact.

The Cessna interests had the wreckage of the Cessna reconstructed in a rented hall. They had the 8-foot segment of the Beechcraft wing mounted on a movable dolly.

The Cessna interests said they wanted to display the mock-up to the jury. The court and Counsel inspected it. The court agreed. Arrangements were made. At ten o'clock on the designated day, the court convened in the hall. The press covered the event. Flash bulbs popped. Reporters scribbled. It was a good show.

Over objection, the court let the mock-up into evidence. Once in evidence, the Cessna interests had their expert conduct a school for the jury. He walked the jury about the mock-up explaining points as he went along.

As a bonus, if any of the jury had sharp eyes and were perceptive, they would have seen blood stains in the cabin area.

The tour around the mock-up and the running commentary of the expert whetted the jury's appetite for more. Lead counsel for the Cessna interests had this planned, too.

He asked his expert to move the segment of the Beechcraft wing mounted on the movable dolly into the place on the Cessna where it had hit and lodged. Counsel for the Beechcraft interests leapt to their feet objecting. They reminded the court that it had previously ruled it would not allow this. The build-up persuaded the court to reverse itself.

The Cessna expert expertly positioned the dolly a distance from the mock-up. Then he pushed it, slowly but inexorably into the precise place where it had lodged on that fateful day. He did not have to ask any juryman to imagine the Beechcraft wing smashing into the back of the heads of two men sitting in the tiny Cessna cabin.

The Cessna expert had recreated the collision exactly as he said the impact marks proved it had happened. As he recreated the event, a look of absolute belief literally came across the jury's faces.

In due time the Beechcraft expert took the stand. The jury listened to him in stony disbelief.

Emphasis can come in less dramatic packages. A critical portion of a medical record can be photographed and enlarged for use on direct or cross-examination. A witness can place objects on a magnetic board as he recounts the events culminating in an accident. The examples are endless. The key is to isolate the points that need emphasis beforehand, and plan how best to create that emphasis.

11.3.4   Demolishing Your Opponent's Version
                of the Facts When It Conflicts Sharply
                with Your Version of the Facts or
                with the Physical Facts Themselves

There are two related but distinct thoughts here.

Your version and your opponent's version of the facts may
sharply differ, but be congruent with the physical facts or the laws
of nature. Or your opponent's version could be opposed to
physical facts or the laws of nature.

In the first situation you must plan demonstrative evidence
of a self-evident top quality, that dramatically and conclusively
overwhelms your opponent's evidence. He may be right but you
blow him out of the water.

In the second situation you must plan demonstrative evidence, also of a self-evident top quality, that proves conclusively
that your opponent's version of the facts does not fit the physical
facts or is opposed to the laws of nature.

Again, the plane crash case illustrates the first situation. For
practical purposes, it illustrates the second point as well—that the
Cessna overshot the proper place to bank, and that if it did the
assumption that a student pilot engaged in aerobatic maneuvers
was a flight into fancy.

Another example illustrates demonstrative evidence fulfilling
the physical facts rule. Plaintiff, a garage operator, bought an
automobile hoist. It consisted of a rectangular framework made of
I-beams with upright posts at each corner. An automobile is driven
into it. A front cross-bar is positioned against the front of the
front tires. The cross-bars were supported by and could move back
and forth on rails. When the hoist lifted the car thus positioned,
the front cross-bar would slide forward a few inches and lodge
snugly against the frame of the car.

While working under a car, plaintiff claimed it slipped off and
fell on him. He sued the manufacturer for design negligence.

Experts for both parties videotaped hundreds of tests with
the same or identical automobile and with the same or identical
hoist. One series of tests dealt with a properly positioned car. In
no case would any amount of pressure, pushing, or pulling cause a

properly positioned car to fall. Another series of tests dealt with a car where the front cross-bar was positioned under the bumper. The car could be lifted but a slight amount of pressure would cause it to fall. Plaintiff admitted that to position a car in this way would be dangerous. He said though that he had positioned the car properly but that somehow it had "jumped out."

Defendant displayed the videotapes at the trial. The jury returned a verdict for the plaintiff.

Defendant appealed. The court of appeals reversed. The court held that countless tests established that misuse rather than negligent design caused the accident. The plaintiff's testimony that he had positioned the car properly, the court said, was of no probative value under the physical facts rule.

An imaginative and altogether first-rate use of demonstrative evidence by defendant's counsel prevented a miscarriage of justice.

11.3.5   Demonstrating the Nature and Extent, or Non-Extent, of Personal Injuries

The predominance of personal injury litigation has given rise to a library of techniques and an industry of devices on ways to elucidate the medical proof and inflate or deflate damages.

By the time of trial, the plaintiff might look like he never had been hurt. Color photographs of the injury would show how severe it was.

On the surface, plaintiff's recovery might seem complete. Modern x-ray pictures could show the misalignment of bones. The injection and photographing of a substance could illustrate the pathology of a bodily system.

The number and variety of medical aids is truly impressive—anatomical charts, transparencies, overlays, skeletons, reproductions of organs, medical illustrations, x-rays, prosthetic devices.

Motion pictures or videotapes play an increasing role. Plaintiffs use them to illustrate a day in the life of a disabled person. Defendants use them to expose claimed injuries as fraudulent.

Enlargements have found their niche. Key portions of the hospital record can be blown up for use on examination.

The crutch used or cast worn by the plaintiff can be produced to dramatize the inconvenience and annoyance.

In a medical malpractice case, a photograph delivered the coup de grace to plaintiff's case. Plaintiff had tinnitus, a condition of ringing in the ears. It bothered her very much. She consulted a neuro-surgeon. He told her that a sectioning of the eighth cranial nerve might cure the condition. He did not urge the operation however because it was so delicate.

A year or so later the patient, in anxiety over her condition, consulted the doctor again. She requested and he performed the craniotomy as a last-ditch effort for relief.

Plaintiff claimed the operation did not cure the tinnitus. She also claimed it caused a right facial droop due to an inadvertent sectioning of the seventh cranial nerve.

The patient's frame of mind worsened. She had to be institutionalized. Ultimately, she died.

Her husband substituted himself as plaintiff in the malpractice action she had commenced against the doctor.

At the trial the husband did not produce expert testimony that defendant had breached the standard of care. Nonetheless, the court did not grant the defendant's motion for a directed verdict but reserved on it.

The surgeon relied on the medical records and called one witness.

The medical records proved that he had warned her about the risks of surgery and the chances of success.

The one witness was a photographer.

When the patient had been institutionalized after the operation, she had had her snapshot taken for her file. The snapshot showed her in a close-up, face on, holding a sign with her name legibly printed on it in large letters. The snapshot depicted her with a pronounced and unmistakable left facial droop.

The photographer testified that because her name was not reversed in the photograph, the snapshot had not been reversed in developing. Thus, as she faced out from the snapshot, her right side was in fact her right side, and her left side in fact her left side.

The court did not grant the renewed motion for a directed verdict. The jury resolved the problem by returning a verdict for defendant.

11.3.6   **Maximizing the Effectiveness of Demonstrative Evidence by Programing It into Your Trial Plan**

This sixth guideline is procedural. To get the most out of your demonstrative evidence, you must plan when to use it during the trial.

If you have impressive demonstrative evidence, you should make it the high point of your case. This often means you should end your case with it. If you have run-of-the-mill demonstrative evidence—for example, ordinary photographs of a scene for use by a fact witness—you do not have such pressing considerations. Even in that instance though you want to use the photographs at the most effective place in the witness's testimony.

You should plan to use your demonstrative evidence when the jury is fresh, early in the morning or right after the noon recess.

You should plan so that your presentation of the demonstrative evidence is not interrupted by a recess. This means you must take into account how long you will need to lay a foundation.

You should include in your planning possible use of demonstrative evidence other than on direct examination.

You might use a blackboard or drawing pad in your opening for simple but illuminating diagrams.

In plotting your cross-examination, you should consider how to use such things as photographs, diagrams, and models. In the case of the Vanishing Damages, an enlarged photograph of the embossing roll revealed a work order number corresponding to the number on defendant's written work order for the job.

Plaintiff effectively brought this out on examination of defendant's chief engineer under the adverse witness statute.

As tape recordings come into increasing use, you may find it necessary to replay tapes of witness statements for impeachment.

You likewise have to plan how to use demonstrative evidence exhibits in your closing argument. If you can weave a summation around these exhibits, you will make a far more lasting impression than if you simply orated.

Finally, you should exploit the demonstrative evidence in the case on an appeal.

Appellate judges rarely will plow through a record. Perhaps one law clerk will do so. Appellate lawyers sometimes wonder how many of the judges on a given panel do more than scan the briefs and appendices.

But even on a scanning, a picture will deliver its message. On oral argument, a picture or a model can capture attention and make a point instantly. In the short time usually given you for argument, this instant insight can be crucial.

11.4   Winning with Photographs—How to Use the Right Type at the Right Time for the Right Purpose

You should become well-versed in the use of photographs. They are the principal form of demonstrative evidence. There are several types:

• The ordinary black-and-white still shot.

• The still shot in color. At times you will need color. As mentioned, for example, a photograph of a wound. At other times, because it is more vivid, you will want color to capture the jury's imagination.

• The three-dimensional still shot. When you need to show the relative height and position of features, use three-dimensional photographs. However, they require a viewer or projector, and cannot be taken by the jury into deliberations.

• Slides. Slides also require a viewer or projector. If you think they are important, have them made up into prints.

• Aerial photographs. You will find aerial photographs invaluable for depicting an area of land or to show the relationship of topological features or objects to each other. In a condemnation case, for example, an aerial photograph could show the condemned land, the sites of comparable sales in the neighborhood, the nature and effect on a landlocking, and so forth. If an accident took place on a cloverleaf, an aerial photograph could show the relationship of the entwined roads.

In most localities, local pilots and photographers can be found to take aerial photographs. Various municipal, state, and Government agencies have series of aerial photographs. Newspapers may have them too.

• The posed photograph. The posed photograph attempts to reproduce the recollection of a witness about the scene. The attitude of the courts varies widely. Some courts permit the posed photograph upon a proper foundation that it fairly and accurately portrays the scene. Other courts take the view that even with such a foundation, the posed photograph represents and reinforces a one-sided portrayal of the scene. Still other courts will permit a posed photograph if it depicts agreed-upon facts.

• Medical photographs. This is a specialty in itself. You might find the photography department of the local hospital as a source of the techniques in this area. To show x-rays, you need a shadow box or positive print. Holding a negative print to the light is unsatisfactory. You also need an expert to interpret x-rays to the jury.

You must plan your photographs. You first must decide what you want the photographs to show and how you intend to use them at the trial. You should then hire a professional photographer to take the shots and use his expertise in the early planning. You should then go with him to the scene or object to be photographed. Once there, you and he can make final decisions on a number of legal and technical matters.

You want to make sure of accuracy for the purposes of foundation. For example, you might want the photographs of a scene to be taken at the proper time of day, and season, and under weather conditions so that angle and intensity of light, shadows, foliage, etc. are the same as at the time of the incident.

Use the photographer for technical points—distant shots and close-ups that capture respectively the perspective and details you want to show; the utility of including a person or familiar object or of putting a ruler or yardstick in the photograph to give perspective and to show depth or distance; when shots should be taken from a height to get a proper perspective.

You should also plan your use of photographs at the trial.

Avoid small photographs. You cannot examine a witness on a small photograph and have the jury see it at the same time. If you pass around copies of the photograph, you are apt to lose the jury's attention as they look at the copies. Features on the photograph often are not distinct. Identifying marks made by the witness do not stand out.

Enlargements or blow-ups solve these problems. The blow-up can be displayed on a stand in full view of the jury. The jury can see the features as the witness points to them with a pointer or places marks on the photograph.

If you plan for several witnesses to mark the same photograph, you have several alternatives. You can obtain several enlargements. You can use transparent plastic overlays. (The overlays should be of the same size so that marks to properly position the overlay on the photograph coincide with each other.)

You should have the original print from which the enlargements were made available. You may need to display the original to show that the enlargement is accurate. For example, you may have a newspaper photograph of an accident scene. The enlargement might have excluded a figure in the original.

Enlargements have become crucial in cases involving the genuineness of handwriting, typewriting, and printing. Photographs of admittedly genuine and allegedly spurious specimens are made. They are enlarged. From the enlargements the expert can make his comparison, pointing out the features on which he bases his opinion. Without the enlargements he would be hard-put to get his points across. If he could not show the jury the visual matters he is describing, he probably would lose them in a welter of technical words.

11.5   How to Bring the Outside World Live into the Courtroom—A Note on How to Use Motion Pictures and Videotapes

You should consider the use of motion pictures or videotapes in two situations especially.

• To capture real evidence. A surveillance film exposing a fraudulent claim of disability. A film of illegal acts during a strike.

A documentary of a day in the life of a disabled person. A newspaper or media videotape of the actual event giving rise to the lawsuit.

• To display a sequence of events. The operation of a piece of equipment. The movement of traffic at a location. How visibility changes as one moves through a location. Tests or experiments that cannot be conducted in court. A demonstration of why an event could or could not have happened at a particular location or in a particular way.

You should work closely with the expert cameraman in planning a film. You must work out a scenario—the events to be depicted, the sequence of the events, the nature of the various scenes, the length of the film, and so forth.

When possible, you should have the witness who will testify about the film help plan the film. In this way you often can arrange the scenes to run about the same period of time as he will take to testify about the scenes. Otherwise, at the trial, you will need a projector that can be stopped so that the film does not outstrip the witness. You also may want him to spend some time on a particular frame.

You should also consider making still shots of important frames for introduction as exhibits. In this way, you have the use of them during the entire trial.

The use of a sound track on the film often encounters hearsay objections.

11.6   Reducing Complex Testimony to Readily Grasped Points with Three-Dimensional Models and Demonstrations

A model is three-dimensional. The observer sees all the pertinent features at a glance. If it is a working model, the observer can see it perform. Consequently, you will find models especially valuable in three situations: Where you want to show the spatial relationship of topographical features. Where you want to show how something works. Where you want to represent a large object or the particular feature of a large object.

There are many types of models—fixed or movable; to scale

or not to scale; detailed or schematic; color-coded to show features or the relationship of movable parts; with cut-aways to expose the inner workings. The test is fairness and accuracy of representation. Within this test, the only limitation on a model is the ingenuity of the model maker.

Models can virtually become toys. They are fun to work with. This is a source of their strength with the jury. However, you must guard against getting carried away by the toy feature, a model for a model's sake. You must always view the model as a means to an end—a demonstration of something to the jury so that the jury can better understand, is impressed, and will remember. So to reiterate the constant theme about demonstrative evidence, you must think through precisely what you want to show. With models this analysis can be especially important because you have such a variety of models to choose from. You might have a hankering for a slick working model but find that a schematic model does the job better.

The word model is a broad term. As far as the principles of demonstrative evidence go, the actual object, or an exact duplicate, or a sample of the object or matter involved in a suit is a model.

In a narrow sense, a model is a representation of some other thing. You can find professional model makers in most cities. Talented hobbyists, artists, machinists, and sculptors can make models, too. You will find some models ready-made. Airplane manufacturers often have models of their products. A number of concerns have anatomical models on the market.

The magnetic board has become a popular form of model in automobile cases. The board has diagrams of streets and intersections. It comes with magnetized models of automobiles, stoplights, and so forth. As the witness testifies, he positions the models on the board. You can use overlays on which the positions are marked to preserve testimony. You can prepare special layouts; e.g., a railroad yard, on which to place models.

Demonstrations, experiments, and tests often involve models. The demonstrations can take place in open court or elsewhere and be brought to the jury's attention. This can be by testimony or by other means; in the case of the Fool-Proof Hoist, it was done by videotape.

The crucial consideration for a demonstration test or experiment is substantial similarity, not identity, of conditions. In the case of the Non-Duplicable Water, however, the court required the latter. Defense counsel wanted to show in court that a vaporizer could not have caught fire in the way plaintiff claimed. The court refused the test. Counsel produced an identical model of vaporizer. The court still refused the test. The reason? Counsel could not come up with what the court said was similar water!

The purpose of a demonstration, test, or experiment is not to prove that a certain result in fact happened given certain conditions. The purpose is to show that a certain result had a tendency to happen or not to happen given substantially similar conditions.

Physical and chemical demonstrations, tests, or experiments as distinguished from mechanical ones can be very effective, and very prejudicial. By their nature, the court has a much harder time passing on similarity. For example, a little girl had been burnt when her dress caught fire. Her counsel purportedly had obtained similar fabric. Subjecting it to a flammability test, he was told that it was as flammable as tissue paper. The court did not permit him to garb a mannequin in a tissue paper frock and put a match to it in the courtroom.

The greatest danger by far, however, is the model that does not work, or the demonstration, test, or experiment that fails. A failure often guarantees a loss. You must try many dry runs before you hazard the real run in court.

11.7 Demonstrative Evidence for the Low Budget Case—How to Get the Most Out of Maps, Diagrams, and Charts

You will find maps and diagrams ideal, low budget tools for depicting locations and the two-dimensional relationship of objects. In planning to use them, you should bear several points in mind.

Keep the exhibit simple. A map or diagram affords impact by presenting the essentials without frills. The more you clutter a map or diagram with details, the more you take away from the central message to be conveyed.

There are exceptions to this. If you need to show topograph-ical features or road networks you will require maps showing these features. In maritime cases, the varying depths of water often figure prominently. The splendid United States Coast and Geodetic Survey Maps ideally suit that purpose.

Work out with the witness who will testify about the exhibit exactly what you want the exhibit to convey. He has to put the exhibit into words. You have to make sure it makes the point.

Have the witness practice free-hand diagrams he will draw on a blackboard or drawing pad at trial. You should see to it that a prepared exhibit made the point you wanted it to make. You likewise should see to it that the sketches of the witness at trial make the point too. Besides, the more the witness practices, the better he will sketch at trial.

So simple a thing as a flubbed sketch can hurt you. In the damages case described in Chapter 2, for example, plaintiff had its plant engineer describe the embossing process and system. At a point, counsel asked him to sketch the attachments and piping at the end of the embossing roll, transmitting the coolant into it. He had testified moments before that he had found the flexible metal tubing intact. This tubing carried the coolant from the fixed piping on the floor up to the roll.

He made the sketch alright. The problem was that he neglected to show an 8-inch piece of pipe affixed to the end of the journal to which the flexible tubing attached. He showed the flexible tubing as attaching directly to the end of the journal.

A minor mistake? Creditabilitywise, no. The jury had to think less of the plant engineer's expertise because of this slip.

Charts have become indispensable in presenting complicated statistical and economic data. The jury cannot grasp or retain a mass of oral figures. They go numb at the sight of single-spaced schedules. They sigh with relief when the economist or statistician unveils his first chart.

A chart does four things very well. It simplifies data. It capsulizes data. It compares data. At a glance, it lets the jury picture what the data means.

You should keep charts simple. If you need to show several functions, use several charts. Prepare schedules of data to back up the charts. Indicate the source of the data. Label the charts accurately. If possible, you want the chart to speak for itself. You at least want it to speak for itself after your expert has explained it. You want the jury to understand it thoroughly in the jury room during deliberations.

Work with an expert in preparing the charts. Different types of data can be better shown in different types of charts. You also want to take advantage of specialized knowledge such as when a logarithmic scale should be used in order that slopes appear visually accurate.

In the fiduciary case, the defendants' economist prepared charts that illustrated key points in his testimony. (See charts and tables on pages 250-253.)

11.8   When You Can Use the Senses of Sound, Taste, Touch, and Smell to Drive Home a Key Point in Your Case

You may be able to use the senses of sound, taste, touch, and smell when you have real evidence, the thing itself involved. In a nuisance case, for example, you might persuade the court to allow the jury to visit the neighborhood of a noxious foundry.

In the case of the Sylvan Rock Band, an Inn in a country neighborhood changed its format. From a family restaurant it became a roadhouse. With the roadhouse came a rock-and-roll band. The band performed with amplification from early evening to early morning.

The neighbors sued to enjoin a nuisance.

At the trial the plaintiffs produced a tape recording. One of the neighbors had placed an ordinary tape recorder on the windowsill of a window in his house. The recorder captured the sounds.

The court allowed the tape recording into evidence to demonstrate the nature of the music—thumpings, varooms, beats, and so forth—to which the witnesses had testified. The court did not allow it in to show volume.

The science of identification by voice prints will increase the recourse to sound in the courtroom. The use of tape recordings to take statements will, too.

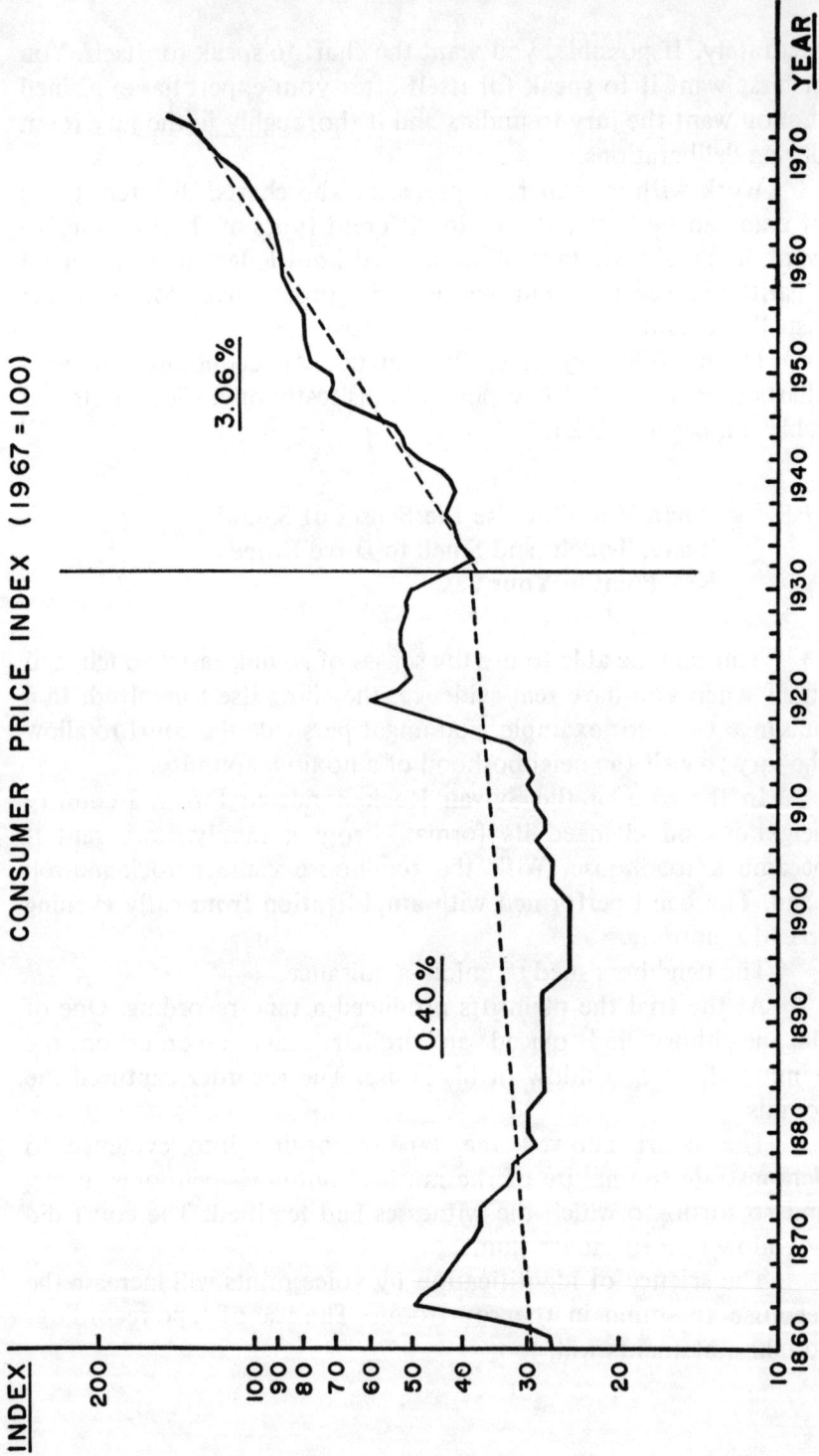

Prepared by Dr. Mark Schupack, Brown University

CONSUMER PRICE INDEX (BLS)
1967 = 100

Year	Index	Year	Index	Year	Index	Year	Index	Year	Index
1860	27.0	1883	29.0	1906	28.0	1929	51.3	1952	79.5
1	27.0	4	28.0	7	29.0	30	50.0	3	80.1
2	30.0	5	28.0	8	28.0	1	45.6	4	80.5
3	37.0	6	28.0	9	28.0	2	40.9	5	80.2
4	48.0	7	28.0	10	29.0	3	38.8	6	81.4
5	47.0	8	28.0	1	29.0	4	40.1	7	84.6
6	44.0	9	28.0	2	30.0	5	41.1	8	86.6
7	43.0	90	28.0	3	29.7	6	41.5	9	87.3
8	41.0	1	28.0	4	30.1	7	43.0	60	88.7
9	40.0	2	28.0	5	30.4	8	42.2	1	89.6
70	38.0	3	28.0	6	32.7	9	41.6	2	90.6
1	37.0	4	26.0	7	38.4	40	42.0	3	91.7
2	37.0	5	25.0	8	45.1	1	44.1	4	92.9
3	37.0	6	25.0	9	51.8	2	48.8	5	94.5
4	35.0	7	25.0	20	60.0	3	51.8	6	97.2
5	33.0	8	25.0	1	53.6	4	52.7	7	100.0
6	32.0	9	25.0	2	50.2	5	53.9	8	104.2
7	32.0	1900	25.0	3	51.1	6	58.5	9	109.8
8	30.0	1	25.0	4	51.2	7	66.9	70	116.3
9	29.0	2	26.0	5	52.5	8	72.1	1	121.3
80	30.0	3	27.0	6	53.0	9	71.4	2	125.3
1	30.0	4	27.0	7	52.0	50	72.1	3	133.1
2	30.0	5	27.0	8	51.3	1	77.8	4	147.7

% Growth Rates

Years	
1860-1931	0.40
1932-1974	3.06

Sources

Years	
1860-1970	Long Term Economic Growth, 1860-1970, U.S. Dept. of Commerce, pp. 222-3.
1971-1974	Statistical Abstract of the U.S.

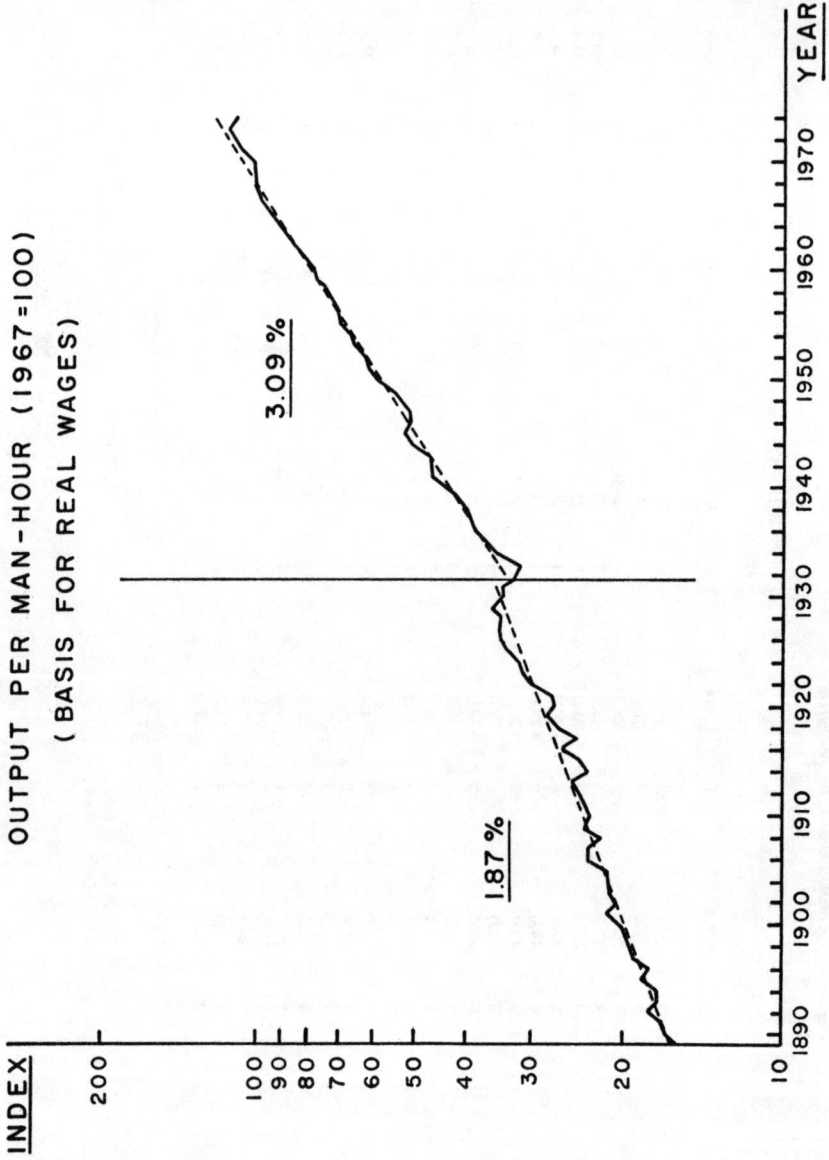

OUTPUT PER MAN-HOUR (1967=100)
(BASIS FOR REAL WAGES)

INDEX

3.09 %

1.87 %

200
100
90
80
70
60
50
40
30
20
10

1890　1900　1910　1920　1930　1940　1950　1960　1970

YEAR

Prepared by Dr. Mark Schupack, Brown University

OUTPUT PER MAN-HOUR
1967 = 100

Year	Index	Year	Index	Year	Index	Year	Index	Year	Index
1889	15.8	1907	23.1	1924	31.8	1941	46.1	1958	74.3
90	16.5	8	22.1	5	33.4	2	46.5	9	76.9
1	16.8	9	23.7	6	34.2	3	47.6	60	78.2
2	17.8	10	23.3	7	34.4	4	50.8	1	80.9
3	17.1	1	23.7	8	34.2	5	52.9	2	84.7
4	17.2	2	24.2	9	35.9	6	51.1	3	87.7
5	18.3	3	25.0	30	34.3	7	51.3	4	91.1
6	17.9	4	23.3	1	34.1	8	53.6	5	94.2
7	19.1	5	24.3	2	32.3	9	55.3	6	98.0
8	19.4	6	26.1	3	31.8	50	59.7	7	100.0
9	19.8	7	24.7	4	35.1	1	61.5	8	102.9
1900	20.1	8	26.8	5	36.8	2	62.7	9	103.3
1	21.5	9	28.0	6	38.9	3	65.3	70	104.0
2	20.7	20	27.1	7	39.0	4	66.9	1	108.2
3	21.1	1	27.2	8	40.0	5	69.9	2	111.8
4	21.1	2	29.8	9	41.6	6	70.0	3	114.8
5	21.6	3	31.2	40	43.3	7	72.0	4	111.7
6	23.3								

% Growth Rates	
Years	
1889-1931	1.87
1931-1974	3.09

Years	Sources
1889-1970	Long Term Economic Growth, pp. 210-11.
1971-1974	Economic Report of the President, 1975, p. 286.

In general, the four senses of sound, taste, touch, and smell have two major shortcomings as pure demonstrative evidence as distinguished from real evidence—the subjectivity of the senses; the difficulty of establishing similar conditions so that the representation is fair and accurate. The subjectivity of these senses, in fact, make it difficult to even tell if conditions are similar.

12

Using
the Pre-Trial Conference
to Get the Upper Hand
at Trial

12.1 Approaching Pre-Trial as a Tactical Weapon to Win Cases

The term pre-trial does not have a fixed meaning. It means different things in different jurisdictions. To get a handle on it the best place to start is with the rule authorizing it, rule 16.

Rule 16 gives the court power in its discretion to call a pre-trial conference with counsel. In six subsections, the rule lists matters for the court to consider. The first five subsections cover specific steps designed to narrow issues and expedite trial. The sixth subsection gives the court power to consider, "Such other matters as may aid in the disposition of the action."

A number of courts have issued detailed local rules. Typically, these rules spell out pre-trial procedures and provide for and present the content of pre-trial conferences and pre-trial orders. Local rules vary greatly. For practical purposes local rules, not rule 16, govern pre-trial procedures.

Rule 16 also requires a pre-trial order embodying the results of the pre-trial conference. This order controls the subsequent course of the action unless modified at trial to prevent manifest injustice.

Different courts have different ideas about the purposes of pre-trial. At least six different purposes can be mentioned: to eliminate surprise at trial through full disclosure; to expedite trials by narrowing issues and stipulating facts; to insure trial on the merits by winnowing issues from the welter of facts disclosed by discovery; to level the economic and professional advantages between parties; as a by-product, to help bring about settlements; to force settlements and thus clear dockets by judicial pressure and burdensome preparation for pre-trial.

Regardless of the rules and the announced or hidden purposes of pre-trial, the approach of the individual judge governs what pre-trial means in his court.

He may meet informally with counsel before trial to discuss settlement, trial dates, scheduling of witnesses, and so forth. He may have been doing this for years, but to be modern he now calls it pre-trial.

He may require a detailed pre-trial memorandum but use it for his own guidance and not for a pre-trial conference or pre-trial order. He may call this pre-trial.

He may require a pre-trial memorandum and use it for a pre-trial conference at which he takes specific steps that he embodies in a controlling pre-trial order. He will call this pre-trial. This is pre-trial in its formal sense. But even this judge may hold a preliminary "pre-trial conference" before formal pre-trial to see if he can settle the case.

When a judge has a case, for all purposes he may hold a series of conferences from the very start. He may use the method suggested for handling complex and protracted litigation; e.g., conferences to hear omnibus motions addressed to the pleadings, the scheduling of discovery, establishing methods for handling documents, setting dates for formal pre-trial procedures, and so forth. Quite properly, he can call this pre-trial.

The case of the Ten-Minute Pre-Trial illustrates how much the attitude of the judge has to do with pre-trial despite what the local rules may say. In that case, two of the three counsel in the case came from out of town. The court issued its boilerplate order prescribed in the local rules calling for detailed pre-trial memoranda and setting down a date for a pre-trial conference.

On the appointed day, a storm drenched the city in an all day torrential rain. Out-of-state counsel fought their way into town, but they were late. The time set for the pre-trial conference had long passed.

Court was still in session. It was in session indeed. From the posted docket, counsel discovered theirs was one of six pre-trials scheduled for the half hour before the court began to hear motions.

Counsel sat through the balance of the motions. When the court had wrapped them up, it convened the pre-trial conference. The conference consisted of ten minutes of informal colloquy in open court to set dates for closing discovery and pre-trial memoranda. As for the super-duper pre-trial memorandum the order required, the court never so much as mentioned it.

The attitude of the judge has a lot to do with the form of pre-trial. It also has as much or more to do with the content of the pre-trial. Specifically, the judge's attitude will determine whether he will dig into the case to help narrow issues, stipulate facts, and so forth. It will determine how strict or lax he will be about pre-trial procedures. It will determine the extent to which he enforces the pre-trial order.

You must determine the judge's attitude because he has enormous power to achieve the purposes of pre-trial. These purposes are broad and varied. The upshot is that the court's power is almost purely discretionary. There is little that is concrete to control that discretion.

For this reason, you must know how the judge at pre-trial in your case regards pre-trial. Even then you cannot be one hundred percent sure because he can be so subjective. But some insight is better than none.

A bird's-eye view of the case law will give you some idea about how sweeping the judge's powers are at trial.

First, the court can compel counsel to attend and participate in pre-trial. If he fails or refuses, the court can dismiss the action with prejudice for failure to prosecute. Local rules often provide for other sanctions.

In one case, however, the appellate court reversed a dismissal with prejudice as too radical a sanction to impose on an innocent party because of his counsel's recusancy.

Second, at pre-trial, the court can take drastic steps to promote the success of pre-trial. To give you some idea, consider the following three holdings:

• The court has the power to compel the parties to agree to "undisputed" facts.

• The court can define the issues in the pre-trial order although a party withholds formal assent to the formulation.

• The court can grant summary judgment against a party who does not produce facts to refute those of his opponent.

Third, the pre-trial order "controls the subsequent course of the action, unless modified at the trial to prevent manifest injustice."

On balance, the courts uphold the binding effect of the pre-trial order at trial by such rulings as: holding a party to the stipulation of facts in the pre-trial order; limiting the trial to the issues stated in the pre-trial order; excluding evidence and witnesses not listed in the pre-trial order; denying a view since it had not been requested at pre-trial; refusing an instruction not contemplated by the pre-trial order.

For example, an aerialist agreed not to sue the circus for injuries sustained during his performances. He sustained an injury during a performance. Despite the clause in his employment contract, he sued.

At pre-trial, his counsel stipulated that the contract had been entered into in Florida. The stipulation became part of the pre-trial order. At trial, the facts indicated that the contract had been entered into in Texas.

The court held that the facts stipulated in the pre-trial order controlled.

You might think the court breathed fire on that one. But did it? In a footnote the court observed that on the issue of the validity of the clause in question, the law of Kansas, Florida, and Texas was the same.

The footnote illustrates that the courts are of two minds about the binding effect of the pre-trial order. Had Texas law allowed the aerialist recovery, and Florida law denied it, what could the court have done? It probably would have modified the pre-trial order to prevent manifest injustice.

You cannot safely generalize about relief from a pre-trial order. Relief largely depends on the circumstances of the case and the attitude of the judge. However, there do seem to be some threads running through some of the cases about relief from the pre-trial order.

A number of courts have interpreted manifest injustice in terms of jeopardizing trial on the merits.

Other courts have evaluated the relief sought in terms of the relative prejudice to the parties.

Still other courts have emphasized whether a party knew of the matter at the time of pre-trial. These courts say that pre-trial will fail if a party cannot approach it openly for fear of excessive rigidity.

Some courts duck the problem. They permit matter outside the pre-trial order by interpreting the language of the pre-trial order to cover it by implication, or because a party did not object to it at the trial.

A case involving "ambivalent jurists" illustrates the subjectivity of the problem. The plaintiff did not indicate he would rely on the doctrine of last clear chance. The pre-trial order did not mention it. The trial court refused to give plaintiff an instruction on it. Defendant won.

On appeal the appellate court reversed. It interpreted the language in the pre-trial order liberally to include last clear chance by implication. It observed that although defendant's counsel was in fact surprised when plaintiff brought last clear chance up, he should not have been.

A year previously the same appellate court had said, "[T]he courts are not to be lenient with counsel who fail to reveal the theory of their case until all the evidence is closed." The court added that the theory of plaintiff's case has much to do with how defendant's counsel will conduct his case.

Consistency is the hobgoblin of little minds.

One last point about approaching pre-trial. It can be a discouraging waste.

As one federal judge has said, ". . . pre-trial procedures have resulted in useless, unnecessary, unprofitable expenditure of time, effort, and expense in the majority of litigation. The average or ordinary case is over-administered, lawyers are put to busy-work resulting in duplication of effort and fruitless preparation and judges have ignored or made minor use of the work product. . . ."

For example, in one case, the local pre-trial rules required proposed requests to charge. The proposed requests of some seven parties to the suit formed a stack of papers 2 inches high. The trial proceeded along the lines everyone anticipated it would. Nevertheless, towards the end of the trial the court required new requests to charge from each party.

The federal judge just quoted concluded by saying, "The forgotten man, the client, is made to foot the bill."

In sum, you must approach pre-trial as it is. If you do you can realize its advantages, exploit its possibilities, and avoid its pitfalls.

12.2   How to Realize the Advantages of Pre-Trial and Exploit Its Possibilities, with a Checklist of the Types of Things You Can Accomplish

You must do 12 things to insure a successful pre-trial.

1. Know the local rules, the interpretations of those rules, and of rule 16, and the attitude and approach of the judge.

2. Prepare thoroughly. Prepare as if for trial. Prepare better than your opponent. At pre-trial you have an ill-prepared opponent at a double disadvantage. He does not know his case. The judge cannot rule on the matters in the full context such as would exist at trial. Therefore, you can often force matters to your advantage. But do not forget, the opposite is also true.

3. Attend pre-trial yourself. Do not turn the responsibility over to someone else.

4. Approach pre-trial in good faith but cautiously.

5. Know the types of things you can accomplish at pre-trial.

6. Know the pitfalls of pre-trial.

7. Assess your case for advantages that you might realize from pre-trial.

8. Assess your case for tactical possibilities you might exploit pre-trial for.

9. Assess your opponent's case for weaknesses.

10. Anticipate how your opponent will approach pre-trial.

11. Study your opponent's pre-trial memoranda. Look for admissions. Spot waffling.

12. Anticipate the steps the judge is apt to take.

The following checklist lists the type of things that you can accomplish at pre-trial. Of course, what you might accomplish in one court, you might not be able to accomplish in another court. However, if you can point to something as having been done in one court, you might persuade another court to do the same thing.

Also, bear in mind that you can realize benefits of pre-trial at all stages of pre-trial—at an informal pre-trial conference; through pre-trial memoranda; at the formal pre-trial conference; at trial by virtue of the pre-trial order.

Simplifying the Issues—Rule 16(1)

You could describe this named purpose of pre-trial more accurately as framing the issues. It includes ascertaining the issues, narrowing them, clarifying them, abandoning untenable issues, eliminating sham issues, and adding new issues developed by discovery.

The theory is that discovery uncovers all of the facts. Out of the facts counsel develop what they conceive the issues to be. From the material presented to it at pre-trial, the court formulates the issues. The official form of pre-trial order in a jurisdiction with a mandatory, full-blown pre-trial procedure recites in part:

"The issues to be tried are formulated by the court as follows:

"Was the defendant negligent in that. . . .

"Was the S/S_____ unseaworthy in that. . . ."

In the case of the *Walloping Window Blind*, for example, a pure notice complaint alleged that on such and such a date "plaintiff was injured through defendant's negligence and the unseaworthiness of the S/S *Walloping Window Blind.*" At pre-trial, the facts were developed. The pre-trial order recited, "Was defendant negligent in that there was a bolonga sandwich on the deck of the ship?"

Amending the Pleadings—Rule 16(2)

This second-named purpose of pre-trial is superfluous. A new or reformulated issue might emerge at pre-trial. However, it would be embodied in the pre-trial order which controls the subsequent course of the action. There is no need to formally amend the pleadings. One court observed that to require an amendment to the pleadings would only add to the paper record. However, if the pleadings go with the jury during deliberations, you must make sure any amendments were included in the pleadings.

Obtaining Dismissals or Striking Defenses

At pre-trial the court has full power to terminate or truncate the litigation. The court can dismiss the action in whole or in part, strike defenses, and grant full or partial summary judgment. The court might be more inclined to take these steps at pre-trial since discovery is completed.

In the case of the Ill-Fated Vacationer, for example, the plaintiff's decedent died when he fell down the stairs at defendant's summer cottage. The complaint standing alone stated a claim.

At pre-trial, defendant moved to dismiss. Plaintiff's counsel said plaintiff's case consisted of the facts in plaintiff's deposition and certain photographs. In the deposition, plaintiff stated she had not seen the decedent fall but had heard him fall near the bottom of the stairs. Plaintiff had no testimony as to the cause of the fall. The photographs disclosed no hidden defect in the stairs.

The court dismissed the action.

In the case of the Target Defendant, a federal judge on his own motion at pre-trial, dismissed the action as to all the non-diverse defendants. This left one diverse defendant in the case. This remaining defendant just happened to be the manufacturer in a products liability case.

In a case of "inapplicable limitations," a suit on a mortgage note, defendant pled as its sole defense the six-year statute of limitations. Plaintiff had commenced the action on the sixth anniversary of the maturity date. The court struck the defense and ordered trial to go forward on damages.

The relationship between pre-trial and full or partial summary judgment is ambiguous. For the latter there must be no genuine issue of any material fact. The courts say that pre-trial is not to be a substitute for trial. But if at pre-trial, a purpose of which is to frame issues and narrow facts, a party cannot come up with facts to sustain a position, the rationale of summary judgment applies.

You must regard obtaining dismissals and striking defenses as a key purpose in your planning for pre-trial. Even if you believe the court would not go that far, you can favorably condition the court by forcefully raising the subject.

Stipulating Facts and Documents—Rule 16(3)

Obtaining admissions of fact and of documents is one of the named purposes of pre-trial. To realize stipulations, you must approach pre-trial vigorously. Pounce on the weak spots in your opponent's case. Press your opponent to be candid. Push the strong points in your case.

How far the court will go to compel agreement on facts depends on the court. With any court, your first step is to bring out that the facts you want stipulated are indisputable.

You should think about getting stipulations in several circumstances.

One is where a stipulation will realize an economy, and there is no tactical reason why you should not stipulate.

Another is where a stipulation could eliminate the testimony of a damaging adverse witness. Through discovery you should know what this witness has to say. If you cannot discredit his testimony, you might ask yourself "why try to" and decide not to cross-examine him. But rather than this mere negative decision, you might try to get the facts he would testify to stipulated. The testimony would then go into evidence as antiseptically as you could hope.

The logic of this thinking could carry you to the point of admitting liability. If you have no real defense on liability and fear that the evidence on liability might enhance damages, admitting liability might be a sound tactic. The converse is also true. If you have a weak witness, you might try to get the facts he would testify to stipulated.

How stipulations are phrased can be crucial. Sometimes you will reach an impasse about whether you or your opponent will stipulate that X is a fact. A way out of the impasse is to stipulate that if A were called as a witness, he would testify that X is a fact.

The tactics of stipulating are complex. You must decide several things beforehand—what you want to stipulate; what you cannot stipulate; what items to set up for purposes of trade-offs; what you think your opponent will try to do.

The stipulating of documents has become a primary pre-trial function. The process varies but generally goes as follows. The documents of each side are given exhibit numbers. Those agreed to completely are marked into evidence. Those questioned are marked for identification. Often, as to these, the parties will agree as to authenticity but not as to relevancy or privilege. When the document for identification comes up at trial, the court rules on it. In the case of important documents, the court could rule on admissibility at pre-trial.

Limiting the Number of Expert Witnesses—Rule 16(4)

There are several ideas behind this subsection of the rule— eliminating unnecessary proof; cutting down on the cost of trial; leveling advantages between parties; preventing a battle of experts.

You can use the rule tactically. By interrogatories and through your opponent's pre-trial memorandum, you can find out about his trial experts. If his experts outnumber or outclass yours, at pre-trial you might seek to limit the number he plans to call. At the least, you will force him to open up on what he hopes to use them for.

At pre-trial you also might try to obtain a court-appointed expert; e.g., a doctor to examine a personal injury plaintiff and report his findings.

Referring the Case to a Master—Rule 16(5)

Subsection (5) of rule 16 mentions the advisability of a preliminary reference of issues to a master for findings to be used as evidence when the trial is to be by jury. Rule 53, which governs the use of masters, states in subsection (b) that reference to a master shall be the exception not the rule, and that in jury cases the reference shall be made only when the issues are complicated.

The tests for a reference to a master at pre-trial are thus (explicitly) complicated issues and (implicitly) the consequent need of the jury for help, or the interests of judicial administration. Cases with a large number of individual items and accountings lend themselves to a reference.

As a practical matter, pre-trial may be very late for reference to a master. By that time you may have done the work. Also rule 1006 of the Federal Rules of Evidence expressly permits presentation of voluminous records in the form of summaries, which should breathe new life into that old rule of evidence.

Obtaining Separate Trials of Consolidated Cases

Patent infringement cases present the classic situation for split trials. The issues on infringement are separate from the issues on an accounting for damage. The accounting would be complicated and time-consuming. The accounting might not be needed if defendant wins on liability.

Representing a defendant in a negligence case, you might seek a separate trial if a heavy plaintiff's case on damages could carry his weaker case on liability.

To illustrate, defendant held a majority interest in Upward, Inc., a mini-conglomerate. He had weaned it to the point where it prospered. He enjoyed a reputation in the business and financial world.

He came into contact with Mutual Growth Fund, a mutual fund. He or the fund or both together surfaced the idea of an exchange of stock. He thought it wise to diversify his holdings. The fund thought shares of Upward, Inc. might be a good investment. After weeks of negotiations, the deal came to pass. He traded X number of personally owned shares of Upward, Inc. at current market worth millions, for Y number of shares of Mutual Growth, at current market also worth millions.

A number of months later, the bottom fell out of the market for shares of Upward, Inc. The stock lost a large percent of its value.

Mutual Growth took a hard look at the deal. It did not like what it saw. Mutual Growth tried to undo the deal. Nothing came of it. The upshot was a suit by Mutual Growth to rescind, based, in substance, on defendant's alleged failure to disclose material information about Upward, Inc. and its components.

During all of this, the feelings of Mutual Growth's principals escalated. One of them allegedly made remarks about defendant. Defendant asserted a counterclaim for slander based on these remarks.

Mutual Growth's counsel did not want Mutual Growth's suit cluttered with a defamation counter-suit. Before trial counsel raised the point, he got the actions severed.

Ascertaining Witnesses and Documentary Evidence

The disclosure of witnesses has become a major purpose of pre-trial. Many local rules require that facts and expert witnesses be listed in the pre-trial memoranda. Some local rules also require that the gist of their testimony be given. When you get your opponent's list, you should check it out for anything unusual—a surprise witness, the failure to list an anticipated witness, unexpectedly narrow scope of testimony for a witness, and so forth.

Many local rules also require a list of all documents to be introduced into evidence in the pre-trial memoranda. You should subject this list to the same type of analysis as the list of witnesses.

Updating Discovery, and Passing on
Reserved Discovery Motions

Before pre-trial you should check whether your opponent has supplemented answers to interrogatories under rule 26(e). In some jurisdictions, a pre-trial memorandum supplying any additional information probably would be deemed a supplementation. Nonetheless, you should routinely ask about supplementation at the pre-trial conference. At pre-trial you should also make sure the court rules on any requests for admissions postponed under rule 36(a).

Obtaining Rulings on Questions of
Law

A variety of legal questions may remain open up to the time of trial. In the days before pre-trial, court and counsel would thresh them out in open court at trial. To a large extent that is still true. Often, however, a ruling of law has a critical bearing on the conduct of the trial; e.g., choice of laws. You should use pre-trial to get a question like that resolved.

Obtaining Rulings on Evidence

You should routinely use pre-trial to get rulings on difficult problems of evidence that will arise at the trial.

In the case of the Exploding T discussed in Chapter 3, a steam line burst in the tenant's premises. The landlord denied control of the premises. However, the landlord was the named insured on the boiler insurance policy. The tenant had authority that this fact was competent evidence to prove control.

The tenant had a problem though. In that jurisdiction, to mention insurance at trial could cause a mistrial. The tenant had two choices. The first choice was to go ahead with the trial, bringing the point up in the appropriate place. The court could have ruled the evidence out. If mention of insurance came in inadvertently, the court might declare a mistrial. The other choice was to bring the point up at pre-trial. The tenant did. The court ruled the evidence admissible. Even if the court had ruled the evidence inadmissible, however, the tenant would have known about the proof he needed on the issue at trial.

The example also illustrates the type of evidentiary problem a court would be inclined to rule on at pre-trial. Generally, the problem must have an important bearing on the conduct of the case. Generally, the problem must be susceptible of being ruled on satisfactorily standing alone; i.e., it does not need to arise in a trial context to be ruled on properly. To take two other examples. At pre-trial in one reported case the court ruled on the admissibility of depositions and testimony taken in another case. In another reported case on appeal, the Court of Appeals directed that on retrial, the trial court pass upon the authenticity of hospital records in a case involving the mental capacity of an insured to change the beneficiary of his life insurance policy.

The Federal Rules of Evidence create two catch-all exceptions to the hearsay rule. Subsections 803 (25) and 804 (5) provide that statements not covered in the specific exceptions in those rules may be admitted under certain broad, discretionary standards. Both subsections require that the proponent notify his opponent of his intention to use the statement sufficiently in advance of trial to give his opponent a fair opportunity to prepare to meet it. As an opponent you should use pre-trial to seek a ruling on the admissibility of this type of hearsay. One of the standards for admissibility, for example, is that the statement is more probative of the point than any other evidence which the proponent can procure through reasonable efforts. In the thick of trial, few courts will spend much time on arguments about reasonable efforts. At pre-trial you could more effectively try to keep the hearsay out.

Obtaining Rulings on Demonstrative Evidence

You should use pre-trial to smoke out the kind of demonstrative evidence your opponent intends to use. If it turns out that what he plans will be prejudicial, you should seek a ruling prohibiting it. Use pre-trial, in other words, to eliminate grand guignol effects.

You should also use pre-trial either to insure or keep down the costs of demonstrative evidence. There is authority that if a party hopes to recoup large outlays for demonstrative evidence in his bill of costs, he should get prior authorization at pre-trial.

Obtaining Rulings on Trial Tactics

You may suspect your opponent has certain tactics planned, for example, the *per diem* argument on pain and suffering. Or you may suspect he will touch on improper subjects in his opening to the jury. You can use pre-trial to get a ruling on these points.

Pinning Down the Rule of Damages, the Elements in the Measure of Damages, and the Amount of Damages Sought

You can use pre-trial to clear up questions about damages. If you represent a defendant, this should be one of your principal aims at pre-trial. You should pin the plaintiff down and get court rulings on the theory of damages, the calculations of damages, the amount of any liquidated damages, elements going into the damage formula, and so forth. For example, representing a defendant you could ask the court to rule whether it will allow lost wages to be calculated before or after taxes.

To illustrate further, in a condemnation case, both parties sought a pre-trial ruling about an element of damage.

The government had taken land by eminent domain to build a dam. The owners of the condemned land sought to recover for the loss of hot-and-cold water springs on adjacent land and also a flow of hot sulphur water below those springs.

A tunnel had been built on land of other owners long after the taking in question. The court found that this tunnel had caused the springs to dry up. The court thus ruled out the loss of the springs as an element of damage. Just compensation, the court said, includes the value of the land taken, and damage to the remainder of the land caused by the use of the portion taken, but not damage to the remainder of the land caused by the use of adjoining lands of others.

The court made a mixed ruling of law and fact on this point. It also made a pure ruling of law. To overcome this first ruling, the owners argued that the tunnel and dam were part of the same project. Interpreting the legal nature and relationships within the project, the court rejected the argument as a matter of law.

You will usually find courts receptive to pre-trial especially receptive to pre-trial rulings on damages. Otherwise it may face tough rulings in the thick of trial. It may even face a disruption of trial by extended arguments, extended efforts to get the testimony in, offers of proof, and the like.

To get a damage ruling at pre-trial, you must present the problem and the right solution so that the court sees that in its interest it should go along with you.

Getting a Fresh Perspective on the Case

Regard pre-trial as a way to realize this intangible benefit. Your opponent's pre-trial memorandum can be a mine of information. Besides the lists of witnesses and authorities, it will contain his version of the facts and the authorities he relies upon. For the first time perhaps, you will see precisely how he approaches the case. If you analyze his memorandum for what he does and does not say, you may hit upon things below the surface.

The give and take at the pre-trial conference can be equally rewarding. You and your opponent each explain the gist of your case, try to shoot holes in the other's case, and try to plug the holes shot in yours. If you handle this adroitly, and press the arguments, you often can force your opponent to open up.

The judge can be a marvelous catalyst in this process. Whether he fills this role depends upon whether he asks probing questions and insists upon responsive answers. If he does, you should gear your approach to get him asking questions of your opponent. You plan helpful points to bring up. When your opponent waffles, you enlist the judge's help to get a responsive answer.

When the judge gives his views, you may be getting a valuable insight. His overall reaction can tip you off on how you and your opponent's cases may come across at trial. His specific comments on strengths and weaknesses can be a signal for you to attack or bolster points. The comments of some judges will be more valuable than others. But even with a lesser judge, you may get a perspective from analyzing why he says what he says.

Requesting Special Verdicts, and
Passing on the Special Questions
and Charges

The rule of comparative negligence requires that the jury attribute percentages to negligence. This can only be done by questions under subsections (a) or (b) of rule 49. Since the court must ask these questions, it may be inclined to ask other questions.

You must monitor the process carefully. For anything beyond simple questions about percentages, the special verdict and the general verdict accompanied by answers to interrogatories are dangerous. Framing issues of fact is not easy. Asking clear questions is not easy. Determining the relationship of questions is not easy. Giving unambiguous instructions to the jury in this context is not easy. The upshot is that consciously or subconsciously, the court can catechize the jury for the result it wants.

The problems can be so complex that you need time to think them through. You need as much lead time as you can get. The court has discretion whether to use rule 49. If you think it will, in order to get this lead time you may have to bring up the subject at pre-trial. Suggest that the questions and the charges be hammered out early rather than in the press of trial. A final touch can be given in light of events at the trial, but the spade work will have been done.

Some courts have worked out simple pattern questions and charges for comparative negligence cases. This minimizes problems. It may eliminate them. You should still regard the area as dangerous though. You should use pre-trial to look the situation over.

The case of the Sole Proximate Cause illustrates the pitfalls or special questions and the need for lead time to think the problems through.

Plaintiff sued for damages due to a defective oven. Besides a count in strict liability, plaintiff alleged counts for negligent design and negligent manufacture. The case was complex. A number of experts testified. The trial took almost three weeks.

Shortly before trial the court told counsel it might use a special verdict. During the trial the court firmed up its decision, and gave counsel a batch of questions it had drafted for comment. Counsel analyzed the questions and gave their views in extensive memoranda. Of course, while doing this they also had to be preparing for the next day of trial.

At the close of the evidence, the court gave the case to the jury on close to 20 questions.

In answer to one, the jury gave percentages to defendant's negligence and plaintiff's contributory negligence. Eight other questions and answers (in summary form) were as follows:

Q. Did defendant negligently design the oven?
A. Yes.
Q. Was the negligent design the proximate cause of plaintiff's damages?
A. Yes.
Q. Did defendant negligently manufacture the oven?
A. Yes.
Q. Was the negligent manufacture the proximate cause of plaintiff's damage?
A. No.

In its charge the court several times spoke in terms of *the* proximate cause or *a* proximate cause. It did not instruct the jury that there could be concurring proximate causes. The court did not review its instructions with counsel beforehand.

Plaintiff contended that there were no inconsistencies in the answers. Even if there seemed to be inconsistencies, plaintiff pointed out that the charge explained how they occurred. The jury followed the court's instructions to the letter. Charged in terms of only one proximate cause, the jury did not find two proximate causes. Thus plaintiff said there was a view of the case that made the answers consistent.

However, the court did not agree and held these answers to be irreconcilably inconsistent.

Requesting a View

If you want a view you should ask for it at pre-trial. Local rules might require that you formally request or move for a view in your pre-trial submission. Some courts have refused a view because counsel did not request it at pre-trial.

Resolving "Housekeeping" Matters

You should take up housekeeping matters at the pre-trial conference. These matters can run the gamut: problems of scheduling; anticipated requests for adjournments; the availability of witnesses; the exclusion of witnesses from the courtroom; the need for an interpreter; the ordering of daily transcripts; arrangements for the view.

Obtaining Settlements

The purists say settlement is only a by-product of pre-trial. This may be fine for public consumption. For the practical lawyer it ignores reality.

The courts bent on moving their dockets may use pre-trial principally to force settlements. Some of these courts require counsel to attend pre-trial with settlement authority. Some courts have ordered clients into court in order to pressure them into a settlement. In courts like these, at pre-trial you can put your opponent's feet to the fire for settlement.

Regardless of the practice though, there are several reasons why you should regard pre-trial as excellent for obtaining settlements:

• It comes after discovery and the investigation so that both sides know the facts.

• If one or both of the parties came into the case fighting mad, he or they have had a taste of combat.

• The prospects of an expensive trial, or even formal pre-trial procedures, may be a sobering consideration.

• If you have a good judge who digs into the case, he may give you valuable help in settling the case.

• You can use the desire of the court to have the case settled to put pressure on your opponent.

• If your opponent has not been taking offers to his client, you can ask the judge to require him to report back. In extreme cases, you could ask the judge himself to ask the client about the offer.

• If you can say the judge recommends a figure, you often can push your own reluctant client into a settlement. In any event, by quoting the judge, you avoid the client's saying, "You sound like the lawyer on the other side" or "Are you afraid to try the case?"

This may be vital to keep his confidence.

However, you run a danger of pressing too hard for settlement at pre-trial. The process can backfire on you in unexpected ways. The judge might get committed. He works out a marvelous compromise. Your client does not accept it. The judge would be superhuman not to harbor feelings for your client which he may subconsciously give vent to at trial.

Another danger is coloring the judge's view of the case. Inevitably hearsay creeps into settlement discussions. The more the talk, the more the hearsay usually. Even if the judge sits with a jury, the hearsay could affect the trial.

The adamant adjuster in the plane crash case illustrates how badly pressing too hard for settlement at pre-trial can backfire. You will recall in that case that a Beechcraft Baron flew into the rear of a Cessna-150. Five people were killed—the student pilot and instructor in the Cessna, and the passenger and two men, Jones and Smith, in the front seat of the Beechcraft. Jones and Smith owned Stonehill Corp., the corporation that owned the Beechcraft.

The Beechcraft had swing-over controls so that it could be flown from either of the two front seats. Jones and Smith were both pilots. The evidence did not indicate which had been flying.

The estates of Jones and Smith faced an impossible trial situation. Each had sued the other and Stonehill Corp., as well as the estates of the student pilot and instructor, and the owner of the Cessna. The latter three parties naturally had counter-suits. Besides negligence, these suits alleged that Jones and Smith had been on a joint venture. If the jury found a joint venture, the negligence of either would be attributed to the other. Thus for the estate of Jones and Smith to prove the negligence of Smith or Jones would be to prove the case against itself for all others.

One insurance carrier was defending for the estates of Jones and Smith, and for Stonehill Corp. The carrier settled the cases of the two estates against each other and against Stonehill Corp.

This resolved the impossible trial situation but left a practical one. The accident had been a rear-end collision. For the estates of Jones and Smith to have a real chance as plaintiffs against the Cessna group, they had to be suing as plaintiffs only, with no death actions against them.

The carrier settled the case of the estate of the student pilot against the two estates. This left the suit by the estate of the instructor as the only death action against them. (For diversity reasons, the suits of the passenger's estate were not part of the consolidated cases.)

The estate of the instructor made a demand within the reasonable range. The insurance adjuster made a low offer. Talks continued but got nowhere. But for the tactical reason mentioned, pressure built to settle that particular case. Finally, a pre-trial conference was arranged with just the judge, defense counsel, and the adjuster.

After the usual preliminaries, the judge got into the situation. The adjuster stuck to his position. The judge began to focus on certain key points. On these key points the conference in substance went as follows:

To the judge's view of the chances of liability in a rear-end collision, the adjuster said that he had never lost a student pilot case yet.

To the judge's comment that the cost of an appeal for a long trial would be very large, the adjuster said he had just paid many thousands of dollars for a record in another case.

To the judge's question about why such a low offer in light of possible damages, the adjuster replied that his offer was enough "for a bunch of immigrants."

The instructor had come from Europe with his parents after World War II.

The preceding covers the major subjects for pre-trial, and many of the minor ones. You can use it as a checklist. You should also use it as suggestive of the types of things you can accomplish at pre-trial. Your case may have a problem that does not fit any pre-cast molds. If the problem is the type of thing that pre-trial can deal with, you should not hesitate to bring it up.

If the court does not conduct pre-trial, you can request that it do so. You should point out why you think pre-trial would be helpful. Bear in mind that a court that does not customarily conduct pre-trial might not be receptive to the more extreme steps that can be taken at pre-trial. You will stand a better chance of getting pre-trial by setting your sights on more conventional steps such as marking documents, clarifying issues, and getting evidentiary rulings.

12.3   How to Guard Against the Pitfalls of Pre-Trial

Your opponent's gain at pre-trial may be your loss. You should also regard the advantages of pre-trial as possible dangers of pre-trial. You should use the checklist not only for steps to take but also for things to guard against.

You should be especially on guard against four principal dangers of pre-trial:

First. The pre-trial order can freeze the case. If something is not in the pre-trial order, it may not get into trial, depending on how the judge feels about "manifest injustice." The problem is that pre-trial is not trial. Prepare as you will for pre-trial, things come up after pre-trial. You do not stop preparing the case. Yet the new idea you have or the new witness or document you find might be precluded. Or you may have to prepare for pre-trial on the basis of a witness's statement. When you interview the witness just before trial, you find he has a different story.

You cannot fully protect yourself against this inherent defect of pre-trial. However, you can take several steps to maximize your protection.

List every witness and document you conceivably might use. You can always not call a witness listed. You cannot always call a witness not listed.

Designate expert witnesses as such and fact witnesses as such. In the case of the Mislisted Witness, a person listed as an expert witness was not allowed to testify as a fact witness.

Try to keep the pre-trial order open-ended with such language as:

> "The parties also reserve the right to call additional witnesses and submit further documents at the trial, provided that the names and addresses of such witnesses and copies of such documents shall be furnished to opposing counsel at least 10 days before the trial."

If you believe a witness may not be available for trial, reserve the right to take his deposition *de bene esse*.

Second. A statement in the pre-trial memorandum can be used as an admission.

In the case just discussed, pre-trial memoranda were filed before the estates of Jones and Smith had settled with each other. In his pre-trial memorandum, counsel for the estate of Jones stated that Smith had been flying the plane and that his negligence caused the mid-air collision. At the trial, the Cessna interests almost persuaded the court to let this into evidence as an admission. On the joint venture theory, this would have *ipso facto* defeated the two estates.

You must be circumspect in stating the facts of your case, and in arriving at stipulations. Insert qualifying language and reserve your right to supplement or correct your statement in light of further facts that might be developed.

Third. The concept of stipulations is fundamentally at war with the nature of a trial. At a trial you are making a presentation. You are bending all of your efforts to persuade the jury. You plan to present evidence so as to make an impression on the jury. You take steps to insure that the jury remembers important testimony.

Then at pre-trial you are asked to stipulate undisputed facts. Nothing, however, can have less of an impact than a stipulation read to the jury. To ask you to stipulate thus may be tantamount to asking you to forsake the crucial consideration about the effect of testimony.

There is another danger, piecemeal stipulations. Evidence must be presented with a theme. A block of evidence must be internally related. A number of blocks of evidence often must be related to each other. To stipulate a bit of evidence here and a bit there could make a hodge-podge of your presentation. You may get facts admitted but find that the jury does not understand what is going on.

Admissions and stipulations, of course, can be important and powerful. Interspersing admissions at key points in a trial is a well-known tactic. The topic here, however, is the risk of stipulations.

The rules-of-thumb for stipulations are as follows:

—Consider the effect of the stipulation upon your presentation at trial.

—Do not necessarily stipulate important facts that you want to impress upon the jury.

—If your opponent seems too generous in his offer to stipulate facts, be careful. He may be trying to steal a march.

Fourth. Impeachment material may be exposed. Be very careful where local rules require all documents to be listed or exchanged, and all witnesses to be listed and (perhaps) the gist of their testimony stated. To do so literally could destroy impeachment as a tool in the search for truth. Some local rules provide that counsel can ask the court to examine impeachment material *in camera* for a ruling whether it should be disclosed. Even if the local rule does not provide for this, you should always ask for such a ruling before voluntarily exposing impeachment material.

13

How to Prepare Your Witnesses
for a Direct Examination
That Will Prove Your Case
and Withstand Cross-Examination—
When Trial Is Imminent

**13.1   Litigation-Tested Techniques for the
Successful Review of Witnesses' Testimony**

**13.1.1   Steps to Take Before the Review to
Insure Its Success**

The purpose of direct testimony is to present
facts in support of your case. Your purpose is to present the direct
testimony so as to make the best possible impression on the jury.

To do this you must pick out the facts to use, plan how to present them, and take every step you can that your witnesses present themselves so the jury accepts their testimony.

You should be working on these goals from the start, the first two especially since they are implicit in much of what you do in preparing the case for trial. Just before trial, however, you must bring these goals into focus. At that time, the third step, preparing the witness for direct and cross-examination, becomes tops on your agenda.

This preparation consists of going over the testimony of the witness with him, orienting him about trial, and giving him pointers on how to testify. When you actually "horseshed" a witness, these three things merge. It is more convenient to discuss them separately.

There are several preliminary points:

1. Prepare the witness before trial commences. You will have time to do a better job. Also your opponent may call the witness under the adverse witness rule.

2. If there is any appreciable lag between the time you horseshed the witness and the time he will testify, brush him up before he testifies.

3. As trial counsel try to prepare the witness yourself. He must get to know you, your mannerisms, how you ask questions, and so forth. You must get to know him. If the two of you get to know each other, you will be able to take him through his direct testimony confidently and meet any contingency with aplomb. When you cannot personally prepare the witness, you should still spend some time getting to know him.

An incident in the case of the Man-Made Cove discussed in Chapter 4 illustrates why this is important. The issue in the case was whether the cove, a large body of water with an opening to Long Island Sound, was natural or artificially made.

Plaintiff lined up impressive proof that it was man-made. The proof established that until the turn of the century, the area had been a salt marsh with a small creek running through it. Then dredging operations commenced for sand. These operations continued at intervals over the years forming the cove.

In the evidence hunt, a young lawyer in the office of plaintiff's counsel found Jolyon Jones, an octogenarian who had spent his life in the area. He remembered the area before and after the dredging. The young lawyer prepared Jones thoroughly on the dates of the dredging, and the key events in Jones' recollection on which he could peg those dates.

A senior partner was to examine Jones at trial. Before putting him on the stand, counsel spent a good deal of time with Jones discussing the case and getting to know him.

At the trial, Jones started out well. He remembered the area as a salt marsh. He told how he had rowed in the creek, and fished and fowled there. He remembered the commencement of dredging. But when he began to tell about the successive waves of dredging, he became confused. He got some dates and events right. He got others backwards or forgot them. He would transpose or drop out decades.

Here, counsel's work paid off. Having gotten to know Jones, he knew how far he could press him to clear up points. He knew when he was pressing too far and risking more confusion. With this in mind, counsel began to reshape Jones' testimony. He took Jones back over it, simplifying it.

Jones responded. He convincingly established the original nature of the area as a salt marsh and the formation of the cove by dredging. If anything, the very rehabilitation after the confusion gave his testimony greater impact.

4. Have the witness go over his deposition, answers to interrogatories, documents, and so forth, to refresh his recollection beforehand. However, do not let him refresh himself on any materials you do not want your opponent to see. Your opponent has a right to inspect anything the witness has refreshed his recollection upon. Be especially careful, therefore, about impeachment materials, and the witness's statement. As mentioned before this is why you should try to avoid giving the witness a copy of his statement when you take it. As trial approaches, he may read it before you can warn him not to.

In a few jurisdictions, you can lay a neat documentary trap for your opponent. On direct examination, you give your witness a document to examine. Your opponent asks to see it. After he has read it, you move that it be introduced into evidence. Under the so-called English rule, when a party calls for and inspects a document during trial, it is treated as introduced into evidence by the party calling for it. See Wigmore on Evidence § 2125.

5. Prepare each witness individually. You cannot accomplish what you should accomplish if you prepare witnesses in a group. Also you run the risk that a witness may tailor his testimony to that of other witnesses. Then on cross-examination he may be forced into a discrepancy. You want to know about any discrepancy before trial. If it is more apparent than real, you may be able to iron it out. If it is real, you want to be able to plan how to handle it.

6. Know the facts thoroughly, in general and as to the individual witness. This sounds preachy but the pressures of practice can tempt you into a piecemeal approach, or into trying to refresh yourself on the case as you review it with the witness.

A main purpose of reviewing testimony of a witness, for example, is to coordinate it with that of others. You do this to insure accurate and effective testimony, and to plan for trial. Witnesses will recall different things about an event they both see. A detail one witness recalls may stimulate the recollection of another witness who does not recall it. Or it could be the other way around. To accomplish things like these, you need the case at your fingertips.

7. Know the law thoroughly. You must plan the testimony in light of the legal principles you must establish. You also need to know the law to take advantage of presumptions. If you have a rebuttable presumption in your favor, you do not need direct testimony on the point except perhaps to lay a foundation. You may still have to prepare testimony on the point for use on re-direct examination or rebuttal.

For example, plaintiff had gone riding with a friend in a motorboat belonging to the friend's father. The friend piled the motorboat up on the shoreline. Plaintiff hit his head against a bulkhead.

By statute the operator of a boat was deemed to be operating it with the consent of the owner, and the owner was responsible for any damage caused by operation of the boat. Counsel did not need to prepare plaintiff for elaborate direct testimony to establish that the friend had the motorboat with the father's consent.

8. Make an outline in chronological or other logical form of the witness's testimony if you have not yet prepared a draft witness sheet to work from.

9. Make a list of the points you particularly want to cover with the witness. You may have jotted down a number of these points already in the trial book. You will get others from the depositions and other materials you review for the conference.

10. Visit the scene with the witness. You should do this to refresh his recollection about details, to make sure that you and he understand each other, so that what you point out on a view dovetails with his testimony, etc.

13.1.2   How to Review the Testimony of a Witness for Greatest Effect at Trial

Purpose

You review testimony with a witness for three reasons:

• To work out the answers he will give on direct examination.
• To decide how to handle the questions he could be asked on cross-examination.
• To make sure that he presents himself and testifies in the best way he can.

General Scope

Cover every topic you will ask, or might ask, the witness about on his direct examination. Sometimes you will think of a point during direct examination which you would like the witness to cover. You know it is down his alley but you have not reviewed it with him. You run a risk if you ask him the question. He may fluster and you may not get the answer you "knew he knew." Rather than run this risk, wait or ask for a recess to go over the point with the witness.

Cover the areas of evidence you anticipate the court will exclude. You will have to make a record of this excluded evidence by an offer of proof under rule 43(c). Usually you make this record by a statement of what you expected to prove by the answer to the objectionable question. Sometimes, however, the court will ask you, or you yourself will want to make the offer of proof by an actual examination of the witness outside the presence of the jury. Or, after you have made a statement, the court may ask the witness questions.

Cover the topics the witness may be cross-examined on. More of this in a moment.

Method

The best method is to discuss each topic with the witness in detail and ask him questions about it. Follow your draft witness sheet or outline in doing this.

Ask clear, precise, and unequivocal direct questions. You want to accustom the witness to the type of questions you will ask at the trial. You also want to hear the witness's response—what he says and how he says it. If he leaves out points in his answers, or does not understand your questions, or displays bad mannerisms, you can take steps to correct the problems. Leading questions do not give you the benefit of this kind of full and responsive answer.

You should use leading questions, however, to help you understand points, and to make sure that you and the witness understand each other. For example, the witness explains something. You then put your understanding of what he said into a leading question to see whether he agrees.

Ask plenty of questions but do not conduct a dry-run direct examination. When he testifies, the witness might try to remember the drill worked out in the dry-run. This could affect his spontaneity. Worse, your opponent could pounce on it in cross-examination to show "rehearsed testimony."

Do not hesitate to suggest more accurate and more effective answers. You and the witness are going over his testimony to develop that kind of answer. If you shy away from making suggestions, you are not doing your job.

Take every step within your power to insure that the witness tells you "the whole truth and nothing but the truth." For this reason, do not assume a gosh darn thing. The witness may have forgotten things. He may be unconsciously suppressing them. He may be deliberately concealing them. He may be inventing them. He may be lying. He may be doing all sorts of things.

You cannot risk that he may not be doing one or more of these things. Consequently, in going over his testimony, insist on clear and complete answers. Do not glide over "minor" inconsistencies. Make sure you thoroughly understand everything. Press the witness if need be. In extreme cases, put the situation to the witness bluntly.

To illustrate the importance of this kind of thoroughness that assumes nothing: An industrial accident involved a piece of equipment which was an integral part of a system in plaintiff's operation. Plaintiff sued the manufacturer of the equipment.

The manufacturer defended, one ground being that plaintiff had altered the system, and to accommodate the piece of equipment to the new system had altered it too. By virtue of the defense, subsidiary questions arose. What design did plaintiff furnish for the equipment? Had the design on the blueprint been orally modified? And there were other questions.

The original order had been placed, and any of these events, if they had taken place, occurred a number of years before. Plaintiff's then plant manager, who had since retired and moved away, began to look like the person who would know the situation best. The current personnel could not answer many of the questions or fine points. Such documents as plaintiff could find did not answer all of the questions either.

Counsel got the retired witness to come on. He appeared to be the proverbial answer to the maiden's prayers. He immediately filled counsel in on a number of points. He ransacked the plant to find old records. He had a facility for refreshing himself on hazy points as he dug into the case. And he projected an assurance of his knowledge that inspired counsel with confidence.

By the time counsel had finished reviewing the case with the witness, the case looked air-tight.

One seeming cloud on the horizon had been cleared up. The witness had been out of work sick for a period of time. From the dates he gave though, he had not been away during any critical period.

On direct examination he did well enough. Some of the points though that had been clear in conference came out fuzzier than counsel had anticipated. But all in all, except for one other point to be mentioned later in this chapter, the witness did a creditable job.

On cross-examination defense counsel began to probe. He developed that the witness's absence from work may have come during a more crucial time than first seemed. He opened gaps in things the witness might be expected to know about. He vigorously attacked the creditability of crucial points in the witness's testimony.

Defense counsel did a good job on cross-examination. Plaintiff's counsel sat through it like good soldiers, impassive.

When cross-examination was over, plaintiff's counsel asked a few questions on re-direct examination. He did not want the jury to think he wished to get the witness off the stand. When the witness did step down, as he passed the counsel table he asked, "How'd I do?" Sensing that the jury may have heard that something had been said, counsel smiled.

This witness appeared to have the credentials. He was honest. He wanted to help. He seemed to know the technical points well. He and the expert witness seemed to agree on these points. It is true that the trial of cases is strewn with might-have-beens. Still, in preparation here if counsel had pressed harder, who knows. He might well have become alerted to the weaknesses.

Mannerisms and Attitude

In reviewing testimony observe how the witness responds.

Watch for mannerisms—a distracting use of hands, a grimace at an unpleasant question, speech shortcomings such as "you know" and "like," and so forth. If the mannerism will hurt his testimony, warn him about it. If the mannerism is harmless, do not tamper with it.

Pay particular attention to how the witness listens to and answers questions. You want to be sure that he understands questions before he answers them. You want to see if he jumps in with an answer before the question is finished. You want to know if he guesses. In short, you must spot any flagrant violations of the canons of good testifying and correct them.

Listen to how the witness expresses himself. Does he use words carefully or loosely? Can he describe things clearly? Is he capable of sustaining an explanation? Has he a vocabulary adequate to express what he has to tell? From your conclusions you will decide how to ask the witness questions. For example, if he has trouble sustaining an explanation you must break his testimony up into little pieces, with precise questions prepared to elicit each piece.

Check how accurately the witness estimates and describes time and distance. From start to finish, for example, an accident may have taken seconds. In that time the vehicles may have traveled many feet. The witness who misconceives time and distance or garbles them in his testimony, or both, can do your case irreparable harm.

Finally, monitor the witness's attitude. Part of being a trial lawyer is being a coach. You must see to it that he goes to trial in the right frame of mind. You may have to buck up the timid witness, tone down the exuberant one, or temper the arrogant one. You may have to fire up the witness whose testimony will win or lose the case. With a steady witness, you may not have to do anything at all. But you must know what you should do. You cannot neglect psychology.

Points to Cover

The following is a checklist of points to cover in the review of testimony, and in some instances to include in the testimony:

• Each substantive topic that the witness will testify to, or might testify to.

• The facts establishing the foundation for the witness's testimony. You must convince the jury that the witness saw what he says he saw and heard what he says he heard.

• The facts establishing the witness's lack of bias and interest in the outcome to present him as an independent witness. You cannot do this with every witness. With those that you can, you must.

• The fact that the witness has been subpoenaed. Subpoena every witness to support the showing of his disinterest. Explain this to the witness, and that a subpoena protects him from his employer. The subpoena assures you that the witness will show up. You should not rely on promises to appear.

• "Warm-up" questions. You want the witness to be at ease when you get to the key parts of his testimony. Most witnesses will not be at ease when they take the stand. Warm-up questions— name, age, education, background, experience, and so forth— accustom him to the scary new experience.

• Derogatory material. Cover derogatory material you know about with the witness. Press him to reveal any derogatory material to you. You then must consider whether to bring out derogatory material on direct examination. The hornbook approach is that to do so is less embarrassing to the witness and less harmful to the case than if the derogatory material is brought out on cross-examination. On the other hand, if you have a sympathetic witness the jury might react against your opponent if he used it to attack the witness. Or your opponent might not know about it.

To illustrate the situation, in a case involving divergent versions of an occurrence, a tap had been set up and used the night before. It consisted of a keg of beer, a tank of compressed air, and a regulator valve with a gauge. The next morning two men came to dismantle the apparatus. The keg exploded injuring both. Both men sued the company furnishing the tap.

The regulator valve operated the opposite way from common valves like water faucets. It turned counter-clockwise to close and clockwise to open.

The second man stated that when the two of them had gone into the room, the first man turned the valve and he (the second man) had seen the pressure rise on the gauge and shouted the warning before the keg exploded.

The first man did not agree with this version of the incident. He had been seriously injured. He was a popular figure in the community. He made a good witness. The problem was that he had had a conviction some years before.

It is not clear how best to handle problems like that. It is clear, however, that you must do your utmost to find out whether they exist. You can then make a decision about how to handle them and not be surprised.

• Demonstrative evidence. You hardly need a reminder about this for sophisticated demonstrative evidence. But do not forget such simple things as scrutinizing photographs and practicing sketches. The flubbed sketch in the damages case discussed in Chapter 11 illustrates that you cannot be too careful. At trial, the plant engineer neglected to include an important part in a schematic sketch he made of a piece of equipment.

Preparation for Cross-Examination

You should prepare a witness for cross-examination carefully. He probably has ideas about cross-examination, most of them not good. If you parade the horribles, warning him of all manner of dire things, you may work him up to the point where he freezes on the stand.

How explicit you become depends on the witness, but do not be deceived by appearances. The little old lady might be a lot tougher-minded than a bumptious salesman. Even expert witnesses need careful preparation. For example, counsel had to use the head of a firm that specialized in investigating industrial accidents as an expert witness. The man had investigated the accident in suit. On the basis of the facts he found, and the conclusions about causation, the party hiring him had brought suit.

From the nature of his job and the years he had been in it, counsel took it for granted that the witness knew about testifying. In discussing the case, he obviously knew what he was talking about. In preparing him for cross-examination, counsel warned him that opposing counsel was a big man physically who took a slam-bang approach to cross-examination. The witness also sat through some early days of the trial and saw opposing counsel in action.

On his own direct examination, the witness did fairly well, not overpowering but adequate. On cross-examination the opposing lawyer started to hammer away searching for weak points. He hit upon a couple of insignificant steps in the witness's investigation. Instead of deflecting the blows with his expertise, the witness froze. Counsel redoubled his attack. It got so that even on unassailable points the witness scarcely gave a creditable answer.

So you cannot tell a book by its cover. You must use your powers of insight to judge the witness.

Try to work much of the preparation for cross-examination

into the preparation for direct examination. Explain and illustrate points as you go along. For example, when you are using leading questions to clear up matters in your preparation for direct examination, take the time to explain leading questions—that they recite facts and suggest answers; that the witness must listen to them carefully to make sure the facts are correct; that he has to think about his answers because a yes or no embraces all the facts in the question.

In one way or another, cover the following points in preparing a witness for cross-examination:

• Explain the purpose and illustrate the techniques of cross-examination. This includes the leading question and the modes of impeachment.

• Tell him/her about your opponent's style of cross-examination. The smooth type who tries to lull the witness into letting down his guard. The aggressive type who tries to scare the witness into ill-conceived answers. The abrasive type who tries to goad the witness into angry retorts.

• Warn about pet cross-examination techniques, especially any your opponent likes to use—jumping around, avoiding any logical or chronological approach; asking double questions so he can exploit a yes or no answer; asking loaded questions such as "Have you stopped beating your wife yet?"; asking incomplete questions, pausing to elicit a response, and then adding tags that change the meaning of the questions.

• Give examples of the trick questions that might be asked, and how to answer them.

• Advise on the best way to testify. This and the preceding point are covered in section 13.3.

• Review every point your opponent could cross-examine him/her about.

This last point is the all-important substantive preparation for cross-examination. You probably will have covered a lot of the points in preparing the witness for direct examination. In preparing for cross-examination, however, you must go into every point the expert *could* be cross-examined on. The key word is "could." You want your witness to be prepared for anything and everything. Your job is to think of these points.

Use the same method of preparation for cross-examination as you did for direct examination, only more so. Discuss the material in detail and press the witness with questions. Use leading questions. Try to trip him up. Keep after him for responsive answers. Do not let him put you off. Even try to get him mad if you think you run dangers along this line.

This method is not the same as a dry-run cross-examination. It is better. You get the benefit of tough questioning and of in-depth discussion. Each supplements the other.

You can hardly go too far in preparing a witness for cross-examination. As an example, back in the days of rent control, a pompous fellow and his wife were tenants in a big house with many rooms, including three bathrooms. The landlord wanted to get his hands on the house to remodel it into a number of apartments.

The landlord offered the tenant an apartment and other inducements to get him to move out. The tenant steadfastly refused. The landlord finally brought an action to eject the tenant on grounds permitted under the rent control statute.

At the trial the tenant insisted he needed all of the rooms. He was not very explicit as to why. The judge, puzzled, asked him why he and his wife needed three bathrooms.

The tenant replied, "Some of us have higher standards of personal hygiene than others."

13.2   How to Orient a Witness for Trial

You must prepare a witness for things that will happen at the trial and how to conduct himself at the trial. This would seem too obvious to mention except for the fallacy of the familiar—because you are so familiar with what goes on at a trial, either you assume that the witness also does or you overlook that he does not.

In the case of the "too willing witness," just discussed, for example, he had spent years in the East living and working in the state where the case was to be tried. On retiring, he had moved to the Middle West. When he came back to consult on the case, however, he had the manner and the garb of a man of the West.

Counsel did a double-take when he met the witness. However, during the days they worked together, counsel became accustomed to him.

The day he was to testify the witness walked into court wearing a fancy shirt with a bolo, a cord, and a slide, instead of a tie. He looked like a rancher in his holiday best. For a trial in the West he would have been dressed perfectly. For a trial in the East he struck an incongruous note.

Counsel had not covered the subject of dress with the witness. He had fallen into the fallacy of the familiar.

Instructing the witness about the ins and outs of trial and advising him on how to testify merge into each other. Regard the first more as general orientation, and the second as concrete tips. The exact points you cover and how deeply you go in the orientation depends on the witness. The following list contains the points you should consider:

- The physical set-up of the courtroom.
- For a client who will be with you the entire time, the stages of the trial from selection of the jury to the jury verdict.
- The scheme of direct, cross-, and re-direct examination.
- Points of courtroom etiquette such as standing up for the judge.
- That he might be called under the adverse witness rule.
- That he should dress conservatively, explaining what this means.
- That he should not talk to jurors during the trial.
- That he could be excluded from the courtroom when other witnesses testify.
- If the court observes the rule, that he cannot talk to you about the case during recesses while still subject to cross-examination.
- Not to react to testimony by making faces or comments.
- Not to slouch, chew gum, be inattentive, whisper, or otherwise distract from the trial.
- Not to take any material to the stand without telling you what he intends to take.
- To leave children at home or in school. If children testify, to make arrangements that they can leave shortly afterwards.

13.3   Tips on Testifying—What to Tell Your Witness About How to Testify

You must give your witness pointers about how to testify. The problem is how.

He will not absorb a long list of technical dos and don'ts about a procedure that he knows nothing about anyway.

You can solve the problem by weaving a number of the tips into the general review, re-emphasizing a few of the crucial instructions at the end.

You also have to guard against the fallacy of the familiar. Here you fall into the fallacy by not illustrating the principles. For example, as mentioned earlier, illustrate a leading question so that the witness can see why it is so important that he listen to it carefully.

The following is a *checklist of points you should cover with the witness:*

"Listen carefully to the question asked."

"If you do not understand or hear a question, ask that it be repeated."

"Watch out for double questions or unfinished questions."

"Do not interrupt to answer a question before the questioner has finished asking it."

"Only answer the question asked."

"Do not volunteer information." (Explain that the purpose of re-direct examination is to give the witness the opportunity to explain points counsel wants explained. The exception to this rule is the witness with the ability to expand on his direct testimony in response to a broad question. If you have such a witness advise him to do so.)

"Answer the question in terms of the facts within your knowledge."

"Try to avoid 'I don't know' answers unless you do not know."

"Do not guess, speculate, or get into opinions."

"Try not unduly to hesitate over an answer."

"When an objection is made, stop testifying and do not speak until you receive instructions on what to do."

"Speak up when you are testifying."

"Look at the jury when you are testifying."

"On cross-examination, do not lose your temper or argue with the cross-examiner."

"Be polite and serious."

"In a negligence case, do not mention insurance."

"In reply or as reactions, do not grunt, make faces, nod or shake your head, gesticulate. Answer in words."

"Beware of certain trick questions on cross-examination such as follows:

Q. Have you discussed this case with anyone?

A. Yes, my counsel.

Q. What did he tell you to say?

A. The truth.

Q. Are you being paid to testify?

A. I'm only being paid my lost wages.

Q. Did you discuss your testimony with your lawyer during the recess?

A. Yes I did, and he said it was perfectly all right."

INDEX

297